ONCE
WAS ENOUGH

ONCE
WAS ENOUGH

Celebrities (and Others)
Who Appeared
a Single Time on the Screen

Douglas Brode

A Citadel Press Book
Published by Carol Publishing Group

A Citadel Press Book
Published by Carol Publishing Group
Citadel Press is a registered trademark of Carol Communications, Inc.

Editorial, sales and distribution, rights and permissions inquiries should be addressed to
Carol Publishing Group, 120 Enterprise Avenue, Secaucus, N.J. 07094

In Canada: Canadian Manda Group, One Atlantic Avenue, Suite 105, Toronto, OntarioM6K 3E7

Carol Publishing Group books may be purchased in bulk at special discounts for sales promotion,
fund-raising, or educational purposes. Special editions can be created to specifications. For details,
contact Special Sales Department, 120 Enterprise Avenue, Secaucus, N.J. 07094.

Designed by Andrew B. Gardner

Manufactured in the United States of America

10 9 8 7 6 5 4 3 2 1

Library of Congress Cataloging-in-Publication Data

Brode, Douglas, 1943–
       Once was enough : celebrities (and others) who appeared a single
   time on the screen / Douglas Brode.
           p.   cm.
       "A Citadel Press book."
       ISBN 0-8065-1735-2 (pbk.)
       1. Motion pictures.   2. Celebrities.   I. Title.
PN1995.B733   1996
791.43902890922—dc20   95-48049
                                                                        CIP

For James J. MacKillop
Educator, author, scholar, friend

CONTENTS

ACKNOWLEDGMENTS

With appreciation to the following people who contributed their time and effort as well as wonderful suggestions: Scott Lecleau, Kathryn Metherell, Peter Violas, James MacKillop, Bob Polunsky, and Tony Regitano; also, to Photofest, Cinema Collectors, Collector's Book Store, and Larry Edmund's Bookstore, as well as to Republic Pictures, MGM, United Artists, Warner Bros., Paramount, Walt Disney Productions, Universal Pictures, and 20th Century–Fox for their generous support and permission to reprint stills from their films.

INTRODUCTION

The gray late-winter day had turned drizzly and uninviting, best friends were off visiting with families, and it being a Sunday, I'd already seen the movies that had opened in town for the weekend: *Moby Dick* at Patchogue's "big show" (the respectable Friday-night film with my parents), a double bill of an Audie Murphy western and a Vincent Price horror opus at the déclassé Rialto with my pals on Saturday afternoon. Sensing my boredom, my father mentioned, "There's a good old movie on TV this afternoon. It shows the gunfight at the O.K. Corral at the end." Welcome news, certainly, to a thirteen-year-old fan of *The Life and Legend of Wyatt Earp* on Tuesday evenings at eight-thirty. Though I'd never even heard of *My Darling Clementine* and was perhaps a bit put off by the hokey-sounding title, there were precious few alternatives, so I gave it a try.

Watching that film shaped my life in many ways. Everyone who becomes intensely involved with motion pictures can cite the film that changed his life, the single movie that first offered a vision of what movies, at their best, can be. In the forty-some years since that rainy afternoon, I imagine I've seen *My Darling Clementine* a hundred times: catching it occasionally on television while still a college student, later screening it on Moviolas to write serious articles for journals like *Cinéaste,* eventually watching it in the company of my own college students when I'd become a professor of film. Doubtless other film aficionados have experienced much the same feeling after seeing John Ford's masterwork; for me, though, there was another, unique aspect to the experience.

"Oh, there's Cathy Downs," my mother mentioned while passing through the living room, glancing at the TV, where Clementine Carter was just then dancing in the arms of Wyatt Earp at the dedication of Tombstone's first church, still half-finished—much like civilization itself in John Ford's allegorical portrait of an American community in transition from uninviting desert outpost to full-blown modern city.

Elizabeth Threatt

"Who is she?" I asked. Suddenly it struck me as strange that I'd never seen or heard of this A film's leading lady before. I did, after all, watch most of the old movies that played on New York airwaves during those early days of television, on showcases like the warmly remembered *Million Dollar Movie,* and had become pretty familiar with the stars who had shined for the previous generation.

"She used to be your baby-sitter when you were little," my mother casually said. "Just before she won a beauty contest and moved to Hollywood."

"You mean," I muttered, barely able to get out the words, "that she's related to the Downs family over on the next block?" It seemed impossible that a queen of remote, almost mythical Tinseltown could have such humble origins.

"She's their daughter," my father said.

I was literally speechless, amazed to learn that, some ten years earlier, when the now-burgeoning town of Patchogue was little more than a whistle-stop on the Long Island Rail Road, the Downs family had owned and operated one of the village's first grocery stores, just across the street from the soda and newspaper shop where my grandfather sold magazines and candy bars to commuters waiting for the train. One day, Mr. Downs had, during a lull in business, rushed over to show my grandfather an official-looking letter that had arrived in the morning mail, and about which he was greatly concerned.

"Do you realize what this is?" my grandfather asked after slipping on his spectacles and studying the document carefully. "A contract from Hollywood. Darryl F. Zanuck is offering Cathy the lead in a major motion picture."

Mr. Zanuck had seen Cathy's pinup pose, which had been syndicated nationally in the newspapers, then conferred with his director John Ford. The two decided that this unknown young woman was precisely right for the title role, that of a schoolmarm who arrives in Tombstone from the East, ushering in the family values, Christian morality, and mainstream American ethos that automatically accompany her presence, unconsciously transforming the wilderness into a garden.

"Looks kosher to me," my grandfather pronounced. Louie Lichenstein may not have been an educated man, but his natural intelligence and worldly wisdom were well-known and highly regarded throughout our little hamlet. His gut reaction was good enough for Mr. Downs, who decided on the spot to give this proposal his blessing. So it was that his daughter Cathy exited our small town, off to Monument Valley, where she would star in what would become one of the most acclaimed motion pictures ever produced.

"What I don't understand," I said after listening spellbound to this tale that personalized for me the stunning woman whose immortal moment on celluloid was ritualistically unfolding for us this lazy afternoon, "is why I haven't seen or heard of her before." It didn't make sense: she was gorgeous, her performance was excellent, and here she was in the arms of Hollywood's finest actor, Henry

Sexy, talented Neile Adams could have been a major star, though she gave that up to become Mrs. Steve McQueen; her only important film was This Could Be the Night. *(courtesy Metro-Goldwyn-Mayer)*

Fonda himself. What had happened to Cathy Downs afterward?

That wasn't so easy to answer. "I don't think she ever did anything else," my father, the house expert on such matters, said. He and my mother exchanged glances and shrugged; so far as they could recall, this had been Cathy Downs's single moment of cinematic fame. The notion fascinated me then, as it has over the years—how could anyone get that far, then prove unable to follow through? The hard part would, it seemed, be breaking in, getting started; but with an auspicious beginning, why the following silence? A dozen theories passed through my mind: she married and lost interest in acting; she offended someone in power at the studio and was summarily dismissed; she chose the wrong follow-up project, it failed to materialize, and her moment had passed; she had become hooked on some forbidden substance and was unable to work.

In point of fact, Cathy Downs, as I later learned, had actually appeared in several B movies over the years. At the Rialto I even caught a grade-Z horror film she had appeared in during the late fifties—that was unmistakably her face, but

Why have an actor play a judge when you can actually have *a judge? Joseph Welch suffers through courtroom histrionics in Otto Preminger's* Anatomy of a Murder. *(courtesy Columbia Pictures)*

the glow was gone, the potential spark of star quality that Ford had seen and briefly lit up had somehow gone out during the preceding decade. Yet in the public's memory, Cathy Downs remains a one-shot wonder, a person who had one major movie role and then, for reasons most people would or could never learn, slipped out of the limelight. What I couldn't get over was that she had once lived right down the block from us, had literally held me as an infant in her arms. That kind of personal connection caused me to try to learn as much as I possibly could about what, for me, turned into a nagging question: Whatever happened to Cathy Downs?

It also explains why, from that point on, I would always watch movies from a unique angle, ever on the lookout for other one-shot wonders—people who had, like my onetime baby-sitter, enjoyed big-league stardom, but only once. Before long I was filling notebooks with entries on the sports stars, glamorous models, celebrities of passing notoriety, TV and show business personalities, singing sensations, and others in the public eye who had parlayed their sometimes fleeting fame into a single screen appearance. Many of those people showed up on TV, in live or filmed appearances. Some appeared in B movies that came and went, walk-ons and cameos in various projects, or had more recently appeared in direct-to-video junk. But there had been one, and only one, theatrical feature with a leading or key supporting role.

This book is the result of that ongoing fascination. Of the thousands of personalities whose names I've jotted down over the years, this selection must be considered a mere sampling, a collection of some of the most fascinating stories I've encountered and carefully documented over the years. When I first suggested the project to my editor, his major concern was whether there would be enough such people to fill an entire book. I assured him then that the problem would be one of selection, and I was right. For each entry included in this final cut, literally a dozen others in the same category had to be shuffled aside for lack of space. Perhaps if this volume proves successful, a follow-up will be in order; after all, Hollywood creates new one-shot wonders every year, while there are plenty from the past I hated to bypass. If readers can think of anyone significant who has been overlooked, or any new one-shot wonder created since the book's publication, please feel free to contact my publisher.

If we do publish a second volume, and your suggestion is included, I'll happily acknowledge your contribution at the opening of the next book.

One other significant note on selection: Two kinds of one-shot wonders are included, which I categorize as actual and perceived. The actual one-shot wonders are those people who have truly appeared in one, and only one, motion picture, then drifted out of the limelight. The others, those "perceived" one-shot wonders, are people who, like my childhood baby-sitter, managed to get into several other films, before or after that moment of glory. But no one remembers those other projects, so these "stars" resemble one-hit wonders of the music business, many of whom actually recorded a second song, or even numerous others, though the follow-ups never hit the charts.

Perhaps another intriguing story—this one far more recent—will suffice to explain that second syndrome. Not long ago, a colleague at the college where I teach (who, importantly, had absolutely no notion of this project) rushed up to me on a Monday morning, eager to talk about a film he'd seen on cable TV over the weekend. It was *East of Eden,* one of his (and my) favorites from the 1950s. As a teenager, he had—like all the rest of us—been mesmerized by James Dean, the actor who touched our generation much as Elvis was just then doing through music, expressing our collective, emerging, then largely unformed point of view through popular art. Now, though, with the passing of time, my colleague had watched the film more objectively, noticing that the young performer playing Dean's brother offered what was, technically speaking, a far superior performance. Dean had charisma; this fellow exuded craft.

"Who *was* he?" my colleague asked, then added, "I don't ever remember seeing him in anything else."

I explained that the actor's name was Dick Davalos, and that he had indeed been in several other pictures of which no one save dedicated film scholars had any knowledge.

"I don't understand," my colleague mused, "how anyone could be so good in such an important film and never get to do anything else of note."

I smiled and informed my colleague I'd just spent the weekend working on a book that would attempt to answer that very question. You are now holding that book.

1
THE PANTHEON

T hese are the true classics of the one-shot-wonder genre: the most memorable of all those diverse stars and unknowns who hit the high note just once, cinematically speaking.

CATHY DOWNS
My Darling Clementine (1946)

A modest critical and commercial success in 1946, John Ford's fanciful version of the Wyatt Earp story has, over the half century since its release, taken on the stature of an American classic: not merely another western about Tombstone and the O.K. Corral, but a symbolic portrait of the forces of civilization gradually taming the frontier. No single image better captures Ford's romanticized vision than that of girl-shy Henry Fonda summoning up his courage to dance during a Sunday-afternoon camp meeting before a half-finished church with the future schoolmarm, Clementine Carter, nicely played by Cathy Downs. Though cast as the title character in one of the ten finest films ever produced by 20th Century–Fox studio, Downs was, just one year later, making the rounds of Monogram, the seediest of all poverty-row companies, searching for work in third-rate items like *Panhandle*. Quite a comedown for the girl from Patchogue, Long Island, who'd sung in her glee club, then moved to New York (accompanied by her mother, as chaperon) to try modeling. By 1943, the picture-perfect (34-24-35), brown-haired beauty could be seen in everything from mail order catalogs to high-fashion magazines. Her unique looks, combining small-town openness with a touch of class, allowed her to appear equally at home in jeans or satin.

Then, on a shoot near Phoenix, Arizona, a Fox scout spotted her sipping a soda at a lunch counter and offered to arrange a screen test. When it proved successful, Downs was spirited off to California where she appeared in *Billy Rose's*

Diamond Horseshoe as the gorgeous Miss Cream Puff. Then followed a walk-on in *The Dark Corner,* a film noir. *Clementine,* which seemed likely to open doors, somehow proved a dead end, despite the fact that Downs's natural, flawless acting put to shame that of the other female lead, Linda Darnell, preposterously cast as a half-Indian/half-Mexican temptress.

Downs's personal life did not go well, either. She married golf pro Joe Kirkwood Jr. (who would go on to play the title character in *Joe Palooka* on TV in the early 1950s), then divorced him claiming cruelty in 1955. Kirkwood was furious that Cathy couldn't play golf, then humiliated her publicly when she tried to learn. The twenty-eight-year-old, willing to accept a token $1 a year just to get away from Kirkwood, married again a year later, hoping Bob Brunson would work out better. In 1962, Cathy—who had, professionally, been reduced to bits in bad B sci-fi films—divorced Brunson, claiming extreme cruelty. Following that, she drifted out of the public eye.

KATHARINE HOUGHTON

Guess Who's Coming to Dinner (1967)

Rarely have the critics savaged a premier performance with such relish as when Katharine Houghton debuted in this softly satiric put-down of racism, in which an upscale white girl brings home the perfect fiancé, who just happens to be black. Director Stanley Kramer never even considered any actor but Sidney Poitier for the latter role. Since the film would reunite the legendary screen team of Spencer Tracy and Katharine Hepburn (playing the kind of cozy married couple they'd never had the opportunity to become in real life), who better for the part of Hepburn's daughter than her then twenty-one-year-old niece, recently graduated from Sarah Lawrence? Houghton had become interested in acting one year earlier, when several filmmaking students from Princeton noticed the classy beauty in a school cafeteria, on the spot offering her the lead in their independent movie. Bitten by the acting bug, Houghton found work in summer stock, then won a role in Garson Kanin's new play *A Very Rich Woman*.

Kramer signed her without even bothering to do a screen test; word spread through the press that a new Hepburn would shortly arrive. Somehow, the initially positive advance publicity transformed into nightmarish overhype. When the film was eventually released, the mood among the public as well as the press had transformed from "I can't wait to actually see this girl" to "You're gonna have to really show me something." Perhaps Houghton's performance was not quite as silly, shrill, and unsubstantial as reported at the time, though Houghton certainly wasn't very good. No other roles were immediately offered, so she retreated to regional theater, only occasionally doing the lead in a minor movie such as 1974's *Seeds of Evil,* or a small supporting role in a big picture such as 1988's *Mr. North.* Before landing her first acting job, Houghton had planned to be a writer. Over the years, she authored nine off-Broadway and regional-theater productions, wrote and starred in a one-woman show (*To Heaven in a Swing*) based on the work of Louisa May Alcott, saw her comedy *Buddha* published in *The Best Short Plays of 1988* (Schilton Books), and finally penned *M.H.G.,* a biography of her historian/labor-activist mother, Marion Hepburn Grant. Living a full, rich, active life, Katharine Houghton was a one-shot wonder only so far as major Hollywood movies were concerned.

GEORGE LAZENBY
On Her Majesty's Secret Service (1969)

The worst thing George Lazenby had going against him was that he didn't happen to be Sean Connery. Albert "Cubby" Broccoli had handpicked the male model and sometime Marlboro Man, who hailed from Queanbeyan, Australia, to play James Bond. He was cast following a highly publicized worldwide talent search, itself the subject of a *Life* magazine cover story. According to Broccoli, Lazenby was precisely right to replace the retiring star of the most popular series of action films to appear during the 1960s, but the public and reviewers were lying in wait for the newcomer. Despite an intense critical drubbing, Lazenby was actually quite

George Lazenby as agent James Bond in On Her Majesty's Secret Service. *(courtesy United Artists)*

charming in the role of 007, occasionally winking at the audience as if to apologize for not being "the other guy." Besides, the film was so imaginatively written and sumptuously produced that it put to shame immediate predecessors and subsequent chapters in the emerging Bond epic. Though box-office returns on this holiday release were not up to expectations, they were in no way embarrassing. So Broccoli decided to stick with Lazenby, hoping the hurdle had been crossed and, with another major release, Lazenby would comfortably slip into the role.

That's when George Lazenby walked. Why? "I think I wanted to destroy my career," he reflected to Dana Kennedy of *Entertainment Weekly* a quarter century after the major misstep. Following his major-star buildup, the actor was convinced by unscrupulous managers that the world was his oyster. Why limit himself to Broccoli and Bond when dozens of other intriguing roles would pour in? Sadly and arrogantly, Lazenby listened to such advice and went off sailing around the world for fifteen months. When he returned home, no desperately hungry coterie of fans was waiting for him, only the realization that—since Connery had returned for the next film—he was a forgotten has-been. After that, Lazenby took small supporting roles in minor movies such as Peter Bogdanovich's *Saint Jack* and kidded his tarnished superspy image in the TV movie *Return of the Man from U.N.C.L.E.* In 1995, at age fifty-six, the recently divorced Lazenby could be found living in L.A., making the rounds of auditions.

MARK FRECHETTE

Zabriskie Point (1970)

World-class filmmaker Michelangelo Antonioni arrived in America to make his first English-language film in the late sixties, when a virtual revolution appeared ready to engulf the country even as a psychedelic mentality overtook Hollywood following the release of *Easy Rider*. Convinced the Establishment would shortly be overthrown, Antonioni fashioned a radical epic in which two free-living hippies help blow up the last remnants of their failed society. For the leads, he insisted on casting unknown nonactors who would live, rather than play, the parts; the roles went to Daria Halprin and Mark Frechette. Frechette subsequently appeared in several low-budget Italian films never released in America, but would not work in another important film. *Zabriskie Point* proved to be a box-office disaster; though *Easy Rider* had been all the rage only one year earlier, *Airport* was now hot at the box office, the public backing off counterculture flicks and instead embracing old-fashioned escapism.

Anyone associated with the failed project was in big trouble, career-wise, though Mark Frechette's unhappy experiences went beyond his inability to find acting jobs. A year and a half earlier, Frechette had been living in a Boston commune, finding occasional work as a carpenter, when Antonioni happened to bump into the teenager on a downtown street and, in broken English, announced that he'd just found the hero for his new film. After the fizzled release, Frechette returned to the Ft. Hill commune, though soon found himself about to be evicted for nonpayment of rent. Desperate for money, Frechette and Sheldon T. Bernard, another resident, attempted to hold up the Brigham Circle branch of the New England Merchants National Bank, managing to kill an innocent bystander before being captured. Frechette was sentenced to a six-to-fifteen-year stretch in the Massachusetts Correctional Institution at Norfolk. Two years later, while in the prison weight-lifting room, Frechette lost control of a 150-pound bar he was pressing; it came crashing down on his throat and killed him instantly.

MICHAEL JACKSON

The Wiz (1978)

The idea must have sounded perfect: match Diana Ross, Motown diva turned movie star, with Michael Jackson, king of seventies pop, for the film version of *The Wiz,* translating everyone's favorite Hollywood fairy tale into the pop idiom of the disco era. Perhaps if director/choreographer Bob Fosse had been signed, it might have worked. Instead, Sidney Lumet—acclaimed for gritty, realistic films such as *The Pawnbroker* and *Dog Day Afternoon*—was allowed to try an all-singin', all-dancin' project for the first time. The results were dreary, dull, even disastrous, *The Wiz* rating as the most leaden musical movie ever based on a lilting Broadway play. Critics proved kinder to Jackson (as The Scarecrow) than to the film itself, predicting he might well have a happy movie career ahead of him. During the early 1980s, rumors endlessly circulated that he would play the title role in a new version of *Peter Pan* to be directed by Steven Spielberg, though when that project finally did reach the screen, Robin Williams had the part.

His full name is Michael Joseph Jackson; born in Gary, Indiana, on August 29, 1958, he was the seventh child of Joe and Katherine Jackson, who whipped their five sons (Jermaine, Tito, Jackie, Marlon, and Michael) into The Jackson Five. Signed by Motown in 1969, they had four No. 1 hits within their first year. Immediately, though, Michael's charisma called out for a solo career; his first link to the movies came when Michael sang "Ben," the title song for the film about a killer rat. After splitting from The Jacksons in 1984, Michael was a pioneer in the music video field: "Thriller" (a horror tale) and "Beat It" (contemporary gangs) were essentially mini-movies, broadcast on MTV, redefining the notion of "a movie" for a new generation. Gradually, though, Jackson was transforming: cosmetic surgery made him appear ever more androgynous, while his color continually lightened. His pioneering efforts in alternative film continued, with *Captain Eo* for the Disney theme parks and *Moonwalker,* which sent a childlike Jackson off on fantastical music-inspired adventures. But the question continued: Would Jackson again appear in a theatrical film? One strong possibility was a remake of *The Seven Faces of Dr. Lao.* The material—a family-oriented fantasy—seemed made to order until all hell broke loose. Allegations that Jackson had molested children brought to his home for "play" seriously curtailed his music career and seemingly derailed forever the possibility of *Dr. Lao* or any other theatrical films.

VANILLA ICE

Cool as Ice (1991)

Like Lincoln said, you can fool all of the people some of the time, and some of the people all of the time, but you can't fool all of the people all of the time. Proof positive, Robert Van Winkle of Florida, who for about a year cajoled the public into thinking he was the new white dude who would be to black rap what Elvis had earlier been to rhythm and blues: taking a highly ethnic and idiosyncratic form of American subculture music and making it palatable to the vast (largely white) mainstream through the force of a remarkable personality and a unique talent. That describes Elvis to a T; Van Winkle, a.k.a. Vanilla Ice, just didn't have it.

Vanilla Ice as Johnny, the rappin' motorcycle dude in Cool as Ice. *(photo by Greg Gorman, courtesy Universal Studios)*

Discovered by Tommy Quon, owner of Dallas's City Lights club, Vanilla Ice cut "Ice Ice Baby" for Quon's local Ultrax label and gradually the song achieved cult status, then became a commercial hit. A well-made video allowed Ice to win airtime on MTV.

Shortly he was a phenomenon, if a short-lived one. His smug smile and nasty eyes beamed out at the public from posters that graced the music stores in malls all over the country. Ice seemed to be on the verge of major-league stardom when he was featured (in a singing-only cameo) in the popular *Teenage Mutant Ninja Turtles II* film. Then came *Cool as Ice,* which was supposed to be the *Viva Las Vegas* of the nineties, and as such the beginning of a series of musical movies designed to do for him what Elvis's popular flicks had done for the King some thirty years earlier. Ice played Johnny, a wandering rugged motorcycle dude with an earring and an attitude. Apparently this was intended as a takeoff on Brando's legendary role in *The Wild One.* But the kids had already sensed Ice's image was only an act, so his career was frozen by the time *Cool as Ice* hit the theaters, where it played to empty houses for one week, then was unceremoniously yanked. No sequel has been announced at the time of this writing.

2
ME, MYSELF, AND I

A unique subgenre of the one-shot wonder is the celebrity of the moment who plays him or herself in a film biography; here's a sampling of the most memorable.

GERTRUDE EDERLE

Swim, Girl, Swim (1927)

New Yorker Gertrude Caroline Ederle, the third of six children born to German immigrants, was interested in swimming from the tender age of eight. She had won herself a place as a member of the Women's Swimming Association at twelve, soon winning short- and long-distance events for a total of 250 victories by the time she reached her teen years as a spritely seventeen-year-old. Still, her greatest fame was yet to come—as a member of the second U.S. women's Olympic swimming team where she won two bronze medals and a gold medal. Always, though, when people think of Gertrude Ederle, they think of one thing and only one thing: she was the woman who succeeded in swimming the English Channel, on her second attempt, which took place on August 6, 1926, covering thirty-five miles in fourteen hours and thirty-one minutes. There were offers to appear in vaudeville, staged swimming exhibitions, and a single movie that capitalized on her brief but intense bout with fame.

The film was *Swim, Girl, Swim,* starring the popular comedienne Bebe Daniels as a Dana College girl named Alice Smith, an awkward swimmer who has always wanted to win a big meet for her team. At one point, she even believes that she's been the victor of an important match, though that's not the case. In this lighthearted comedy-drama, Alice enlists the aid of—who else?—Gertrude Ederle, who gives the heroine those key coaching hints that will propel her to success in the film's final moments. Not, however, before Gertrude Ederle has the opportunity to rescue an overly dressed and rather dour fellow, Mr. Spangle (William Austin), from drowning. About Gertrude's only screen appearance, the *New York Times* reviewer noted that "Miss Ederle may not be an actress, but she is emphatically graceful when it comes to diving and giving an exhibition of her crawl stroke."

DOUGLAS CORRIGAN
The Flying Irishman (1939)

Long before Andy Warhol created his legendary "famous for fifteen minutes" phrase, a young man named Douglas Corrigan lived out that idea, fleetingly enjoying national—even international—fame. Though he was forgotten even before this synthetic RKO exploitation film could be hurriedly prepared for mass consumption, his nickname—"Wrong Way" Corrigan—remained part of idiomatic American English long after he'd drifted into obscurity. Screenwriters Ernest Pagano and Dalton Trumbo (the latter to be named as one of the Hollywood Ten a decade later, accused of socialist thinking despite the jingoistic American-dream theme of this script) took the bare bones of Corrigan's life, fleshing it out into a makeshift Horatio Alger fantasy. The fact-based movie concerned an indomitable young man who sticks to his guns and personal vision, eventually overcoming all odds, achieving his aim through pluck and luck.

When Doug Corrigan was only nine, his parents separated; he moved to Los Angeles with his mother and brother and sister where she struggled to support them. Following her early death, Doug took on the responsibility of caring for his siblings, even putting his brother through college. But his great obsession, flying, had already emerged, so he began scrimping and saving (while working numerous jobs) to eventually buy himself an antiquated plane. Corrigan then began barnstorming the country in his old crate, that being a popular rural event in Depression-era communities during the Dust Bowl days of the 1930s. Hoping to win a job as a transport flier, Corrigan overcame all the many obstacles that stood in his path. Finally, he won his incredible nickname with a wrong-way flight across the Atlantic. The movie concluded with Corrigan taking off from New York on his nonstop to Los Angeles, but mistakenly flying over to Ireland, then finally receiving a hero's welcome in his native San Antonio. As for his performance in the title role, *Variety* unkindly noted that "before the camera, [Corrigan] is decidedly amateurish. He's self-conscious to an extreme delivering dialog in a nasal monotone." There were no further film offers beyond this stint at playing himself.

Elsa Maxwell in a role only she could play: as the world's foremost party animal, offering advice to ambitious young women including Lynn Bari in Hotel for Women.

ELSA MAXWELL

Hotel for Women (1939)

Elsa Maxwell transformed the hobby of throwing parties into a high art form. "The odd thing," she once ironically admitted, "is that parties have never meant anything to me." What meant a great deal to the woman born in an opera box in Keokuk, Iowa, in 1883 was music; a child prodigy, she could play any instrument instinctually. Growing up in California, Elsa performed Puccini's music for the composer himself without ever taking a lesson or even peeking at the score. She was hired to improvise mood music on an old piano to augment silent movies at her local bijou. Then it was on to a career accompanying the likes of Caruso, as well as knocking off hundreds of songs (many published) and entire musical revues. Her show business experiences were varied: Elsa toured Europe with a Shakespeare troupe, then performed rowdy numbers in South African music halls. Her reputation preceded her to Paris, where the smart set showered her with party invitations. When—despite an abundance of wine, women, and song—such soirees grew boring, Elsa saved the day (or, more correctly, night) by staging elaborate charades.

Before long, she was hired to run a nightclub on a barge in Venice's Grand Canal, then stolen away by the prince of Monaco to shake up the staid scene in Monte Carlo with risqué high jinks. A hefty 196 pounds at a mere five feet, the world's most prominent party animal returned to America in 1938. Soon there was *Elsa Maxwell's Party Line* on the radio, a syndicated gossip column, and several cameo appearances in the popular comedy shorts of the period. There was also the lead in a single feature film, *Hotel for Women*. In it, she lorded over gorgeous young girls (Linda Darnell, Ann Sothern, Lynn Bari) intent on snagging millionaire husbands. "Miss Maxwell plays herself," *Time*'s critic commented, "popping out brisk remarks, decanting an occasional drop of the Maxwellian philosophy, which undoubtedly seems headier after 2 A.M." She was a natural, so when Marie Dressler dropped out of her famed *Tugboat Annie* series, the buzz had it that Elsa might assume the role, though it never transpired. With her self-consciously mannish hairdo suggesting a personal as well as fashion statement, Elsa never married, living instead with best pal Constance Bennett. In the late 1950s, she was a semiregular on TV's *Jack Paar Show*, though by this time her chitchat seemed more nostalgic for the bygone prewar era than any kind of cutting commentary on the current scene.

JACKIE ROBINSON

The Jackie Robinson Story (1950)

In the late 1940s and early fifties, the worlds of sports and movies were simultaneously embracing the emerging civil rights movement. Pioneering films like *Home of the Brave* portrayed the forced desegregation of the U.S. Army during World War II's final hours, while Jackie Robinson revolutionized baseball by becoming the first African American to play in the major leagues, beginning the integration of pro sports. Although plenty of fine young black actors were around at the time—Sidney Poitier and James Edwards most notable among them—director Alfred E. Green wisely decided that Robinson had become such a distinguishable (as well as distinguished) national figure that no one but Robinson himself would be completely convincing as Jackie Robinson. Happily, this was one of those rare times when such a gamble paid off handsomely.

Though Jackie appears slightly nervous on-camera, his strength of character, essential geniality, and aura of human decency come through beautifully, especially in those scenes with Louise Beavers as his supportive mom. The film simply but eloquently followed the athlete's path from Cairo, Georgia, where he was born into a family of sharecroppers, to California, where he excelled at sports in high school and college. It covered his now-famous stands against racial discrimination while in the U.S. Army and his Negro League experiences with the Kansas City Monarchs (inexplicably called the Black Panthers in the film), to the final breaking of the color barrier when Branch Rickey persuaded Robinson to play for him, first with the minor-league Montreal Royals, then for the Brooklyn Dodgers. The

11

An American folk hero plays himself: Jackie Robinson steps up to bat in The Jackie Robinson Story.

uncontested king of base stealers was, in 1947, named the very first Rookie of the Year for all of baseball; in 1949, he hit .342, ranking him at the top of the National League. An interesting footnote: Ruby Dee, who played Jackie's wife, Rachel Isum Robinson, in the film, portrayed Jackie's mother in the TV film *The Court-Martial of Jackie Robinson* forty years later, featuring André Braugher as Jackie.

WOLFMAN JACK

American Graffiti (1973)

In *Have Mercy,* an autobiography published almost simultaneously with his sudden and unexpected death in the summer of 1995, Wolfman Jack recalled the way in which he'd won a key role in a classic movie. During the early seventies, he was broadcasting daily on L.A.'s KDAY, syndicating his old radio shows around the country, and hosting NBC's new late-night Friday musical show, *The Midnight Special.* One day, he was contacted by people from Universal, asking him to stop by and take a look at a script that a then-obscure film-school graduate, George Lucas, had concocted with several equally young and unknown writers. The Wolfman and a friend drove to the studio, where a secretary handed them a script featuring a character named Wolfman Jack. Fearful that *he* would be asked to pay *them* for the great publicity this would generate, Wolfman was amazed, upon meeting Lucas, to learn he'd be paid $3,000 to appear as himself in the movie, an ensemble comedy-drama about various teenagers who, on graduation night in 1962, leave the prom and drive off for diverse misadventures, each discovering something significant about himself.

Tying all those story threads together would be a disc jockey the kids listen to and rely on as the only adult they truly trust. Several years earlier, Lucas had religiously listened to the Wolfman on XERB; in Jack's words, "sometimes the signal would go in and out, which gave it a kind of mystical, ethereal quality. Some of the kids thought I was flying around in a plane while I did the show, just staying out of reach of the authorities." Brilliantly blending escapist fun with a rite-of-passage serious intent, the ultralow-budget film—shot just north of San Francisco—became a smash hit, launching young actors (Richard Dreyfuss and Harrison Ford among them) toward superstardom while setting the style and tone for films of the seventies. Suddenly, the man who had been born Bob Smith in Brooklyn, spending his teenage years as a juvenile delinquent until a Mexico radio gig revealed his true calling, was transformed into the country's most famous DJ, with the possible exceptions of Kasey Kasem and Dick Clark. In later years, Wolfman did brief cameos in minor movies including *Motel Hell*. But thanks to *American Graffiti*, he'll always be remembered as the disc jockey who introduced white-bread kids to the joys of black soul music in that last moment of American innocence before the Kennedy assassination plunged us into the ongoing nightmare of contemporary life; in actuality, the Wolfman wasn't heard on California airwaves until the late 1960s.

EVEL KNIEVEL

Viva Knievel! (1977)

Robert Craig Knievel spent his teen years in Butte, Montana, raising hell until that day when he caught Joey Chitwood's daredevil act at Clark Park and knew he'd found his calling in life. That night, the boy creatively focused his criminal inclinations by stealing a motorcycle and practicing dangerous stunts. Over the years, he ran (and played for) a semiprofessional hockey team, broke records as a life insurance salesman, and tried his hand at safecracking. While working as a Honda dealer in Moses Lake, Washington, he built a racetrack and performed wild rides through walls of fire and over live rattlesnakes. Despite endless injuries, Evel finally went professional, barnstorming rural fairs in Western states, achieving national prominence when, on New Year's Day, 1968, he zoomed his cycle a full 141 feet over the lavish fountains in front of Caesars Palace in Las Vegas. Two years later, Evel beat his own distance record by jumping nineteen adjacent automobiles for a 150-foot flight.

Actor/producer George Hamilton, fascinated by "the last gladiator of the New Rome," befriended Knievel and made a biographical film about him. *Evel Knievel* was a surprise hit, scoring huge box-office returns on the drive-in circuit while winning surprisingly positive reviews. But Knievel—a good-looking, glib, flamboyant con man whom *The New Yorker* once described as a combination of "Robert Mitchum, Elvis Presley, Captain Ahab, and an astronaut"—believed deep down that no one could play Evel but Knievel. He finally got a starring gig as himself in a considerably less ambitious movie, 1977's *Viva Knievel!* Though veteran director Gordon Douglas rounded up a strong supporting cast of solid actors—Gene Kelly, Lauren Hutton, Leslie Nielsen, and Red Buttons among them—the fictional plot was routine and con-

In full regalia, Evel Knievel simultaneously performs a daredevil stunt while shooting at drug-smuggling slime in Viva Knievel! *(courtesy Warner Bros.)*

trived. In Mexico, Knievel (wearing his trademark red, white, and blue tight-leather jumpsuit) performs daredevil exploits, earning money to help his favorite nuns run an orphanage; all the while, assorted villains try to kill him off, then use his equipment truck to smuggle drugs into the United States. Apparently, Evel Knievel had hoped this amateurish opus might launch a series of stunt movies akin to the Presley musicals; when the film floundered, so did Knievel's dream of movie stardom.

MUHAMMAD ALI

The Greatest (1977)

The man who had been born Cassius Marcellus Clay Jr. in Louisville, Kentucky, and gone on to defeat Sonny Liston with a technical knockout in the sixth round on February 25, 1964, joining the Black Muslims the following day and changing

14

his name, played himself in this disappointing biopic. Ali was surrounded by a stellar cast that included Ernest Borgnine, Robert Duvall, and James Earl Jones (with Roger E. Mosley as Liston), as well as a sound track that boasted George Benson's "The Greatest Love of All," but none of that compensated for filmmaker Tom Gries's lack of conception of what to focus on in Ali's life or what he hoped to say through this rather bland vehicle. Employing the techniques of a routine made-for-TV flick, Gries merely ran Ali through the paces of a synthetic, cleaned-up version of his life, showing all the obvious elements—preparing for a big fight, dealing with the dirty and financial sides of the fight game—while completely failing to dramatize

Muhammad Ali, a.k.a. Cassius Clay, confers with his coach (Ernest Borgnine) in the disappointing biopic The Greatest. *(courtesy Columbia Pictures)*

what was, indeed, one of the most remarkable lives of our century. Clay's moral and spiritual transition to Ali could have made for an important social drama, and perhaps someday a first-rate filmmaker like Spike Lee may just choose to tell that tale.

Most surprising of all was that Ali, such a performer/poet in the ring, did not come off terribly well as an actor. If, in televised interviews, Ali often took on a mesmerizing quality, that was precisely what was missing from his portrait of himself, since in the film he always seems awkward and self-conscious, as if concerned about the camera closing in on him. In fact, Clay had already played himself once. In the 1962 film version of Rod Serling's Requiem for a Heavyweight, he can be glimpsed during the opening three-minute ring sequence as the young fighter who kayos Anthony Quinn as "Mountain" Rivera. Also, in 1979, Ali appeared in the TV special Freedom Road, based on Howard Fast's novel about a former slave who achieves political prominence during Reconstruction. But the unhappily named Greatest remains his only starring film role.

3
ALL THE BLAND YOUNG MEN

They were young, handsome, and pleasant; but, as time would tell, thoroughly unmemorable, making their premier performance their final curtain as well.

GREG McCLURE

The Great John L (1945)

"Selznick had nothing on us," Bing Crosby once laughingly reflected about his work behind the camera on *The Great John L,* "in his search for Scarlett O'Hara." Der Bingel was referring to his own exhaustive quest to find the proper person to star as the legendary boxer Sullivan, in a film biography that Crosby had long planned to produce. Knowing full well that the public still possessed a vivid image of the title character, the crooner/actor turned moviemaker felt compelled to pass by the usual method—casting some Hollywood star who bore at best some fleeting resemblance to the character—and determined to find an unknown who looked precisely right and, hopefully, could act to boot. Crosby eventually settled on a twenty-six-year-old six-footer who weighted 185 pounds and was married to a woman named Marge; they had a twenty-month-old child, Teri-Ann. His real name was Dale Easton, though Crosby insisted on giving him a monicker that sounded Irish.

Born in Atlanta, McClure had spent most of his life in Oakland, then moved to Hollywood, where he found work as an extra on the MGM lot and, like hundreds of others, continued to hope that he might be "discovered." Most critics felt that McClure comported himself respectably opposite Linda Darnell in the moderately successful feature, certainly looking the part and appearing athletic enough in the ring sequences. Still, no other offers were forthcoming. Some twenty-five years later a young man was driving cross-country and happened to stop for

Bing Crosby's own discovery, Greg McClure, as John L. Sullivan in The Great John L. *(courtesy Crosby Productions/United Artists Corp.)*

a drink and bite to eat at a humble roadhouse. To his surprise, a 16-mm projector was running an old film, which the regular clientele informed the visitor was the property of the boss, a now threadbare copy of the only film he'd ever starred in, which played endlessly here. There, on a makeshift screen, was the young Greg McClure, forever dashing as John L. And there, behind the bar where he was mixing drinks, stood an aged, overweight flesh-and-blood incarnation of the same person.

DICK DAVALOS

East of Eden (1955)

"Aaron is everything that's good in the world," James Dean (as Cal) says, smirking, cruelly imitating his cold and aloof father (Raymond Massey). Then he shoves Aaron into the arms of the local brothel's elderly madam (Jo Van Fleet). "Aaron, meet your mother," Cal shrieks with laughter before slamming the door on them and running off in Elia Kazan's classic rendition of John Steinbeck's biblical allegory, relocated to northern California during World War I. Today, Dean's charisma still comes through, though in retrospect, his acting appears somewhat mannered (and derivative of Brando). Though no one took notice at the time, the performance by the young actor playing Dean's brother is, technically speaking, far more accomplished and satisfying. His name was Dick Davalos, yet another perceived rather than actual one-shot wonder. Davalos had become a professional actor while still in his teens; working with the Chapel Theatre Group, he appeared in plays staged for grade-school kids in the New Jersey area. Davalos learned dance from Martha Graham and eventually married one of her dancers, Ellen Van der Hueven. He ushered at the Trans-Lux theater in New York while waiting for his big break, which came when Kazan cast him in the sought-after and, everyone presumed, star-making role.

After *Eden,* Davalos took a small part in *The Sea Chase,* but was soon dropped from Warner Brothers for "being difficult." He shifted to Broadway, playing the young Italian immigrant in Arthur Miller's *A View From the Bridge.* The play was acclaimed as a modern classic, bolstering the career of everyone associated with it except Dick. There were small roles in such minor late-1950s films as *I Died a Thousand Times* and *All the Young Men,* then the rebel role in TV's Civil War show *The Americans,* but ratings were disappointing and it lasted only half a season in 1961. Following that, Davalos worked only occasionally, playing leads in very bad movies such as *Pit Stop* and bit parts in good ones such as *Cool Hand Luke.* He can be glimpsed in the Clint Eastwood World War II action-comedy *Kelly's Heroes* as a crazed rifleman. But to the public at large, he is the actor they remember for only one role: Aaron in *East of Eden.*

WENDELL BURTON

The Sterile Cuckoo (1969)

Liza Minnelli stepped comfortably into superstardom playing Pookie, the charmingly eccentric student in this quietly appealing film, based on John Nichols's acclaimed novel. Making his debut was Wendell Burton, the handsome, clean-cut

Wendell Burton (left) *relaxes on the beach with director Alan J. Pakula and his* Sterile Cuckoo *costar, Liza Minnelli. (courtesy Paramount Pictures)*

youth (he resembled Brandon De Wilde of a generation earlier) who provided a refreshing contrast to the shabby young men then dominating *Easy Rider*–era youth films. Part of the appeal of *The Sterile Cuckoo* was that this 1969 movie seems altogether out of time, the story of a young love that, however deep and sincere, cannot last owing to the essential mismatching of the boy and girl.

During his younger years, Wendell Burton planned to enter politics. While a student at San Francisco State college, a teacher suggested he take an acting class, since an effective politician needs to perform. He did and was bitten by the acting bug, working in a regional-theater production of You're a Good Man, Charlie Brown. When director Alan J. Pakula held open auditions to find an unknown for Cuckoo, Burton tried out and won the role. "I never seemed to be right for the parts," he sighed when asked why nothing much ever happened afterward, an era in which Robert De Niro, Jack Nicholson, and Al Pacino were creating a new breed of mean-streets hero. In fact, Burton did play roles in two other films—Fortune and Men's Eyes and Goodnight Jackie—though both were such total busts that they were shelved. He worked occasionally on episodic TV dramas such as Medical Center and Kung Fu, as well as several above-average made-for-TV movies, Go Ask Alice and The Red Badge of Courage. He also won stage work, including Gower Champion's musical version of the Thornton Wilder chestnut Our Town, perfect for him since it concerned wholesome types. Burton (who eventually married in 1978 and has two children) turned to religion for solace; he became a Christian in 1974, making his newfound faith a cornerstone of his career. He wrote ten songs for his debut Lamb and Lion gospel album.

4
SMALL SCREEN, BIG SCREEN

Television celebrity would seem the perfect jumping-off place for the movies; yet movie-star status has proven elusive for some of the most famous of all TV people.

DAVID FROST

The V.I.P.s (1963)

Following *Cleopatra,* Elizabeth Taylor and Richard Burton—the Lunt and Fontanne of sixties la dolce vita chic—chose a contemporary romantic melodrama, laced with comedy, about jet-setters not unlike themselves, stranded at a fogbound London airport. The film, originally to have been titled *International Hotel,* updated the old *Grand Hotel*–style ensemble piece. The modern twist made it necessary to show the characters being hounded by the press, much in the manner of Liz and Dick in their daily lives. For the role of the chief reporter, a young and relentlessly aggressive type, there was only one person, so far as Burton, director Anthony Asquith, and screenwriter Terence Rattigan were concerned: the ubiquitous David Frost, who had recently transformed himself into a household name via his much-talked-about Saturday-night BBC program.

That Was the Week That Was, a revue composed of blackout sketches, irreverent songs poking fun at current political problems, and no-holds-barred satire, quickly became the program of choice for most people in Great Britain. As for the master of ceremonies, David Frost, people who liked him considered the commoner who had attended Cambridge on scholarship to be witty, urbane, and civilized; those who did not found him pompous, smug, and abrasive. Those alternate sets of qualities were on view stateside in 1964 when NBC imported Frost and company for a watered-down American version. Shortly, Frost was jetting back and forth across the Atlantic, appearing in *The Frost Report* for the BBC and the syndicated

Connie Francis as the young show-biz hopeful who wins a spot on The Tonight Show *with Johnny Carson in* Looking for Love.

David Frost Show for Westinghouse in the United States. Most observers felt his greatest hour came when Frost interviewed a post-Watergate Richard Nixon about his failed presidency.

JOHNNY CARSON

Looking for Love (1964)

Throughout his long, happy history on TV, Jack Benny regularly made self-deprecating gags about his motion picture performances, particularly *The Horn Blows at Midnight,* implying it was the worst movie ever made. Benny was a personal hero to Johnny Carson, the Iowa-born, Nebraska-bred comedian who in the 1960s combined Benny's droll deadpan humor with a sexy-schlepp quality not unlike that of the young Jack Lemmon. It made sense that, picking up a cue from his idol, Carson would continually crack jokes about his filmdom failure. In 1964, he had unwisely allowed himself to be talked into appearing opposite fading songstress Connie Francis in *Looking for Love,* a dim-witted combination of songs, romance, and comedy.

Francis plays a sweet young thing taking a shot at stardom and romance, hitting the big time on everyone's favorite late-night chat show. The big surprise was how stiff, awkward, and uncomfortable Carson appeared. This, despite the fact that beginning with his five-year run as host of ABC's daytime *Who Do You Trust?* (1957–62) and throughout his subsequent stint as the most popular of all *Tonight*

21

Arthur Godfrey (right) *clowns with fellow all-American institution Doris Day on the set of* The Glass Bottom Boat. *(courtesy MGM)*

Show hosts, Carson always appeared relaxed, easygoing, and totally spontaneous—despite the fact that many supposedly "improvised" bits between Carson and guests were scripted and rehearsed! Film proved to be his nemesis; the moment Carson became aware that his performance would be recorded forever on celluloid, this world-class entertainer unaccountably froze in his tracks. Though his role in *Looking for Love* called for little more than a rehash of his *Tonight Show* persona, Johnny came off like a bad Carson impressionist who repeats the famed mannerisms without projecting the legendary warmth and wit.

ARTHUR GODFREY

The Glass Bottom Boat (1966)

In 1966, two American institutions were brought together: Doris Day, last bastion of old-fashioned virginity in a world rapidly embracing free love, and Arthur Godfrey, veteran broadcaster who had built a virtual empire on informal folksy chatter. Rod Taylor played the scientist whose biography freelance writer Day has been hired to pen; Godfrey played her father. As pilot of the title boat, he whisks tourists around the old family river while warbling little ditties and accompanying himself on the ol' banjo. Though this was Godfrey's only major movie, he'd been honing his act for a quarter century.

Despite his abiding rural image as an adult Huck Finn, Godfrey was born in New York City in 1903. A runaway from his New Jersey home at age fourteen, he found work as everything from a coal miner to an architect's assistant, finally joining the Navy, where he was assigned to radio technical school. Later, he whimsically took a shot at on-air performance in Baltimore. Local success caused him to approach CBS, where as an announcer he stunned the nation by allowing his voice to register disgust at overwritten advertisements. Luckily, listeners were impressed

Florence Henderson had her only film role in what at moments appeared to be The Sound of Music *transplanted to Scandinavia:* Song of Norway. *(courtesy Cinerama Releasing Corporation)*

by what they perceived as his "honesty." When the emerging medium of television went mainstream in 1948, Godfrey became to CBS what Milton Berle was to ABC: an emerging TV network's first mainstay. But some always claimed that beneath his informal aura of genial cracker-barrel philosopher, a petty, smug personality lurked. The ruthless barefoot broadcaster boy played by Andy Griffith in *A Face in the Crowd,* who cynically manipulates public opinion and basks in his power to do so, was widely believed to be based on Arthur Godfrey.

FLORENCE HENDERSON

Song of Norway (1970)

Born the tenth and last child of a tobacco sharecropper in rural Indiana, Florence Henderson attended a Catholic school where her singing talents were nurtured by Benedictine sisters. Then a well-to-do family friend financed her move to New York City, where, at age seventeen, she won a role in Joshua Logan's short-lived 1951 musical, *Wish You Were Here.* Richard Rodgers spotted her scene-stealing work in that show and immediately cast Florence as Laurey in his road-company production of *Oklahoma!* As soon as that run was completed, Henderson played the title character in *Fanny* opposite Ezio Pinza. Still, despite being hailed as the next Mary Martin, she remains best known for her TV sitcom part as Carol in *The Brady Bunch* from 1969 to 1974, plus a brief-lived, barely remembered 1977 update called *The Brady Bunch Hour.*

There was also one movie, *Song of Norway,* in which Henderson was likewise cast as a fawning wife. Florence played Nina, spouse of composer Edvard Grieg (Toralv Maurstad), in a film version of the 1944 Robert Wright–George Forrest operetta. Andrew and Virginia Stone, disgusted by the direction in which

23

mainstream movies were going following the abandonment of the old studio Production Code, produced the film as a halfhearted alternative to the X-rated likes of Midnight Cowboy. Though the values were reminiscent of *The Sound of Music*, most critics found the movie's quality to be considerably less impressive. But mature viewers, starved for old-fashioned entertainment, made it a surprise box-office hit. Nonetheless, Henderson did not receive another film role until her brief cameo appearance in The Brady Bunch Movie a quarter century later.

DICK CAVETT

H.E.A.L.T.H. (1979)

Nebraska-born, Yale-educated Dick Cavett moved to New York in hopes of becoming an actor. When roles weren't forthcoming, he talked his way into a comedy-writing job with Jack Paar of *The Tonight Show*. After the temperamental star stormed off the set in April 1962, Cavett wrote for Groucho Marx, Jerry Lewis, then finally returned to his old spot at NBC, this time providing comedy lines for Johnny Carson. After a stint as a stand-up comic (Cavett attempted to become the WASP Woody Allen), he went up against Carson in the late-night slot, to some degree succeeding where others (Merv Griffin, Joey Bishop) had failed by offering an alternative rather than similar, inferior competition. Whereas Carson always emphasized mainstream entertainment for the vast canvas of America, Cavett created an urban-oriented show, appealing to more educated viewers. His coda—"ideas don't have to be dull"—allowed for frank discussions of the Vietnam War, the emerging counterculture, and civil rights, as well as serious literature.

But in his heart of hearts, Cavett still wanted to be an actor. Over the years, the format of his show has been used in many movies, with Cavett providing cameo appearances as an interviewer in, most recently, *Forrest Gump* and *Apollo 13*. Only once, though, has he portrayed himself in a central role. Dick provides the opening and closing bookend scenes, as well as the narrative perspective through which Robert Altman's *H.E.A.L.T.H.* is filtered. The film is set at a Florida hotel where an outlandish health-food convention is taking place. Diverse characters have arrived to partake of the events, each armed with his or her own agenda. Among the players were such noted performers as Carol Burnett, James Garner, Glenda Jackson, and Lauren Bacall, though it is Cavett who for once stands center stage throughout, mimicking his own televised tendency to be brash and buoyant at the same time.

CHUCK BARRIS
The Gong Show Movie (1980)

When people with half a brain happened to catch *The Gong Show* while spinning the dial in search of something decent to watch, they assumed that the producer/host, Chuck Barris, must have been one of those show business schlocky types willing to do absolutely anything for money, agreeing to create and appear in the most banal, inane show that pandered to the lowest common denominator of popular taste for however much money he could get. What an incredible shock, then, to catch the self-serving, self-righteous *Gong Show Movie* and realize Chuck Barris did not perceive himself that way at all. Instead of the expected collection of nostalgic clips and sentimental reminiscences about the daytime series for NBC (1976–78) that later continued in syndication, Barris and the film's cowriter, Robert Downey (Sr.), portrayed Barris as the Woody Allen of television, a gutsy, intellectual little guy who stood up to the middle-brow censors by trying to maintain standards, integrity, and a personal vision that was always

Chuck Barris, so often typed as a symbol of television at its very worst, portrayed himself as a courageous champion of groundbreaking entertainment in The Gong Show Movie. *(courtesy Universal City Studios)*

on the cutting edge of popular taste. In Barris's view, he had not been commercially turning out mindless trash all those years, but had rather been courageously fighting against all odds to get his brand of guerrilla television to the people.

Barris began his show business career as the writer of hit songs (including "Palisades Park" for Freddie Cannon) and later tried his hand as a novelist (*You and Me, Babe*) before moving into television. There, he helped to create such well-remembered (if not necessarily well-respected) shows as *The Dating Game, The Newlywed Game, Treasure Hunt, The $1.98 Beauty Show,* and *Three's a Crowd.* Barris also composed the theme songs for most of those shows. In *The Gong Show Movie,* Barris played himself in docudrama re-creations of his misadventures with network big shots and included segments from the series that had been considered too risqué for broadcast back then. Perhaps someday his vision of himself as a champion of offbeat television will be justified, and he will come to be seen as a pioneer of inventive, groundbreaking entertainment rather than the vulgarian he has generally been written off as.

25

Dr. Ruth Westheimer

One Woman or Two (1985)

In this Gallic variation on Howard Hawks's classic comedy *Bringing Up Baby*, Gerard Depardieu plays a stuffy paleontologist who discovers the fossilized bones from the very first prehistoric Frenchwoman. Sigourney Weaver is the calculating capitalist eager to exploit the situation in order to sell large quantities of her chichi perfume. That the two will fall in love rather than kill each other is insured by the presence of a teensy little lady with the voice of a giddy bird and the wisdom of a secular saint. Ostensibly a philanthropist eager to solve a sticky financial situation, the elderly third wheel ends up dispensing the same sort of sage sexual advice associated with the woman playing her. Dr. Ruth Westheimer—nicknamed Grandma Freud by the press owing to her popular radio show in which she insisted on the need for "good sex," without guilt—had become America's most famous media therapist since Dr. Joyce Brothers. Like her predecessor, Ruth was chastised by colleagues less for what she had to say than for her "vulgar" popularity with the general public.

Born Karola Ruth Siegel in Frankfurt, Germany, in 1928, the little girl had early on been drawn to things sexual in nature, secretly slipping into her dad's den to study his "forbidden" books. When the Nazis came to power, Ruth's parents sent her to safety in a Swiss school, where she freely dispensed sexual advice to her female classmates. Ruth's parents died in Auschwitz, after which she was among those lost European Jewish children who eventually ended up in Palestine. Growing up there, she trained as a sniper for the Israeli underground movement, also teaching kindergarten on a kibbutz. One marriage brought her to Paris, another to New York; all the while, Ruth studied psychology, eventually earning a doctorate. While lecturing to broadcasters about the need to promote "sexual literacy," she attracted the attention of one woman in the audience, an FM station's community-affairs manager. Dr. Ruth was invited to be a guest on WYNY's Sunday talk show. When audiences responded beyond anyone's expectations, she was given her own show, which immediately became a ratings success. Then it was on to superstardom via a nationally syndicated radio show, a lucrative publishing deal with Warner Books, and a nightly live spot on then-emerging cable TV's Lifetime network, prominent celebrities showing up to "ask Dr. Ruth" about their problems. "I dispense common sense [about sex] with a smile," Dr. Ruth cooed. That's precisely what her character did in Ruth's single film.

5
THE WIDE WORLD OF SPORTS

Athletes from around the world have attempted to turn their star turns on the playing fields into screen careers; most often, lightning strikes but once.

JOE LOUIS

Spirit of Youth (1938)

It had been a long haul from a windowless mountain shack without electricity in Lafayette, Alabama, to Hollywood, California. Still, Joe Louis slam-banged himself there by way of Detroit, where he began boxing at a local athletic club, dropping his actual last name, Barrow, so that his mother wouldn't be embarrassed by the violent sport he'd entered. Under the tutelage of trainer Jack Blackburn, Louis learned that style and skill were as significant as weight and muscle. Though he was defeated by Germany's Max Schmeling in 1936, Louis came back the following year to defeat Schmeling, winning the world heavyweight title and thereafter defending it successfully twenty-five times. Nicknamed the Brown Bomber, Louis was one of the first African-American boxers to become immensely popular with white fans, helping to break down existing barriers in pugilism much as Jackie Robinson would do for baseball in the early 1950s.

Understandably, then, Louis was picked for the lead in a 1938 motion picture that would be marketed by Grand National Company directly to those theaters that then played exclusively to black audiences, while the company also hoped and trusted that the movie—like its star—might exert crossover appeal. *Spirit of Youth,* written by Arthur Hoerl, typecast Joe as prizefighter "Joe Thomas," who almost muffs his chance at the title by forsaking his disciplined training and understanding girlfriend (Edna Mae Harris) when an alluring roadhouse siren (Cleo Desmond) spirits him off for some hot times in her irresistible arms. In true redemption-saga form, the hero temporarily stumbles but in time makes his comeback, doing the right thing with his stand-by-your-man woman as well as in the ring. Joseph F. Coughlin, critic for the *Motion Picture Herald,* noted in the January 8, 1938, issue that "when [Louis] gets into character and the ring, Joe is naturally convincing and in his own element. However, when the lines must be recited, Louis' famed deadpan expression becomes as uncomfortably heavy as some of the wooden words he must speak and as a result the situation at times becomes unintentionally humorous." Five years later, Sgt. Joe Louis requested the public to support their country by buying bonds in a cameo in Irving Berlin's patriotic grab bag, *This Is the Army.*

ALTHEA GIBSON

The Horse Soldiers (1959)

The civil rights movement, which swept society after school integration made this cause a national priority in 1955, hit Hollywood hard, impacting even on the work of older, traditional directors. While John Ford's cavalry trilogy of the late 1940s and early fifties had ignored the accomplishments of black soldiers, *Sergeant Rutledge* focused specifically on their plight. Naturally enough, when Ford decided to film a Civil War story, he considered it important to feature an African-American character who, though a slave, would project great dignity. For that role, the personal servant (and best friend) of Southern belle Hannah Hunter (Constance Towers), Ford chose a nonactor whose accomplishments made her perfect for the part.

That was Althea Gibson, who might be described as the female counterpart to Jackie Robinson. Just as he had pioneered the movement of black athletes into baseball, Gibson had done the same for tennis. Gibson had been raised in Harlem in New York, where as a teen she'd played paddle tennis on the street. After entering (and winning) the Park Department's annual Manhattan girls' competitions, Gibson realized she might have major talent. While a student at North Carolina's Industrial High School at Williston, she honed her craft and, in 1948 (at age twenty-one), won the National Negro women's singles contest, successfully defending her championship for the following nine years.

Attending Florida Agricultural and Mechanical University on an athletic scholarship, Gibson was in the right place at the right time. In 1950, former woman's tennis champion Alice Marble composed a vigorous essay for *American Lawn Tennis* magazine, complaining about what she called a "de facto color line" long overdue for removal. Althea Gibson was accepted into the national championships, the first African American to play against what was otherwise all-white competition at the National Singles in Forest Hills, Long Island. What sportswrit-

Ingemar Johansson was "introduced" in All the Young Men. *(courtesy Columbia Pictures)*

ers tagged her "slashing style" quickly established Gibson as a player to watch, though throughout the early fifties Gibson lost numerous matches and seriously considered early retirement from competition. Then, in 1955, Gibson was picked by the State Department as one of four American tennis players to tour Asia on a goodwill tour and came into her own.

Her crowning moment of glory occurred in July 1957, when she won the women's singles finals at Wimbledon, during which she defeated fellow American Darlene Hard, after which Gibson was presented to Queen Elizabeth II. Shortly thereafter, she was introduced to John Wayne and William Holden, with whom she would costar in her single movie. In it, Gibson projects all the warmth, intelligence, and courage that Ford needed for that part.

INGEMAR JOHANSSON

All the Young Men (1960)

Though integration of the U.S. Army belatedly began during the waning years of World War II, it was not until the Korean conflict that segregation was eliminated from our armed services. The interracial conflicts arising from that change were dramatized in *All the Young Men,* starring Alan Ladd as a rugged company commander attempting to maintain a sense of serenity within his outfit's ranks. Sidney Poitier portrayed a black soldier overcoming prejudice, while the whitest of the whites was played by Sweden's first-ever heavyweight world champion, Ingemar Johansson. Columbia Pictures had signed the handsome twenty-eight-year-old six-footer to a long-term contract shortly after his defeat of Floyd Patterson on June 26, 1959.

Actually, Johansson's life could provide ripe material for a movie. A native of Göteborg, Sweden, Johansson had dropped out of school at age fifteen, aimlessly wandering until that day when a visiting cousin, Ring Larson, described his bouts as a lightweight in America. Young Ingemar was inspired to start training. He fought for the first time in 1947, traveling to America for a Golden Gloves competition during which he knocked out Ernest Fann in Chicago. Then, at age nineteen, he fought Eddie Sanders at the Olympic trials in Helsinki, but was disqualified when officials insisted Johansson was refusing to fight.

Johansson was banished from amateur boxing, though he always claimed he'd been following his coach's advice to let his opponent spend himself first. Refusing to retire in disgrace, Johansson instead went professional, fighting a series of matches culminating in his knockout of Europe's reigning heavyweight, Franco Cavicchi, in Bologna. Then came the Patterson match, which Johansson won in the third round with what he himself called his "mystic" right-hand punch. Still, the hint of scandal continued to dog him. Allegations that the Patterson-Johansson match had been arranged by underworld figures led to a full investigation by the New York district attorney Frank Hogan. Though it turned out that racketeers were involved, this time Johansson himself escaped unscathed and moved on to his only film.

CAROL HEISS

Snow White and the Three Stooges (1961)

When Carol E. Heiss of Ozone Park won the world's championship skating crown in 1956 at age sixteen, she was the second-youngest international titlest ever, Sonja Henie having done it at age fifteen a quarter century earlier. No wonder, then, that Hollywood looked at the pretty, petite (five-foot-two-inch) blonde and wondered if she might become the next generation's Sonja Henie, starring in a succession of romantic musical skating movies. Unfortunately for Heiss, these were different times. The generation weaned on *The Wild One* and *Rebel Without a Cause* could hardly sit still for studio-bound, sweet-spirited concoctions about a vivacious girl who breaks men's hearts like so much thin ice. Still, Hollywood had to give Carol Heiss at least one shot, which they did, if halfheartedly, with *Snow White and the Three Stooges*.

The less-than-extravagant film was shot in 1960 after Heiss won the Olympics. This was one of several attempts to revive the theatrical careers of the Stooges, their zany shorts from the 1940s having been syndicated on television, creating a whole new generation of fans. But earlier filmmakers had sensed that a little bit of the Three Stooges went a long way, wisely relegating them to short subjects. Heiss was charming enough as Snow White on skates, but when the film

Carol Heiss shows the poise (and great legs) that helped her become an Olympic champion.

emphasized her character, the Stooges' die-hard fans stayed away in droves, while lovers of skating chose to pass owing to an aversion to the Stooges. All told, the matchup was not a happy one, but Heiss had already announced her decision to withdraw from competition after the 1960 Olympics. Despite her worldwide renown (though forgotten today, she was the Nancy Kerrigan of her time) she refused to go professional. When it became clear that a film career was not going to happen, Heiss took it in stride, announcing her intentions to continue her "education and marry and have a family." That was precisely the course she pursued.

JEAN-CLAUDE KILLY
Snow Job (1972)

In February 1968, Jean-Claude Killy won a triple Olympic crown, receiving the gold medals for downhill, giant slalom, and slalom events at the Grenoble Winter Olympics. He was only the second man in history to do so, Tony Sailer having swept all three back in 1956. Naturally, some enterprising people concocted a little item called Snow Job. One more of those then-popular Continental heist movies, George Englund's film was in the tradition of Rififi and Topkapi though not in their class so far as plot was concerned. A group of thieves steal $250,000, planning to escape by spiriting the money away on a forsaken ski trail. This device allowed Killy to show off his considerable athletic skills. His acting was something else entirely, and though veteran actor/director Vittorio De Sica was also in the cast, along with American performer Cliff Potts, the best anyone could come up with for a leading lady was Danielle Gaubert, a beautiful but vacuous Garbo

31

Jean-Claude Killy (right) *romances Danielle Gaubert. (courtesy Warner Bros.)*

look-alike who had appeared in Camille 2000, a soft-core remake of that legendary actress's most famous role. Snow Job may not have launched Killy on a film career, but he was already so busy that it didn't matter. He had recently grown interested in auto racing and was deluged with offers to appear in television specials, to serve as spokesman for companies that produced ski-related items, even to supervise his own line of ski equipment.

Not bad for a boy who never finished high school, and who would probably never have gone skiing in the first place were it not for a trick of fate. The eventual World Cup winner began life in a Paris suburb, but when his parents divorced, Killy's father won custody of the three children. So Jean-Claude, with his younger brother and sister, went off with Robert Killy when he opened a seventeen-room ski lodge in Val d'Isere in the French Alps. Robert decided to get to know his oldest son better by taking him up on the slopes and teaching him the fundamentals; imagine Dad's surprise when he realized Jean-Claude possessed remarkable talent. Before long, teenager Killy was skipping school to attend meets in places like Mont Blanc, eventually becoming a champ and, as a result, winning a single shot at movie stardom.

PANCHO GONZALES

Players (1979)

Dean-Paul Martin (himself a one-shot wonder) played a young tennis pro in this maudlin sports melodrama. His teacher and coach was played, in a case of perfect typecasting, by Richard Alonzo Gonzales, a.k.a Pancho. In fact, their scenes together are some of the best in the movie, whereas Martin's romantic moments with "older woman" Ali MacGraw are maudlin and tedious. For a nonprofessional actor, Gonzales was remarkably restrained and subtle as the onetime champ who helps his young protégé survive some humiliating defeats on the court. A Los

Angeles native, born in 1928, Gonzales was the most popular tennis player in the country during the late 1940s and fifties, handily winning the national singles championship in 1948 through his world-famous ultrapowerful drive; at the time, this qualified him as the second-youngest player ever to do so.

Intriguingly, Pancho began playing tennis when his mother became worried about football and other rough body sports that her son engaged in while a student at Edison Junior High, scrimping to buy her twelve-year-old a used fifty-cent racket for a Christmas present. A fellow teammate gave him the nickname Pancho and it stuck. He openly admitted that his perennial weaknesses were smoking, poker playing, and Mexican food. Pancho always scoffed at the routine of training and, though easygoing enough, remained an outsider even when at the top of his sport. Early on, Pancho learned the game by watching others play and never took a lesson throughout his life, though he assimilated enough skills and technique to effectively play young Martin's teacher in Players.

BRUCE JENNER

Can't Stop the Music (1980)

Ordinarily, a sports star makes his film debut in some movie designed to effectively exploit his athletic abilities. Not so Bruce Jenner, who here played a music-business executive overseeing the careers of the Village People, those gayly costumed princes of the late-1970s disco scene. Jenner hoped to appear as brash and charming on-screen as he had on the tracks and fields of the world's most demanding competitions, doing so within the context of Hollywood's first mainstream-homosexual backstage musical–romantic comedy– pseudo biopic, but came off looking confused, embarrassed, and woefully out of place: in a word, inept.

Descended from Edward Jenner, the Englishman who'd discovered the virus for smallpox, William Bruce Jenner excelled at various sports while attending high school in suburban Connecticut but showed a great propensity for waterskiing. While in college, he was encouraged to train for the decathlon and, excelling at the difficult ten-event/two-day competition, entered the Olympic trials. He competed respectably in the 1972 Olympics and then, in 1976's Montreal competitions, won the gold medal, setting both a world record and Olympic record in the 1,500-meter race. Upon his return home, Jenner was flooded with offers to appear on TV as a product spokesman, and there were a reported two dozen film offers. But "The World's Greatest Athlete" proved, by picking Can't Stop the Music, that he was far from the world's greatest chooser of film projects. The film, which cost more than $30 million (an incredible amount at the time), resembled an updating of one of the cheaply made 1950s rock-'n'-roll exploitation flicks, except that it cost a wad and appeared in theaters after the mercifully brief craze for the Village People had long since peaked. Jenner turned down the other opportunities then open to him, rather than risk further humiliation in Hollywood.

PELÉ

Victory (1981)

Pelé in action in his only major theatrical film, John Huston's Victory. *(courtesy Paramount Pictures)*

In Brazil, soccer is called "football" and it's the most popular sport, as it is virtually everywhere in the world but America. Players who win the hearts of ecstatic fans are invariably awarded some easily identifiable nickname. So it was that Edson Arantes do Nascimento came to be called Pelé, a nonsense term whose origin and meaning not even he can explain. Pelé hailed from provincial Brazil where his father played minor-league soccer. Before long, Pelé was skipping school in Bauru to practice with a makeshift ball he'd fashioned from old, discarded socks. Dropping out after completing fourth grade, he determined to be the world's best at a game he devotedly loved. Playing inside left forward for the Santos Football Club beginning in 1956, he led that team to two world championships, in 1962 and 1963. "Within a year," *Reader's Digest* reported, "Pelé had become a legend throughout his own land. . . . Loping or sprinting, he could drag the ball from one foot to the other as if it were a yo-yo on the end of an invisible string." Shortly, the onetime street kid was the most immediately recognized athlete in the world, at least outside of the United States. However, a cult for soccer had belatedly begun to grow here in the 1970s, making the game—and Pelé—marketable stateside.

One possibility was movies, especially if he was allowed to play the role of a soccer star. In 1981, John Huston gave Pelé that opportunity, offering him a role in *Victory*, a cross between *The Longest Yard* and *The Great Escape*. In it, a team of Allied POWs must decide whether to flee their German captors given the opportunity or stick around long enough to finish a climactic soccer game in which they can trounce the Nazi team, thereby disproving Hitler's theory about the white superrace. Pelé, top-billed alongside Michael Caine and Sylvester Stallone, managed to virtually steal the show with a technique perfectly described in *Sports Illustrated*: "When he rushes through the offensive zone toward a goal, Pelé captures the imagination in a way that only the most dramatic of athletes can." His sweet, silly, highly captivating on-screen personality later led to roles in two small-budget movies, 1983's *A Minor Miracle* and 1986's *Hot Shot,* though neither was ever released theatrically in the United States.

SUZY CHAFFEE

Fire and Ice (1987)

In the mid-1970s, everyone agreed that Olympic skier turned model Suzy Chaffee was as pretty as a movie star. The question was, would it be possible to find the kind of vehicles for her that had, in the old days of Hollywood, transformed ice-skating star Sonja Henie into a true queen of the silver screen? In fact, could skiing prove as photogenic as ice-skating? This was, of course, the era of women's liberation, and so Suzy's athletic abilities, coupled with her blond good looks, might just allow her to have it both ways: attractive enough to become an old-fashioned clean-cut sex symbol, while also a fitting role model for the modern sensibility that required images of strong women. She made her acting debut in *Ski Lift to Death,* a 1978 made-for-TV mystery in which Suzy costarred with such minor-league names as Deborah Raffin, Charles Frank, and Don Galloway. Suzy provided a brief respite from the tedium surrounding a murder at an isolated ski lodge, showing off her considerable skills—at skiing, not acting.

Still, her name recognition was as "Suzy Chap Stick," spokesperson for the popular product that kept people's mouths kissable even when exposed to the rough winds in wintertime. Then, filmmaker Willy Bogner announced his intention to feature the freestyle champion in a $3-million sports musical that would propel her to true, full-blown stardom. Fans waited and wondered; what they got was a short (eighty-three minutes) yet long-winded and annoyingly disjointed compilation of skiing footage, accompanied by inappropriately dubbed in music and mindless narration. Suzy Chaffee played Suzy, a lady skier who fantasizes while freestyling on some German slopes, wondering if she'll ever meet Mr. Right Ski Guy. Meanwhile, John (John Eaves) is doing much the same thing, hoping to meet the perfect Ski Lady. The film cuts back and forth between images of the two; when they do finally meet, the viewer is too bored to care. Barely released to theaters, the movie was eventually dumped on home video, but no one cared to rent it, nor did anyone ever suggest hiring Suzy Chaffee for another film.

6
MAKE MINE MUSIC

Having created the music that made the whole world feel good for many years, they were tapped for acting roles in major movies.

LEOPOLD STOKOWSKI

100 Men and a Girl (1937)

A rarity among highbrow music makers, Leopold Antoni Stanislaw Stokowski was always fascinated by the popular cinema and its ability to convey excellent music to the masses, if presented in easily accessible middlebrow entertainment. That helps explain why he was the sole maestro who agreed to work with Walt Disney on the *Fantasia* project, in which he actually shared the podium with Mickey Mouse at one point. It also allows us to understand why he would agree to act in a light-comedy vehicle for Deanna Durbin, one of the goody-goody debutante starlets so popular with young people during the latter days of the Great Depression. In this upbeat musical, Durbin played Patricia Cardwell, the organizer, manager, agent, and soprano for a group of out-of-work musicians who included Adolphe Menjou and Mischa Auer among the scene-stealing cast of character actors. Making "the impossible seem only moderately improbable," as Frank S. Nugent put it in the *New York Times,* Durbin's Patricia managed to find a sponsor for her "one hundred men," then charmed the country's greatest maestro into becoming their conductor after slipping into his country retreat with the entire entourage and having them captivate the genius with their rendition of Liszt's second Hungarian Rhapsody.

Perhaps in real life he might have called the police; no matter, for this was the fantasy world of movies during Hollywood's golden age, and optimism was still the byword. Stokowski had been born in London, England, in 1882 and graduated

36

Leopold Stokowski gets ready to film a scene for 100 Men and a Girl. *(courtesy Universal Productions)*

from Queens College, Oxford University. Arriving in America in 1905, he served as music director in Cincinnati and Philadelphia, later touring the country as conductor of the All-American orchestra. Attracted to the very mass media that others of his ilk found repellingly déclassé, Stokowski decided to upgrade the quality of the airwaves by accepting a position with the National Broadcasting Symphony Orchestra in 1941, allowing him to build on his previous film experience. Three years later, he founded the New York City Symphony Orchestra, then moved on to a position with the New York Philharmonic. His happy acceptance of film, radio, and TV as possible means of communicating classical music to the public may have been responsible for the title of a book in which he explained his attitudes, *Music for All of Us.*

FRANK LOESSER

Red, Hot and Blue (1949)

When that brassy blonde Betty Hutton was cast to play Eleanor Collier—a screachy aspiring singer trying to break into show business in *Red, Hot and Blue*—director John Farrow needed proper types to perfectly portray the Runyonesque tough guys surrounding her. So William Demarest was cast as fast-talking Broadway press agent Charles Baxter, whose job is to get her plenty of press coverage, a tactic that goes overboard when Eleanor witnesses a gangland killing. As mob kingpin "Hairdo" Lempke, who kidnaps Eleanor as the finger woman, Farrow settled on Frank Loesser, arguably the most successful songwriter in Hollywood at the time though hardly an accomplished actor. Yet under Farrow's masterful guidance, Loesser turned in an appealing comedic take on the traditional Hollywood version of a Manhattan wise guy.

Loesser had been born in New York City on June 29, 1910. From the time he was a child, Frank was never interested in anything but writing songs. Early on, he drifted into jazz, penning lyrics for the Fats Waller composition "I Wish I Were Twins" in 1934. Then Loesser headed for Hollywood and a movie songwriting career. His first major break came when legendary director John Ford accepted his lyrics to "Moon of Manakoora" as accompaniment for Alfred Newman's haunting score to *The Hurricane*. Then came collaborations with Hoagy Carmichael and Jule Styne, until Loesser finally broke out on his own, turning out melodies as well as words. That began with "Praise the Lord (and Pass the Ammunition)," the most popular of all World War II pieces of pop-music propaganda. Later hits included "Spring Will Be a Little Late This Year" for *Christmas Holiday* (1944) and "Baby, It's Cold Outside" for *Neptune's Daughter* (1949). Following *Red, Hot and Blue,* Loesser abandoned films for years, heading back East where he became one of Broadway's best suppliers of hit scores for a succession of big shows including *Where's Charley?, Guys and Dolls, The Most Happy Fella,* and *How to Succeed in Business (Without Really Trying)*. A workaholic and chain smoker, he died of cancer on July 28, 1969.

ROBERT MERRILL

Aaron Slick From Punkin Crick (1952)

From Ezio Pinza to Placido Domingo, opera stars have regularly appeared in movies, but Robert Merrill almost lost his standing with the Metropolitan Opera Company as a result of his desire for mainstream film stardom. In 1951, Merrill found himself in a precarious position, having signed to do a Paramount picture during the summer, though also contracted with the Met to appear in their annual spring tour. Merrill bolted for the West Coast, causing managerial director Rudolf Bing to announce the Met's beloved baritone had violated his agreement and would not perform when the new season opened in the fall. *Aaron Slick From Punkin Crick* was not a full "book" musical but a late minor entry in the "rube comedy" genre: the cinematic predecessor to TV's *Green Acres* and *Petticoat Junction*. Merrill played a big-city crook who, with the help of his gun moll (Adele Jergens), takes a sweet young widow (Dinah Shore) for all she's worth, until a decent bumpkin (Alan Young) comes to her rescue. Merrill mugged it up like a handsomer Sheldon Leonard and sang several songs, none memorable.

What could he have been thinking of? To understand, it's worth recalling that Merrill did not initially dream of opera stardom, hoping during his Brooklyn boyhood to someday be a popular crooner, much in the manner of Bing Crosby. His immigrant mother, who had performed opera during her youth in Russia, wisely let young Robert go his own way, playing baseball and working in his father's shoe store, while also providing training for the obviously talented boy soprano. In 1935, when Robert turned sixteen, she took him to see *Il Trovatore* at the Met, positive he would be inspired by the performance. He was, though for the next several years Robert opted for moneymaking gigs in the Catskills, appear-

ances on NBC radio, and recording sessions for the Red Seal label. With seven hundred thousand copies sold, his 1949 recording of "The Whiffenpoof Song" nearly hit gold status. Hollywood proved to be the ultimate test of loyalties. When *Aaron Slick* opened to virtually no business, then quickly closed, and Paramount made no further overtures, Merrill humbly approached Rudolf Bing at Austria's Salzburg Festival. His one-time mentor took the penitent prodigal back, but only if Merrill began by working on the upcoming spring tour, to compensate for the one he'd missed two years earlier. Merrill hastily agreed, accepting that his lot in life was to be a tony opera star, never trying his hand at Hollywood again.

"Lee" Liberace charms Dorothy Malone in Sincerely Yours, *his only leading role.*

LIBERACE

Sincerely Yours (1955)

In January 1952, a then thirty-three-year-old unknown pianist from Wisconsin, billed simply as Liberace, made his television debut on Los Angeles TV station KLAC, when that fledgling operation desperately needed an inexpensive filler for an afternoon slot. An overnight sensation with the area's middle-aged housewives, the ever-grinning Liberace (real name, Wladziu Valentino Liberace) became convinced his show could go network. When no national sponsor was forthcoming, the undaunted impresario arranged to have his performances filmed and mailed directly to stations around the country, helping to create the now-popular concept called syndication. Shortly, Liberace was seen on more stations than *Dragnet* and *I Love Lucy*.

Hailing from a musical family, "Lee" (who initially billed himself as Walter Busterkeys) always hoped to make music pay off big-time. He recalled seeing a lighted candelabra on a grand piano in *A Song to Remember,* the film biogra-

Oreste, touted by Paramount as their sexy new discovery, in The Vagabond King *with Rita Moreno. (courtesy Paramount Pictures)*

phy of Chopin, and borrowed that bit for his act, also favoring the sequined costumes of a Vegas performer. The result—a middlebrow misconception of classy music that appealed mainly to little old ladies from Pasadena—was ridiculed by intellectuals as kitsch.

Only one major attempt was made to turn Liberace into a movie star, the embarrassingly overwrought *Sincerely Yours,* a reworking of the dated George Arliss vehicle *The Man Who Played God.* Director Gordon Douglas cast the less than imposing musician opposite one of the most strongly sexual women then on the screen, Dorothy Malone. In their creepy love scenes together, she appears ready to devour him whole. On the big screen, and with his uncertain voice lilting in full stereo sound, Liberace's lines elicited laughter, though the ambition had not been to make a comedy. Wisely, he forsook a Hollywood career, sticking to a Columbia Records contract and concert tours, though he did later make several cameo appearances in films, including a brief bit as a fruity funeral-home tour guide in *The Loved One* (1965).

ORESTE

The Vagabond King (1956)

Throughout the 1950s, Hollywood producers clung to the belief that filmed operettas, so popular two decades earlier, would still work, if presented in modernized versions featuring color, wide-screen projection, and stereo sound. So they tried, and failed, with updated versions of *Rose Marie, The Desert Song,* and *The Vagabond King.* For the latter, Paramount decided it had to have an exciting new star, with a grand tenor voice and a charisma that could captivate the women of the world. They thought they'd found their man in Oreste Kirkop, "discovered" by their London representative, Richard Mealand, who screen-tested Oreste performing with the full London Philharmonic, then shipped the results to Hollywood. Aware that several British filmmaking companies were also wooing

Oreste, Paramount rushed him to America and signed the thirty-year-old performer to a contract, keeping him under wraps for nine months while coaching him in the niceties of screen performance. In the film, Oreste played François Villon, legendary poet-philosopher, a dazzler with words as well as sword and a hellion with the women, who fought to make France free for all men of good faith.

Rudolf Friml went so far as to create seven brand-new songs for Oreste to sing, in addition to his original score. The film was directed by the esteemed Michael Curtiz, but nothing could offset that Oreste was bland and, the high quality of his singing aside, couldn't act to save his life. The son of a French ship chandler and an Italian mother, Oreste was born on the island of Malta, qualifying him as a British citizen. During endless bombing by Germany during World War II, he, his parents, and his eight brothers and sisters hid in the island's rocky caves that had been dug centuries earlier, during the war with the Turks. Though he'd never taken a lesson, Oreste loved to sing; his brothers had bought a mouth organ, and later an accordian, to pass the time in the caves. Their neighbors appreciated the makeshift serenades, so after the war, Oreste was accepted as a member of the local opera company. The Carl Rose Opera invited him to audition in London, so soon he was performing at Convent Garden. When *The Vagabond King* opened and quickly closed, Oreste wisely beat a hasty retreat to his first love, live theater.

MAHALIA JACKSON

Imitation of Life (1959)

Born in New Orleans in 1911, Mahalia Jackson cut her teeth on gospel at an early age and, during most of the sixty-one years of her life, worked hard at making her unique genre of American music accessible to the public. Fans of popular music were always hoping Mahalia would embrace jazz and blues, expanding the range of material that she performed with her stunning contralto voice. But Jackson would have none of it. Rather than become the next Bessie Smith or another Billie Holiday, Mahalia Jackson remained the person she wanted to be, earning her reputation as the greatest gospel singer of all time. As a young girl growing up in Chicago, she even turned down an offer by Earl Hines to join his popular music group, continuing to work as a maid while singing with church choirs. To survive financially, Mahalia tried everything from running a beauty salon to a flower shop, finally securing a contract from Decca Records in 1937 to cut gospel albums—and *only* gospel! Even when she played the Newport Jazz Festival in 1957, Mahalia had agreed to appear only if she could sing "The Lord's Prayer."

She can be seen as well as heard performing gospel in several films, but tried a full-fledged acting role only once, in the 1959 remake of Fannie Hurst's durable potboiler *Imitation of Life*, about two women friends, one white and one

As a tenement drug addict, Ella Fitzgerald is menaced by her ruthless pusher (Ricardo Montalban) in Let No Man Write My Epitaph. (courtesy Columbia Pictures)

black, and their difficulties in raising teenage daughters. Lana Turner and Sandra Dee played the white women; Juanita Moore and Susan Kohner were their black companions, though the tragedy of Kohner's character was that as a light-skinned black woman, she attempted to pass for white, precipitating calamity for all. This misguided action ultimately causes the premature death of her own mother. At the funeral, Mahalia Jackson—playing the mother's best friend—mournfully sang "Trouble of the World," adding a moment of simple solemn integrity to a film that was otherwise full of overwrought sentimental emotions.

ELLA FITZGERALD

Let No Man Write My Epitaph (1960)

In *Let No Man Write My Epitaph,* novelist Willard Motley told the tragic story of Nick Romano Jr., living with a drug-addicted mother after the execution of his young father, the subject of an earlier book, *Knock on Any Door,* which had been Hollywoodized in 1949. *Epitaph* was finally filmed in 1960, with singing star James Darren as Nick, Shelley Winters as his pathetic mother, Ricardo Montalban as her pusher/lover, and first lady of song Ella Fitzgerald in the role of an addict. Despite an excellent performance, she instead concentrated her energies on nurturing a natural talent as the world's most acclaimed "scat" singer, a term coined to describe the combination of a breathless pace and nonsense-syllable improvisation that allowed Fitzgerald to sing in such diverse genres as Dixieland, calypso, swing, and pop ballad, while always endowing each number with her unique stamp while maintaining the essence of the individual song.

  Born in Newport News, Virginia, in 1918, Fitzgerald early on came to New York to live in a Yonkers orphanage, then at age fifteen entered an amateur talent contest at the legendary Apollo Theatre, where she was spotted by jazz drummer Chick Webb and was immediately offered the job as vocalist with his band. They collaborated on "A-Tisket A-Tasket" in 1938, based on Ella's concept for an implicitly naughty riff on the innocent old childhood rhyme. With Webb, then later on her own, Ella broke down the color barriers; her natural elegance, coupled with enormous talent, enabled her to cross over to middlebrow white audiences. Her vocal talents made her a natural for jazz movies, so she sang specialty numbers in *Pete Kelly's Blues* (1955) with Jack Webb as the title artist, and in *St. Louis Blues* (1958) starring Nat King Cole as W. C. Handy before playing her single dramatic role in *Let No Man Write My Epitaph*.

ODETTA

Sanctuary (1961)

In William Faulkner's 1931 novel *Sanctuary*, about a rape and murder in rural Mississippi, the Southland's answer to Shakespeare created his most fully realized African-American character, the tortured Nancy, who succumbs to madness, murdering a child in a desperate attempt to salvage the reputation of her white mistress. When British-born Tony Richardson set about filming an uncompromised version in 1961, he could envision only one person in the role: the acclaimed folksinger Odetta. Her contemporary interpretations of blues, ballads, and spirituals caused critics to enthusiastically hail her as the logical heir to Mahalia Jackson and Bessie Smith.

Odetta (Holmes) was thirty-one when she shot the film; she was already a legendary performer. Born in Birmingham, Alabama, to a steel-mill-worker father and working-domestic mother, Odetta experienced firsthand the plight of the working class, which she would later crystallize in concert performances. When she was six, Odetta's family moved to California; several years later, her high school voice instructor was thrilled to discover in her glee club a young woman who might just be the next Marian Anderson. Odetta herself believed her calling was classical; then, she won a role in a touring company of *Finian's Rainbow*. While in San Francisco, Odetta visited the fabled club hungry i, immediately sensing she'd found her calling. Soon her musical performances were sandwiched in between beat-generation poets reading their verse. Odetta recorded an album for Tradition Records in 1956. Like her mentor, Harry Belafonte, Odetta insisted on a middle ground between the extremes of commercial folk (The Kingston Trio) and of absolute authenticity (Cisco Houston), performing in a style just mainstream enough to catch on with the general public, yet always true to the music's origins and intentions. Her strong, sincere contralto voice added the proper tragic touch to her single screen role.

Maria Callas
Medea (1970)

Though she would have seemed the logical candidate for leading roles in opera movies, Maria Callas's single film role was in a nonmusical: the title character in eccentric Italian director Pier Paolo Pasolini's 1970 screen adaptation of Euripides' Greek tragedy *Medea,* following the horrifying later days in the life of adventurer Jason's wife. Medea punishes her sexually errant husband by killing all their children, the ultimate vengeance of a woman scorned. Critics marveled at Callas's conviction and complexity in bringing one of the most difficult roles ever written to vivid life on-screen, making Medea not only understandable but even sympathetic as she enacts what can only be considered the most unimaginable crime a mother can commit. Relying mainly on her penetrating eyes, Callas accomplished her goal without depending on that remarkable

Despite her operatic gifts, Maria Callas's only film role was a straight dramatic one, playing Jason's wife who kills their children as an act of vengeance following his infidelity.

soprano voice that had amazed and enraptured a generation of opera fans, not to mention a certain Greek tycoon.

Born in New York City in 1923 (real name, Maria Kalogeropoulos) to a hardworking druggist and his nonmusical wife, Maria was intently listening to opera on the family Pianola at age three, taking singing lessons at eight, and performing recitals at P.S. 164 at nine. At thirteen, she was studying at the Royal Conservatory in Athens, Greece, on a scholarship, where Spanish soprano Elvira Hidalgo became her mentor. Years later, Hidalgo recalled that in addition to a strikingly individualistic voice, the child's "willpower was terrific." Making an acclaimed debut in *Cavalleria Rusticana* at the age of fourteen, young Callas wowed all of Europe, then returned to America, her presence insuring the success of the Chicago Opera's first (1954–55) season. Callas moved on to the Metropolitan in New York two years later at the urging of Rudolf Bing. Arrogant and abrasive, Callas refused to pay her dues (it was always leading roles or nothing for her), also

44

refusing to pay agents their 10 percent. Gradually, she shed many of the 210 pounds that initially constrained her career, charming the Italian millionaire Giovanni Batista Meneghini (twenty years her senior) into marriage. After a Met performance of *Tosca* in 1965, Callas set her opera career aside to serve as Aristotle Onasis's full-time mistress, a dubious occupation that conflicted with Ari's eventual desire to pursue and marry Jacqueline Kennedy. When the ugly fireworks were through, she accepted Pasolini's offer. Though Callas's stunning debut in *Medea* suggested an entire new career lay before her, the notoriously temperamental star turned down all other screen offers. She died on September 16, 1977.

Teresa Stratas

La Traviata (1982)

"The new Callas" is how opera critics described Teresa Stratas when, in 1959, she debuted as the Met's new star, for physically as well as in emotional temperament she resembled Greek opera star Maria. Stratas, perhaps best known for her role in *La Bohème* but in fact a remarkably versatile soprano, had been born in Toronto in 1938 on the dining room table of the small, dingy apartment over a Chinese laundry in which her destitute parents lived. So as to run their diner unencumbered by the child, little Anastasia's mother would hand the child a quarter for the movies; she would return mimicking Betty Hutton's musical roles. Shortly, Teresa sang semiprofessionally at neighborhood weddings, then went on local TV to perform pop songs, finally turning to serious music after being awarded a scholarship to Toronto University's Royal Conservatory of Music. Initially ignorant of opera, even considering it a phony form of show fit only for rich snobs, Teresa had to be dragged to a Puccini production, where she was stunned to find herself swept up by the magic.

From then on, Teresa Stratas was dedicated to the form. Despite her instantaneous fame, notorious beauty, and impressive talent, she appeared in only one studio movie, of all things, a B western! Teresa played a bit part as a frontier woman in *The Canadians* with Robert Ryan, little seen at the time, almost never revived afterward, all but lost today. Burned by the bad experience, Stratas stuck with American and European stage roles until Franco Zeffirelli's 1982 *La Traviata*, Verdi's operatic version of the legendary love story *Camille* by Alexandre Dumas *fils*. Stratas—who always appeared at her best when playing women of immense, intense character but dubious reputation—was the doomed Violetta, with Placido Domingo her forlorn lover. At once true to the source yet supremely cinematic, the film is rightly considered one of the best (if not *the* best) opera movie ever made.

7
CENTERFOLD GIRLS

M arilyn Monroe was a movie star when she posed for the first issue of *Playboy;* ever since, the gatefold girls in that magazine, and its chief competitor, *Penthouse,* have been trying to go the other way.

CHINA LEE

What's Up, Tiger Lily? (1966)

In the early 1960s, Woody Allen was the darling of *Playboy,* writing humorous articles for the magazine, appearing in advertisements for various products such as Smirnoff gin, even showing up for an occasional pictorial in which he comic-ally posed with the pretty girls, living out the fantasies of every guy who gazed at the magazine and wished he could trade places with that lucky nebbish who also hap-pened to be a literary and cinematic genius in the making. It made sense, then, that when Allen shot one of his first films during the swinging sixties, he cast one of *Playboy's* highly popular models opposite himself, doing a kind of cinematic replay of those humorous pictorials. Having been burned while working on the big-budget project *What's New, Pussycat?* in 1965, Allen believed that he might achieve more freedom on a B film, so he agreed to create an entirely new and com-ical voice track for one of those imported Japanese-made imitations of the James Bond films. Now, whenever one of the Asian characters opened his mouth to speak, the voice of Woody or one of his friends was heard instead.

For some new footage, Woody played himself—the writer/director/ "auteur" of the project—attempting to work on his intellectual endeavors while a breathtaking Asian beauty tempted him with a striptease. She was Chinese, not Japanese, though nobody worried about that very much. China Lee had been *Playboy's* August 1964 centerfold. Born in New Orleans, the five-foot-four-inch beauty worked as a "training bunny in Chicago," teaching other girls how to wag their tails and appear to be on the verge of popping out of their bodices while serv-

46

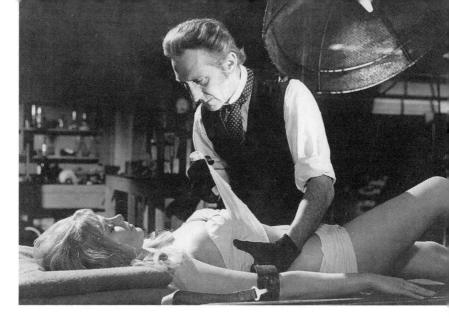

Dr. Frankenstein (Peter Cushing) creates a woman, who, in the person of Playmate Susan Denberg, becomes more dangerous than his famed monster. (courtesy Warner Bros.)

ing drinks to businessmen at the various Playboy Clubs, then at the height of their popularity. An equestrian and a swimmer, she apparently had a taste for intellectual comics; China Lee married a contemporary of Woody's, political satirist Mort Sahl, and retired from show business with only this one film to her credit.

SUSAN DENBERG
Frankenstein Created Woman (1967)

In the midsixties, when Austrian and German beauties such as Elke Sommer and Senta Berger were all the rage in Hollywood, another such import appeared likely to hit the big time: Susan Denberg, a perfectly proportioned blonde who hailed from Klagenfurt, Austria. From her childhood days, friends and relatives had told Susan she was gorgeous enough to be a movie star, so she set out in pursuit of what would prove to be an elusive dream, first heading to London, where she danced in the chorus line of the sexy Bluebells. That led her to Vegas, where she also danced, this time at the Stardust. Scouts for *Playboy* spotted her and offered Susan a centerfold spot; she was Playmate of the Month in August 1966. One look at her layout convinced Warner Brothers that they ought to put Susan Denberg under contract. But for reasons known only to themselves, they felt it necessary to change her name.

So they held a contest, in which the public was encouraged to send in ideal names for this future star, the winning entry to receive $500. Of the over five thousand entries, none seemed right, so eventually executives decided the perfect name for Susan Denberg was Susan Denberg. She was slipped into a decorative bit part in *An American Dream,* a dismal film version of Norman Mailer's acclaimed novel. Then came her leading role, in the British-lensed *Frankenstein Created*

Woman, Hammer's most bizarre variation of the Mary Shelley classic. Terence Fisher, chief director of their series of subdued, color horror films, helmed this story in which the venerable doctor (Peter Cushing) puts a madman's brain into the body of a beautiful young blonde, who then seduces and murders—rather than merely maims—Dr. Frankenstein's enemies. There were no further Susan Denberg films. What went wrong? In 1975, Denberg—living in London—issued the following statement: "I held out for top scripts and turned down a dozen [pieces of junk]. I should have kept working. Instead, I lazed around my expensive flat, squandering my money on clothes and jewelry."

CONNIE KRESKI

Can Hieronymus Merkin Ever Forget Mercy Humppe and Find True Happiness? (1969)

Connie Kreski, *Playboy*'s January 1968 centerfold, also named Playmate of the Year in June 1969, met actor-writer-director-composer Anthony Newley in a lift at the London Playboy Club. She was twenty-one at the time, and Newley was stunned by the vivacious blonde's presence. Though their conversation was brief, Newley remembered Kreski when he began work on a sexy screenplay for himself and then-wife Joan Collins. The film would be a Fellini-esque fantasy about a Newley-like performer. He envisioned it as an X-rated cinematic version of his hit play *Stop the World (I Want to Get Off),* combining allegory and autobiography in a symbolic tale of a song-and-dance man, his estranged wife (in fact, Newley and Collins would shortly separate), and the dream girl who continually passes through his consciousness. Kreski's abundant nude scenes qualified this as one of the first mainstream movies to earn the recently established X-rating, though it's tame by today's standards.

A native of Wyandotte, Michigan, Kreski was of Polish ancestry; her father worked in a Detroit steel factory. Kreski was a psychiatric nurse, modeling part-time, when on a date with a doctor she'd met at the hospital she went to the racetrack and was introduced to one of his friends, a sports editor for *Playboy,* who suggested she send in her picture, which she did. Kreski used her centerfold money to go to London, where she modeled, also receiving a seven-year contract from Universal Pictures. They promised to develop her as an important star, but nothing happened movie-wise until the Newley film; when that flopped, so did her hopes for screen stardom. The 34-23-35 blonde met actor James Caan at the Playboy Mansion and entered into a four-year, highly volatile relationship with the star. Afterward, Kreski continued modeling for several years, then found work at the Playboy Studios West working behind the camera, as a stylist for the next generation of centerfold girls.

MARY AND MADELEINE COLLINSON
Twins of Evil (1972)

An all-too-willing victim is seduced by the title characters, played by Mary and Madeleine Collinson, in Twins of Evil. *(courtesy Universal Pictures)*

Natives of Malta, the Collinson twins were eighteen years old and living in En-gland when they were tapped to be *Playboy*'s first twin playmates, gracing the pages of that magazine's October 1970 issue. They made a cameo appearance in *The Love Machine,* a big-budget bomb, before they went on to the single film in which the two received star billing: *Twins of Evil,* one of the stylish period horror movies that Hammer had been turning out ever since their 1959 remake of *Dracula* (*Horror of Dracula* in America) proved a sensation. Hammer was famous for bringing a new realism to the horror film, eliminating all of the clichés that had become basic to the genre ever since Universal began churning out black-and-white thrillers during the early 1930s. The public, which had in the early days of sound been terrified at the sight of Karloff, Lugosi, and Chaney skulking about on fairy-tale-like studio sets, with dry-ice fog drifting in and melodramatic music blaring away, now found such images rather charming when those films showed up on TV.

Needed was a new approach, so Hammer's filmmakers opted instead for subtle acting by Shakespearean veterans, full-color photography that provided a lush and sensuous appearance, and on-location filming in actual villages and castles. They also beefed up the elements of sex and violence, which in their films of the early-to-mid-1960s were notably more vivid than anything seen before, yet still within the limits of the then-existing Production Code. When that value system disappeared late in 1967, Hammer went all out, offering a kinky mixture of flowing blood and abundant nudity, making clear for the first time what had always been suggested by this genre: in vampire films, sex and death are closely linked. In addition to Christopher Lee's *Dracula* series, there were Carmilla Karnstein films, in which the beautiful vampire woman dominated both men and other women through the evil power of her eroticism. *Twins of Evil* was one of Hammer's most successful variations on this theme, also playing off the "evil twin" ploy: it was impossible for anyone to tell which of the two seemingly angelic young women on-screen was actually the predatory vampire.

8
MODEL BEHAVIOR

From Lauren Bacall to Lauren Hutton, an occasional model really did become a movie star; more often, though, the status lasted for a single stint at top billing.

FRANCES RAMSDEN

The Sin of Harold Diddlebock (1947)

Since the parents of Cambridge, Massachusetts, native Frances Ramsden divorced early on, the girl spent her early years in an Ohio Episcopalian convent and, by age sixteen, had determined to become a nun. Her mother superior insisted she consider other options first, just to be sure, so shortly Frances was instead living in New York where she worked as a Conover model. During a visit to Hollywood, she was invited to lunch at Paramount, where she met the inimitable director Preston Sturges, who immediately noticed that Ramsden's bangs caused her to look like another, younger Colleen Moore, the actress whom Sturges had written screenplays for some fifteen years earlier. He invited Ramsden to stop by the studio for a screen test, but she failed to take him up on the offer, instead marrying Paul de Loqueyssie, a French Army officer who had come to America to escape the Nazis.

De Loqueyssie wanted to be a writer, but since nothing he turned out was published, the couple had to live on money Ramsden borrowed from friends. Bored and nearly bankrupt, the actress called Sturges one day; he had not forgotten her appealingly elfin face. She asked if the screen-test offer was still open, he insisted it was, but at the last moment she got cold feet and failed to show. Then, she and de Loqueyssie divorced after he brutally struck her. Ramsden planned to return to New York, where her agent had obtained for her a small role in the upcoming play *Flamingo Road*. She went out to the Players restaurant to celebrate, unaware it was owned by none other than Preston Sturges. He stopped by the table, making one final offer for a screen test. The following day, she read for the female lead in an upcoming film headlining legendary funnyman Harold Lloyd. She was so convincing in the role of Miss Otis, youngest of the seven sisters Lloyd's character loves throughout his lifetime, that she was awarded the role on the spot. Though critics lauded her work, the mystery lady quickly retreated from the spotlight, never appearing in another film.

VERUSCHKA
Blowup (1966)

Anyone searching for the single film that bridges the traditional commercial story-driven picture with the experimental, reality-based avant-garde modern cinema need look no further than *Blowup,* the first of Michelangelo Antonioni's movies to play mainstream theaters rather than the art-house circuit. David Hem-

Veruschka strolls through "mod" London on the way to a modeling session.

mings, perfectly incarnating the post-Beatles style of contemporary hipness, was the photographer caught in what might or might not be a case of murder, his situation halfway between Hitchcock and Kafka. What everyone remembered most vividly was the opening sequence, in which "Thomas" photographs several models in his studio, as snapping pictures turns into a perverse substitute for sex. Most noticeable among the girls was Veruschka, the six-foot beauty who had recently revolutionized glamour and so seemed the perfect symbolic choice for this thriller set against the back alleys of ultramod London.

She'd been born Vera Lehndorff in 1940, daughter of Prussia's Count Heinrich, who was executed during the war when he joined in an attempt by officers to assassinate Hitler. The surviving family members wandered Europe after that, and Vera would habitually slip off into the forest and embrace trees, hoping to meld with nature. After studying art in Hamburg and Florence, the teenager was stopped in the street and asked to model. Shortly, she decided to conquer New York, where her pose as the mysterious "Veruschka" (Russian for "little Vera")

51

attracted *Vogue*'s editor in chief, Diana Vreeland, who put her on the cover eleven times. Still, she continued her attempts to merge, posing for body paintings in which she appeared to be transforming into a leopard. Although in the public imagination she's a one-shot wonder on film, there were in fact appearances in several forgettable movies; look quickly, and you'll spot her as a countess attending Sting's party in *The Bride* (1985). Mostly, though, Veruschka drifted out of the limelight, though she regularly posed for the German artist Holger Truizsch, who would arrange her with heaps of old rags and paint her body until it was impossible to tell where Veruschka left off and the surroundings began. In fact, that was what she'd been attempting to do all her life.

JEAN SHRIMPTON

Privilege (1967)

Jean Shrimpton, London's top model in the 1960s, was cast as Vanessa, the mysterious beauty commissioned to paint a larger-than-life portrait of a singing idol (Paul Jones); but she falls in love with him and encourages the lad to rebel against government agents using him to manipulate the masses. Though the movie was set several years in the future, the film could only have been made during the days of psychedelia. The Shrimp was then not only the most photographed face alive (scoring a record twenty *Vogue* covers), but truly a living symbol for the Carnaby St. era, much as Clara Bow had become for the Roaring Twenties. The daughter of a wealthy English builder, the five-foot-nine-inch Shrimp had decided to give modeling a try. She was discovered by photographer David Bailey, just then making waves as the visual "voice" of an emerging generation of trend-setting publications. Shortly, she was his favorite subject, in front of the camera and in private life.

In no time, Shrimpton was being paid $120 an hour, then the highest fee ever for a mannequin. After breaking with Bailey, she became involved with actor Terence Stamp, another sixties icon. It seemed no one could unseat her, not so long as the sixties kept swinging along. But then came Twiggy; almost immediately, Jean slipped into oblivion, though not before bringing her vacuous brand of beauty to this strange and unsettling if ultimately unsatisfying film. With fame and fortune behind her, Shrimpton briefly took up with the Old Etonian rebel-writer Heathcote Williams, lived for a time in Wales with a Budd-hist poet, then moved far from the madding crowd, heading for Cornwall where she tried, and failed, to establish herself as a photographer. But she met Michael Cox, an accountant's son. They borrowed money from both their parents to buy and refurbish the Abbey Hotel (built in 1620), then (with their son Thaddeus helping), doing all the cooking and cleaning themselves, attended to their dozen guests.

"Getting old," Shrimpton sighed in 1981, "isn't easy."

SAMANTHA JONES

Wait Until Dark (1967)

A tall, stunningly beautiful young woman in a lynx fur passes through customs at JFK Airport, carrying a seemingly innocuous "McGuffin" that actually contains a stash of heroin. Her breezy self-assurance turns to terror upon realizing she's being stalked by killers who want what she's got. Before long, the sought-after item will have been passed, Hitchcock-style, through a series of hands until Frederick Knott's clever script has the object of everyone's desires in the Manhattan apartment of a lonely blind woman (Audrey Hepburn), who must defend herself against clever psychokillers (Alan Arkin, Richard Crenna, Jack Weston). Despite all the memorable moments and tingling thrills, audiences did not soon forget Samantha Jones in her brief but showy role as the epitome of the chic midsixties la dolce vita lifestyle.

Jones had been born Lind Manhart in a working-class section of Ottawa in 1943, where her mother supported the two of them as a secretary. The tall, gangly girl emerged as a beauty while in high school, changing her name and heading for Toronto to pursue an acting career while supporting herself as a model. Shortly, she was modeling hats in Mexico (and falling in love with a bullfighter who appeared in the same commercial), displaying haute couture in Paris, gracing the covers of *Vogue* and *Cosmo*. But Sam's situation had begun to resemble Monica Vitti's character in any of a number of Michelangelo Antonioni films; deciding that she suffered from existential ennui, Jones forsook her sophisticated but superficial lifestyle to trek across India in search of the Dalai Lama and spiritual salva-

tion through Buddhist self-contempla-
tion. Nobody thought to tell her that
on such a trek for inner understanding
and psychic peace, you weren't supposed to wear microminis that would
have shocked the denizens of jaded
New York, much less the conservative
masses of New Delhi. When she finally came face-to-face with her intended
guru, the walking mannequin realized
she didn't have a thing to say to him.

Instead of achieving nirvana,
Samantha Jones returned to the
United States, married stockbroker
Larchezar "Lucky" Christov, and had a
daughter, Eden. Believing that modeling was too chimeric a career, Jones
pursued acting. When producer Mel
Ferrer saw the first-day rushes from
Wait Until Dark, he offered her a four-
year studio contract, with full star
buildup. But Samantha Jones, wanting
to remain in control of herself and her
career, turned him down flat. She
filmed three low-budget pictures that
were so terrible they couldn't be
released. Having made her stunning
premiere in a megahit, Samantha Jones
was never again seen in a theatrical
release.

Though this looks like a scene from a Beach Party
*youth-exploitation flick, it's actually Christina
Ferrare being serenaded by admirer Chad Everett in
a major production,* The Impossible Years.

CHRISTINA FERRARE

The Impossible Years (1968)

David Niven here played a harried psychiatrist unable to deal with the fact that
his own "little girl" has begun to date. Based on a popular Broadway play of the
early 1960s, this attempt at a suggestively sexy "cute" comedy was hopelessly
dated owing to the social and cultural changes that had racked society at middecade. The film arrived on theater screens even as young people were experiment-
ing with drugs, sex, and radical politics, making the movie's supposedly "contem-

porary" problems seem as if they were taking place in some vaguely remembered, remotely distant period-piece setting called the Kennedy era. Niven's precocious daughter was played by the most popular teen model of the time, eighteen-year-old Christina Ferrare, who would achieve far greater fame through her marriage to auto entrepreneur John DeLorean than she would through films.

The Cleveland-born blonde had been briefly married early on, to her personal manager Nick Thomas. Earning a then-whopping $3,500 a fashion shoot, she still had ambitions to do movies, though after the debacle of *The Impossible Years,* the best Ferrare could get was a bit in *J. W. Coop,* a lackluster, minor-league 1972 rodeo yarn (written, directed by, and starring Cliff Robertson) that was never widely released; she there played a jaded debutante who enjoys a short fling with the Westerner. Christina then married DeLorean, twenty-four years her senior, the following year, becoming half of what she later called "the golden couple, living the high life" in New York, invited to all the best parties. But what seemed an elegant phantasmagoria of endless upscale living turned into a nightmare when DeLorean was arrested and tried for smuggling $24 million worth of cocaine into the United States. Ferrare stood by him throughout the ordeal, then split moments after he was acquitted. She had been stunned by the couple's quick fall from grace with their "elite" social set, and (while still insisting on his absolute innocence in the drug case) the realization that he'd been dishonest throughout their marriage, which she now believed had been an elaborate sham, she merely the trophy wife. Ferrare married Tony Thomopoulos of the ABC broadcast group only weeks after the divorce from DeLorean was final. Understandably enough, she was soon cohosting ABC's *Incredible Sunday* with John Davidson, as well as the syndicated *Home Show* with Rob Weller.

CHRISTIE BRINKLEY
National Lampoon's Vacation (1983)

Throughout the 1980s, any ordinary person considering the life and career of Christie Brinkley would have reached the conclusion that this woman had it all: a supermodel whose ongoing relationships with Cover Girl cosmetics and *Sports Illustrated* made her the most easily recognized beauty in the world; wife of piano man Billy Joel; and subject of such beloved pop ballads as "Uptown Girl," composed by her talented husband, apparently out of absolute adoration. Few could guess that, beneath the surface of success, a sense of failure was mounting.

That failure would not become obvious in her personal life until 1994, when an April 1 helicopter crash in Colorado's San Juan Mountains almost claimed her life, precipitating the rapid end of her nine-year marriage, then revealed to have been in disintegration for some time. Also injured was noted mil-

Christie Brinkley as the mystery blonde who drives cross-country in a flashy red Ferrari, then enjoys a late-night tryst with Clark Griswold (Chevy Chase) at an out-of-the-way motel. (courtesy Warner Bros.)

lionaire/philanthropist Ricky Taubman, whom Brinkley had secretly been visiting. Brinkley's career disappointments had become obvious a full decade earlier, beginning with the negative critical reaction to her performance in *National Lampoon's Vacation,* an otherwise successful 1983 comedy written by John Hughes.

Chevy Chase and Beverly D'Angelo played the Griswalds, a typical American suburbanite couple, tromping cross-country with their kids toward a fabled West Coast theme park. On the road, Clark is continually attracted by a mystery blonde who zips by them in her red sports car. Unfortunately, in a film that was otherwise marked by vivid characterizations, Brinkley's performance sounded the single sour note. She played the part as if uncertain whether she was supposed to be a real human being who just happened to be gorgeous or some Greek goddess come down to earth. As a result, Hollywood was not quick to make any other offers. Brinkley then tried television, but her much ballyhooed CNN series, *Living in the '90s,* was canceled after an embarrassingly brief three-month run. The marriage to Taubman fared only slightly better, faltering after seven months.

9
POP GOES THE MUSIC

They are the women and men who sang the songs that made the whole world sing; they starred in a single film apiece.

JOHNNIE RAY
There's No Business Like Show Business (1954)

Though partially deaf since childhood, Johnnie Ray overcame that handicap to become a top pop star in the early 1950s, just before the advent of rock 'n' roll rendered him irrelevant all but overnight. Still, he filled that awkward gap between Sinatra and Presley, giving bobby-soxers something to scream about by nearly tearing off his shirts during dramatically overwrought renditions of songs like "Cry" (backed by the Four Lads), causing TV comics to mimic and mock him. At middecade, 20th Century–Fox put him in their superproduction musical film as Steve Donahue, a member of a venerable vaudeville family who gives up the boards to become a Catholic priest. Ethel Merman was his mom, Molly, and Dan Dailey was Terry, the dad; Donald O'Connor played Tim, the breezy brother who falls for sultry showgirl Vicky (Marilyn Monroe).

Ray's spirited rendition of "Alexander's Ragtime Band" won over several critics who had previously scoffed, and whatever one thinks of his unsubtle approach, Ray was in fact a musical pioneer who ought to be credited with bringing something of black rhythm and blues to the fast-fading white-bread big-band sound. Lest we forget, his LP *The Big Beat* introduced that term, the original moniker for rock 'n' roll, to America's vast middlebrow audience. But then, just as Ray appeared to be coming into his own, there was Elvis of the gyrating pelvis on TV. Teenage girls had someone new to scream about, while serious music fans still didn't care enough for Ray to categorize him in the Sinatra/Tony Bennett/ Nat King Cole slot of respected pop-standard elder statesman. A decade and a half later, during the height of the camp-nostalgia craze, Ray enjoyed a minor revival, particularly in England.

Though he can also be glimpsed singing in A Certain Smile, *Johnny Mathis* (at piano) *had his only acting role in cult director Hugo Haas's* Lizzie, *as a jazz artist who befriends the title character, played by Eleanor Parker* (at the center of the crowd). *(courtesy Metro-Goldwyn-Mayer)*

JOHNNY MATHIS

Lizzie (1957)

In 1957, psychoanalysis hit Hollywood, thanks to the success of *The Three Faces of Eve* starring Joanne Woodward as a woman harboring a trio of distinct personalities. The critical acclaim lavished on that film caused a similar, if lesser, movie to go all but ignored: *Lizzie,* an intriguing if uneven adaptation of Shirley Jackson's novel *The Bird's Nest*. Eleanor Parker starred as a woman with the exact same problem as Woodward's Eve, Richard Boone had the psychiatrist role that Lee J. Cobb played in the better-known movie, and third billing went to mellow-voiced balladeer Johnny Mathis as a piano player who befriends the title character, offering a sensitive shoulder for her to cry on. Kirk Douglas, in one of his rare ventures at producing a film in which he did not also star, picked Mathis for the part after catching one of his live performances, coming away impressed by a young artist who insisted on continuing in the Nat King Cole tradition, even as most performers were scrambling to record in the newly popular rock-'n'-roll style. Mathis publicly stated that he would very much like to become a "singing actor" on the order

58

of his personal idol Cole, or Frank Sinatra. This was not to be the case.

The following year, Mathis performed the title song for the Paramount film *Wild Is the Wind* but did not appear on-screen, then sang the title song in *A Certain Smile* and was glimpsed briefly in the background as a Parisian cafe pianist who serenades as older man Rossano Brazzi attempts to win college student Christine Carere away from classmate Bradford Dillman. *Lizzie,* however, remains Mathis's only true acting role. There were no future movie offers, perhaps owing to the singer's "choirboy" image and high falsetto voice, though Mathis's endlessly successful career as a Columbia recording artist, concert performer, and TV guest star quickly established him as a millionaire, as well as a household name for four decades.

KEELY SMITH

Thunder Road (1958)

During the 1950s, the studio system gradually crumbled when the big-league players such as Kirk Douglas, Burt Lancaster, and John Wayne incorporated themselves, beginning the age of the independent star-producer. All their movies were major deals, fitting their superstar status. Intriguingly enough, though, another A-list actor, Robert Mitchum, tried his hand as producer-star only once, and in a cheesy (if irresistibly so) drive-in flick. Mitchum was the guiding force behind *Thunder Road,* which effectively elevated a backwoods, Deep South moonshiner to the level of legendary outlaw. It was a cult film, particularly among rural rubes and intellectual college students, before anyone ever came up with that term. Mitchum even sang the title song, while his son James played the hero's younger brother. As the moonshiner's girlfriend, a roadhouse singer who stands by her man to the very end, songstress Keely Smith played her only dramatic film role, though she can also be glimpsed as a singing guest star in several long-forgotten minimusicals, *Senior Prom* and *Hey Boy! Hey Girl!* with her then-husband Louis Prima.

Hailing from Norfolk, Virginia, Smith always sang her blues and ballads (most notably, "That Old Black Magic") with a poker face and stoic stance, while hubbie Prima provided a perfect complement, dancing wildly around her. They were the Sonny and Cher of the pre-rock era, though her most famous duet was with Frank Sinatra in 1958, when they enjoyed a joint hit with "How Are Ya Fixed for Love?" In the sixties Smith moved over to the Sinatra camp and from that point on recorded for Sinatra's Reprise label. Sinatra was so impressed with Smith that he made her a bona fide member of his legendary Rat Pack, though Prima was never invited to join. That awkward situation may have caused the rift that hastened the couple's divorce in 1961. Physically, Smith resembled a popular beat-era actress, Carolyn Jones, though Smith's awkward delivery of dia-logue (as compared to her inspired rendition of lyrics) rendered her a cinematic one-shot wonder.

59

ANDY WILLIAMS
I'd Rather Be Rich (1964)

Andy Williams, the agreeable and soft-spoken pop singer and relaxed TV host, romanced everyone's favorite girl next door from the 1950s and early sixties, Sandra Dee, in I'd Rather Be Rich. *(courtesy Universal Pictures)*

Like Perry Como, whom he resembled both in looks and style, Andy Williams seemed as well suited for television as he was essentially wrong for motion pictures. Williams projected the kind of genial, gracious personality the public felt comfortable inviting into their homes on a weekly basis; he lacked the intense charisma and threatening edge so essential to movie stardom. Williams first began singing in the Presbyterian church of the small Iowa town where he'd been born in 1930. His railway mail-clerk father had visions of his four sons performing as a choir, so shortly Andy (at age eight, the youngest of the Williams brothers) was doing just that. A contract to appear in MGM pictures had to be passed by when Andy's older brothers were drafted for military service. He headed for New York, where an audition for Steve Allen led to a two-and-a-half year stint as a regular on *The Tonight Show*. Shortly, Cadence Records signed Andy, and in 1962 he was picked to headline his own variety series, which would run for the following nine years on NBC.

In 1964, Williams and another popular singing star, Robert Goulet, competed for the hand of Sandra Dee in *I'd Rather Be Rich*. A diminutive Doris Day for the younger set, Dee was here cast as the desirable granddaughter of Maurice Chevalier in an agreeable if forgettable remake of *It Started With Eve*. Incorrectly believing the old fellow is dying, and wanting to please him by marrying, Dee tries to choose between the two innocuously appealing men in her life. Unfortunately, neither Williams nor Goulet (who appeared in ten films) could really act, and the ill-conceived film did not call upon either to do what they both did best: sing. Shortly, Williams returned to TV, a medium that appreciated, even demanded, his relaxed, casual, good-natured manner.

TONY BENNETT

The Oscar (1966)

All the best qualities of Richard Sale's biting, unsparingly honest insider's view of an Oscar competition were scrapped for filmmaker Russell Rouse's glossy, upscale trash-film version of the admirable novel about an ensemble of recognizable Hollywood types vying for the coveted award. Instead, the film focused on a cynical antihero whose entire life is recalled by a onetime best friend. The lead was played by Stephen Boyd, while the best buddy—half-Jewish, half-Irish press agent Hymie Kelly—was acted by Tony Bennett, the unmistakably Italian singer. Perhaps the producers recalled Sinatra all but stealing *From Here to Eternity* back in 1953, winning a Best Supporting Actor Oscar. Could it happen again? Sadly, the answer was no. Bennett had been nicknamed the Method Singer by fellow vocalists in admiration of his ability to virtually live a song's emotions rather than merely perform the lyrics technically. But Bennett offered no notable competition for Marlon Brando as our leading Method actor; he looked confused and embarrassed, never attempting to act again.

That allowed him to concentrate on his remarkable talents as a live performer and recording artist. Born in Queens, New York, in 1926 (real name: Anthony Dominick Benedetto) to a tailor father (who died when Tony was eight) and a mother who afterward supported them as a seamstress, Tony began singing with military bands while overseas as an infantryman during World War II, then attended the American Theatre Wing under the GI Bill following the war. Supporting himself as an elevator operator by day in Manhattan's Park Sheraton Hotel, then accepting low-paying nightclub gigs in the evening, Tony eventually won a TV spot on *Arthur Godfrey's Talent Scouts*. The audience picked him as runner-up to Rosemary Clooney, leading to a high-prestige Greenwich Village gig with Pearl Bailey. Bob Hope caught their show, hiring Bennett for a national tour and anointing Tony with his professional name. Bennett's classic recordings—from the early "Boulevard of Broken Dreams" and "Because of You" to his later, more mature, magnificently mellow "I Left My Heart in San Francisco" and "The Shadow of Your Smile"—offered an easygoing vocal attitude augmented by jazz-inspired pacing, allowing Bennett to be favorably compared with Old Blue Eyes himself as a singer—though never, ever as an actor. It would be thirty years before Tony would even agree to a cameo, appearing as himself (singing the national anthem at a baseball game) in *The Scout*.

Pop diva Dionne Warwick as the beautiful black woman who eventually enslaves her supposed white master (Stephen Boyd). (courtesy Theatre Guild Films)

DIONNE WARWICK

Slaves (1969)

In the pre-*Roots* era, the most ambitious film about the dark days of slavery was cowritten and directed by a white moviemaker, Herbert J. Biberman, who even cast his wife, Gale Sondergaard, in her first film role in twenty years. She had been blacklisted during the McCarthy era for her supposedly "radical" politics, which actually amounted to nothing more than believing in civil rights. The leading role was played by Dionne Warwick, cast as the slave mistress to her white master (Stephen Boyd). Warwick was ironically right not only for the role as written, but the production itself, considering her upbringing and previous career. Raised in an integrated, middle-class New Jersey suburb, Marie Dionne Warwick had never been subjected to any serious prejudice, much less abject poverty, which so many black female vocalists have known, which perhaps explains why she became a pop, rather than blues, singer. In 1960, the twenty-year-old met and married Burt

Bacharach, just then at work creating the new mainstream pop sound for the upcoming decade. Soon, she would be the key interpreter of the airily empty songs this composer-arranger (along with lyricist Hal David) created. Her hits, including "Don't Make Me Over," "Walk on By," and "Message to Michael," appealed more to white audiences than blacks, who preferred Motown.

Warwick radiated more style and less soul than any other black female vocalist of her generation. Her chosen career path led her away from the raunchy realities of the Apollo Theatre, instead to the polite quiet of posh supper-club rooms, eventually even the Copacabana, where (decked out in Dior gowns) a perfectly polished Warwick entertained upscale (mostly white) audiences with her dazzling renditions of passingly pleasant ditties. However impressive her technical virtuosity might be, audiences began to detect an iciness beneath the elegance. Warwick eventually took up a new career, promoting psychics on TV, occasionally doing a cameo in forgettable flicks like *Rent-a-Cop*.

AL MARTINO

The Godfather (1972)

When Francis Ford Coppola began work on *The Godfather*, every Italian singer who'd ever hoped in vain to emerge as the next Frank Sinatra—from Bobby Darin to Frankie Avalon—fought for the role of Johnny Fontanne. No wonder, since it was widely reported to be based on their idol, the Chairman of the Board himself. In the film, Johnny—a 1940s pop singer whose career has faded during the early fifties—convinces his godfather, Don Corleone, that a strong role in an important movie will put him back on top. When the film's producer (John Marley) fails to respond after being made "an offer he can't refuse" by Corleone's lawyer Tom Hagen (Robert Duvall), the Hollywood hotshot wakes up in bed one morning to find the head of his favorite racehorse beside him. In short order, Fontanne has been cast in the "big studio project" and, presumably, goes on to win a Best Supporting Actor Oscar much as Frank Sinatra did for his role as Maggio in *From Here to Eternity*. Eventually, Coppola announced that Vic Damone had been cast. When Damone suddenly backed out, there was much gossip that Vic's friend and mentor Sinatra had suggested that playing Ol' Blue Eyes in such an unfavorable light was an offer that Damone could, and should, refuse.

Eventually, Al Martino was cast in the Johnny Fontanne part. The Philadelphia native (born Alfred Cini in 1927) with a pleasingly gentle but always masculine voice had a huge hit in 1952 with the ballad "Here in My Heart," then was quickly eclipsed in the late fifties by emerging rock 'n' rollers. Martino made a comeback a decade later with "Spanish Eyes," then all but disappeared once again when the British invasion began. Since then, he has been a staple at Vegas and as a featured performer on "music of your life" radio stations. Martino repeated the Johnny Fontanne role for an extremely brief cameo in Coppola's 1990 film, *The Godfather, Part III*.

JOHN DENVER

Oh, God! (1977)

The music scene became so grungy in the early 1970s that a clean-cut country boy with minimalist backup might have seemed woefully out of place. Then again, millions of people didn't care for heavy metal and acid rock, so Henry John Deutschendorf tapped into that market with his soft, sweet ballads. Earlier, John Denver had as a songwriter provided Peter, Paul & Mary with a huge hit, "Leavin' on a Jet Plane"; now, he was recording his own material, breaking with the Chad Mitchell Trio to go solo with such sentimental songs as "Sunshine" and "Thank God, I'm a Country Boy." Hailing God Himself turned out to be a good idea, because director Carl Reiner heard that song and, as a result, put Denver in one of his best-received films of the era, a Capraesque fable that took movies in the same retro direction as Denver's music.

The eternally amiable George Burns played the Lord, come down to earth to encourage an average young man (Denver), not very different from James Stewart's Mr. Smith and Gary Cooper's Mr. Deeds, and help him make it through troubled times. Though the film was a huge hit with those very people who had stayed home listening to John Denver records ever since American films had moved in the direction of *Taxi Driver,* Denver was never able to parlay his first screen success into an ongoing Hollywood career. There were a few TV roles, then Denver's brightness faded after his beloved wife, Annie (subject of his most adoring composition), left him, leading to late-night drunken-driving altercations with the police in his adopted Colorado hometown, though through it all he kept on singing—if not acting.

DONNA SUMMER

Thank God, It's Friday (1978)

Donna Summer became so associated with Giorgio Morodor's disco sound during the midseventies that most music critics severely underrated her talent. In truth, though, La Donna Adrian Gaines had sung gospel as a child in Boston, rock in the German production of *Hair,* and show tunes in the Vienna Folk Opera's rendition of *Porgy and Bess*. Still, when "Love to Love You Baby" made her name synonymous with a quarter hour of simulated orgasm for a superficial dance number, Summer was immediately typed as the reigning disco diva. This led to her type-

John Denver as the Capraesque hero, a common man who with divine inspiration rallies other ordinary folk around him at the moment of direst need; Teri Garr was his wife. (courtesy Warner Bros.)

casting in Robert Klane's slight, silly, superficial film about an ensemble of people whose lives intertwine during one long night at a disco. No one associated with the production apparently ever stopped to consider whether people who attend a disco could be interesting enough to sustain an audience for the length of an entire film.

Jeff Goldblum played Summer's boss, the autocratic owner of the establishment who manipulates both his employees and customers to his own ends, only to be humiliated in the final reel. Summer played an aspiring singer who sees how badly the boss treats even his star disc jockey (Ray Vitte) and pretends to be a waitress, while always waiting and hoping for the big chance to perform and show everyone just what she's got. Donna did get to sing "Last Dance," which became a major hit and even won the Oscar for Best Song. In time, duets with Barbra Streisand and a switch to David Geffen's record label allowed Summer to show more substance than in her disco days, songwise; no one has, to date, given her another chance as a movie actress.

Neil Diamond, in the role of Yussel Rabinovitz, was able to come to terms with his conventionality as a recording artist. (courtesy Associated Film Distribution)

NEIL DIAMOND
The Jazz Singer (1980)

When Neil Diamond appeared on-screen in *The Last Waltz,* Martin Scorsese's 1978 documentary of The Band's final performance, he seemed strangely incongruous. Here was a talented pop music personality, recently playing New York's Winter Garden and Vegas' Aladdin Hotel in sequined costumes, going slightly grungy while attempting to pass himself off as one of the rockers like Bob Dylan, Neil Young, and Eric Clapton. Though Diamond had surged to popularity during the late 1960s, he never felt at home in that era of flower-power rebellion or the music such attitudes inspired, deriving his inspiration as a writer/composer from the likes of Alan Jay Lerner and George Gershwin rather than Lennon and McCartney. His devotion to Tin Pan Alley would eventually lead him to record *Beautiful Noise,* a 1976 album that lovingly recalled the history of pop in the twentieth century, effectively carrying the listener through the entire history of such mainstream music. Diamond's true soul mate was that legendary Yiddish performer gone commercial, Al Jolson; so it made sense that Diamond would eventually re-create Jolson's most famous film role.

But not before an earlier, unrealized shot at movie stardom. When producer Marvin Worth began preproduction on *Lenny,* Worth was struck by Diamond's physical resemblance to the controversial comic, suggesting a screen test. By all reports, Diamond's first attempt to act was going well enough until he reached Bruce's infamous "rough words" in the script, stumbling awkwardly whenever he was required to say anything foul. The experience unleashed deep introspection, causing Diamond to question his conventionality for the first time. Even as Dustin Hoffman walked into the role, Diamond entered psychotherapy. Eventually, he made peace with himself and found a part more suited to him, playing Yussel Rabinovitz, son of a cantor (Laurence Olivier), who must choose between sacred and secular music. "There were so many connections between it and me," Diamond mused. But when the film's sound track sold more copies than the movie did tickets, Diamond read the handwriting on the wall. He took his act to TV, where his specials were greeted with an overwhelmingly happy response from middle-American viewers.

10
"THE BRITISH ARE COMING!"

T he English—as well as their Australian cousins—bring their accented appeal to American movie screens, though not everyone proves as durable as Errol Flynn or Mel Gibson.

FRANKIE VAUGHAN

Let's Make Love (1960)

In 1960, Marilyn Monroe—fresh from her final hit, *Some Like It Hot*—found her career crashing down around her; at age thirty-five, she could no longer play pouting sexpots, but the public didn't want to see her as anything else. Her personal life suddenly took a nasty turn as well. The marriage to Arthur Miller was in trouble for many reasons, one being that on the set of her new film, she fell in love with her leading man, seductively Gallic Yves Montand. The film was *Let's Make Love;* directed by the esteemed George Cukor, it was intended to begin a new era in which Monroe would emerge as a mature, sophisticated comedienne. But the overly long (118 minutes) movie was not a success, and Monroe would act in only one other film *(The Misfits)* before dying on August 5, 1962. *Let's Make Love* was MM's last completed comedy, and time has been kind to it. She projects just the right amount of bubbly blonde ditsiness as her character, Amanda Dell, is cast in a new play satirizing a prominent billionaire, Jean-Marc Clement (Montand). He rushes to the theater, planning on complaining, but the director—mistaking him for an actor—casts him in the part of Clement, unknowingly guiding the real thing toward a parody of himself.

Clement agrees because he has spotted Amanda and is smitten with her. He's upset, though, because in rehearsals, Amanda is romantically linked with performer Tony Danton (Frankie Vaughan). Clement fears their romance may continue offstage. "You think of the millions of chappies who dream about being mauled by Marilyn Monroe, and here I am," Vaughan said on the set. Being cast

opposite MM seemed like a dream come true for the British performer, unknown in the United States but billed in London as "Mr. Showbusiness" and "Mr. Personality," owing to his ability to sing, dance, and tell jokes, something he'd been doing in nightclubs and on "the telly" for years. He recorded the British cover versions of the American pop hits "Tower of Strength" and "Green Door," but never charted in America. Like Richard Burton before him and the Beatles a few years later, Vaughan believed that international stardom lay in wait for anyone who would conquer America. The good news was that he won the key role opposite Monroe; the bad news was that the film bombed at the box office. The best Vaughan could do afterward was a role in a barely released junk movie called *The Right Approach* in which he and the likes of Gary Crosby swapped ideas for picking up young girls. Then it was back to Britain where he remained a music-hall superstar for years.

GERRY AND THE PACEMAKERS
Ferry Cross the Mersey (1965)

Gerry Marsden played lead guitar and performed the vocals, with backup from Les Maguire on piano, Les Chadwick on bass, and Gerry's older brother Freddie on piano. They called themselves Gerry and the Pacemakers, one more of the seemingly endless groups emulating the Beatles back in the midsixties. This relatively fab foursome had an edge over most of the competition: all but Maguire were from Liverpool, plus they were the second group signed (after the Beatles) by Brian Epstein. The Pacemakers alternated between Brit rock 'n' roll ("Don't Let the Sun Catch You Crying") and mainstream pop ("You'll Never Walk Alone").

Since the Beatles had played a romanticized version of themselves on film, so, too, did Gerry and Co. In *Ferry Cross the Mersey,* they actually performed the title number on a ferry as they cross over to London where the group appears in a talent contest, which, according to the film, is how they broke into show business. There were several more hit songs, though the film work had apparently sparked Gerry's interest in acting. In 1967, he quit the group to appear opposite Anna Neagle in the play *Charlie Girl* at London's West End. Several years later, the Pacemakers re-formed to milk the nostalgia craze.

TERENCE COOPER

Casino Royale (1967)

Sean Connery, Roger Moore, and Timothy Dalton; those are the best-known James Bonds. Aficionados can also tell you that George Lazenby played the role in one movie, Barry Nelson was Bond on TV back in the 1950s, and Pierce Brosnan is finally playing the part. Few recall, however, that there was another Bond, truly the forgotten 007: Terence Cooper, a ruggedly handsome Irishman who starred in *Casino Royale*. That book had been the first Bond novel to be optioned for a possible movie. When "Cubby" Broccoli and Harry Saltzman opted for a Bond series in the early sixties, it was the only Fleming novel for which they could not procure the rights. After their Connery films became an international phenomenon, the people who did own *Casino Royale* embarked on their project. In 1964, Charles K. Feldman had a huge hit with *What's New, Pussycat?*—an elaborate pop-art parody for the swinging sixties starring Peter Sellers, Ursula Andress, and Woody Allen (who also scripted). Rather than compete with the Broccoli Bonds on the level of tongue-in-cheek intrigue, Feldman made the decision to go over the top, doing *Casino* as a *Pussycat* spoof, the problem being that Allen did not pen the script this time around. The elaborate, expensive film was a flat, unfunny farce that had audiences recoiling in horror.

The running gag was that Sellers, Andress, Allen, David Niven, and all other cast members were James Bond imitators; the "real" James Bond was incarnated by Cooper, a veteran of London stage and music-hall productions. He had attended Oxford University as a student of architecture but, after appearing for the fun of it in several amateur campus theatrical productions, found himself hooked. Cooper studied drama and eventually appeared in *Paint Your Wagon* at Her Majesty's Theatre, Haymarket. Then, when Sellers was glancing through photos of various pretty girls who were scheduled to appear in the upcoming film, he noticed a male model in the shot with one of them. "Who's the guy with her?" he later recalled asking. "He's a young Gregory Peck." At Sellers's suggestion, Feldman interviewed Cooper and told him, "You remind me of Errol Flynn." After *Casino Royale* flopped, Cooper made a lucrative living by appearing in local Australian film productions, as well as the New Zealand–lensed TV show *Mortimer's Patch,* and occasionally made cameo appearances in direct-to-video junk movies such as Cheech Marin's *Shrimp on the Barbie.*

LEONARD WHITING

Romeo and Juliet (1967)

When Franco Zeffirelli set out to film Shakespeare's tragedy of star-crossed lovers for the 1960s youth generation, he cast the youngest people ever to appear in *Romeo and Juliet,* at once being true to the actual ages of the characters as written while also making the classic more accessible to his contemporary audience. For Juliet, he picked Olivia Hussey, who would continue on with a modestly successful screen career. For Romeo, the director interviewed 350 applicants before settling on Leonard Whiting, who would never again be seen by the mainstream American moviegoer. Sixteen at the time, Whiting was already the veteran of four years of acting on British stage and television. He'd played the Artful Dodger in the London production of *Oliver,* but avoided Shakespeare, insisting he hated the works of the Bard. Whiting had also played the lead in a minor British film, *Young Dick Turpin,* that never received theatrical distribution in America.

Zeffirelli downplayed histrionics and theatricality, cutting much of the ornate dialogue, allowing his young actors to do the roles realistically. Whiting created an ingenious and appealing Romeo and, at the time, was the object of affection for teenage girls. He seemed, for a moment, to be poised on the edge of major stardom. He filmed three other pictures—*Say Hello to Yesterday, Rachel's Man,* and *Royal Hunt of the Sun*—but the studios took one look at the finished products, concluded they lacked commercial potential, and allowed them to slip into oblivion. In 1971, Whiting married American model Cathee Dahmen; the union lasted six years, resulting in one daughter. His acting career going nowhere, Whiting threw himself into writing, turning out four novels and two books for children, but could not find a publisher. Finally, he focused his energies on a script called *Romeo and Juliet 2,* in which the two deceased lovers come back to life and try again; that film has yet to be made. In 1992, at age forty-one, Whiting was living in a modest four-room Victorian row house in Camden town, a less than trendy district of London.

GEMMA CRAVEN

The Slipper and the Rose (1976)

The world needed another film version of *Cinderella* like it needed a sequel to *Gone With the Wind.* But back in the 1970s, the Sherman brothers (Robert B. and Richard M.), who had provided the delightful score for *Mary Poppins,* decided an all-new musical version of the venerable fairy tale was in order. Disney wasn't interested, since their animated version couldn't be improved upon. Instead, the Shermans sold their idea in England, where TV personality David Frost, intrigued

70

by moviemaking, agreed to serve as executive producer. Old pro Bryan Forbes was signed to direct, Richard Chamberlain would play Prince Charming, so all that was needed was the right girl to play "Cindy."

After a long search, everyone agreed that Gemma Craven was their best choice. She had been hoping for a career in film musicals all her life, having been performing live since childhood. Born in Dublin in 1952, Craven had won a local singing contest, then tried acting in a school production of *Thumberline* (a.k.a. *Thumbelina*). Her family moved to England's east coast, where she completed her traditional education, then attended dancing school. Gemma made her stage debut in local theater and was shortly on her way to England's West End, where she starred in *First Impressions,* a musical version of Jane Austen's *Pride and Prejudice,* did *The Threepenny Opera* at the Old Vic, and appeared on British TV in *Dick Whittington* and *The Harry Secombe Show.* But *Slipper* was the ultimate dream come true. Unfortunately, it might better have been a stage musical, as most of the inordinately long running time (128 minutes, mercifully cut from the 146-minute British version) featured static images of the two leads singing to each other. Children found it slow and boring, adults considered it pleasant but uninvolving. Everyone missed Jacques and Gus-Gus; shortly thereafter, Gemma Craven returned to her London stage work.

11
No Business
Like Show Business

From magicians to dancers, ventriloquists to entrepreneurs, these are the show business personalities who also landed major movie roles along the way.

Victor Borge

Higher and Higher (1943)

Victor Borge escaped the Nazis, who came searching for this Jewish artist in his native Copenhagen in 1940, by a stroke of good luck: the pianist-cum-comedian was on tour in Sweden. Since his wife, Elsie Chilton, was an American citizen, Borge persuaded the U.S. counsel in Stockholm to provide a visa for him to accompany her home. The counsel, who had seen and enjoyed Borge's show, happily agreed, but only if Victor promised to continue his unique form of entertainment upon arrival. Borge had become fascinated with the concept of mixing highbrow art with low-jinks humor when, as a teenager, he performed in a concert at the Royal Danish Conservatory and, on a whim, began winking at the stuffed shirts in the front row who were falling asleep. Borge became a great favorite on the Broadway stage (his *Comedy in Music* is listed in the *Guinness Book of World Records* as the longest-running one-man show in theater history) and on TV during the 1950s, where he became a regular on Bing Crosby's show.

Fans considered his act droll and sophisticated, though naysayers insisted that elements of cruelty and bitterness in Borge's approach lent it a nasty ring. But while Borge had appeared in several Danish-language films that never made it to America, he was cast in only one Hollywood movie. *Higher and Higher* featured Leon Errol as a once-wealthy man who, in the company of his former servants, devises a bizarre scheme to raise money, with Frank Sinatra (in his starring debut) as the singing youth who helps them out. Borge was cast as the key blocking character, a crooked Englishman who causes trouble for the heroes, specifically when he wants to marry the leading lady before Young Blue Eyes can propose. Borge's delivery of the Brit lines proved so awkward and overdone that there were no other movie offers. In his defense, Borge later asked, in his characteristic style, "How can I cultivate an accent that has taken centuries of head colds to produce?"

SPIKE JONES AND HIS CITY SLICKERS

Fireman Save My Child (1954)

Originally, this film was to have been yet another period-piece comedy vehicle for Abbott and Costello, who bolted when they became convinced that the material—about a pair of loonies working at a San Francisco fire station, circa 1900, on the day when a new mechanized engine arrives—was not coming together. So Buddy Hackett was abruptly substituted for Lou, Hugh O'Brian (shortly to achieve fame

Spike Jones conducts his collection of zanies as, in their only acting appearance, they play Stooge-like, turn-of-the century firemen saluting the arrival of a new, modern engine. (courtesy Universal Pictures)

as the lead in TV's *Wyatt Earp*) for Bud, along with the most outrageous band in the country as their kooky colleagues. The film was anything but subtle—hardly a surprise, considering their work up to that point—but, in its own silly and slap-stickish way, *Fireman Save My Child* worked nicely as a vehicle for the only group that ever served up their songs in a style that was clearly reminiscent of the out-landish antics that Mack Sennett and Hal Roach had specialized in during the silent cinema.

Lindley Armstrong Jones had begun working as a serious drummer in radio orchestras, then put together his own group, emphasizing loud, noisy, clut-tered (everything from cowbells and pistols to foghorns and slide whistles adding to the commotion) sounds to create genially dumb comedy routines, which tend-ed to overshadow the fact that Jones and his musicians were all first-rate. Their numerous hits included "All I Want for Christmas Is My Two Front Teeth," and they were popular guests on TV variety shows during the early 1950s, eventually hosting NBC's *Club Oasis* in 1958 as well as several different versions of *The Spike Jones Show* between 1954 and 1961, with Spike's wife, songstress Helen Grayco, classing up the act. Though there were several performance-only appearances in other films, *Fireman Save My Child* marked the band's only outing as comic actors in the silent-film tradition, as well as above-the-title headliners.

BERT PARKS
Shining Star (a.k.a. *That's the Way of the World*) (1975)

When Bert Parks died in 1992 at age seventy-seven, he was remembered mainly for his twenty-five-year stint as the host of TV's Miss America pageant. Some recalled that Parks had also starred on Broadway, replacing Robert Preston as Prof. Harold Hill in *The Music Man*. And die-hard media junkies likewise remembered that, in addition to annually singing "There she is . . ." at the climax of the country's most popular beauty pageant, the Atlanta native had also been the regular singer of note on radio's *The Eddie Cantor Show,* later emceeing *Break the Bank,* then hosting TV's *Party Line, The Big Payoff, Giant Step, Masquerade Party,* and *Yours for a Song.* But when it comes to movie acting, most people—even Parks fans—draw a blank, other than warmly appreciating his celebrity cameo appearance as himself in *The Freshman,* in which Parks performed a marvelous piece of self-satire by singing "There she is . . ." to an oversize lizard about to be devoured by corrupt gourmets.

In fact, though, Parks once played a legitimate character role in an ambi-tious, if less than successful, motion picture. *Shining Star,* written by *New York Times* reporter Robert Lipsyte, was intended as the first no-holds-barred exposé of the con-temporary music scene, involving dishonest executives who prey on legitimate cre-ative artists by promoting second-rate "commercial" groups. Here, the unknown

group with obvious talent was played by Earth, Wind and Fire; the worthless white-bread musical family, combining the worst qualities of the real-life Osmonds and fictional Partridge Family, was the Page Family. The group's patriarch and key performer, Franklyn Page, was portrayed by Parks. The overly sweet grin, which had always seemed close to self-mockery, was effectively employed here to suggest a character who comes on as smarmily sentimental but is cynical to the core. The film, originally marketed as *That's the Way of the World,* was eventually released briefly in New York as *Shining Star.*

TWYLA THARP

Hair (1979)

Had *Hair* been filmed in the late 1960s or early seventies, it might have served as a valuable record of the counterculture that emerged during the era of antiwar/pro-drug protest. Had it been made into a movie during the mideighties, it could have created a wave of nostalgia for that bygone period of flower power. Unfortunately, it was filmed by Milos Forman at a most awkward moment between the two extremes, therefore lacking either a sense of immediacy or an angle of perspective. But if the film is a failure, it at the very least rates as a fascinating one, filled with grand moments as Forman attempts to translate the dated James Rado–Gerome Ragni–Galt MacDermot play about the Age of Aquarius into totally cinematic terms, with a game cast including John Savage as an ultrastraight Midwestern youth who decides to join Treat Williams and his tribe of hippies (including Beverly D'Angelo) in Central Park.

    Also on view was Twyla Tharp, playing the queen of the flower children during the film's dance sequences, which she also choreographed. The role was absolutely perfect for Tharp, who had been a kind of proto-hippie long before anyone even came up with that term. The Portland, Indiana, native (born in 1942) had come East to study at Barnard College where she majored in art history, but took an interest in dance, studying with the likes of Richard Thomas, eventually joining the Taylor Dance Company and forming her own group in 1965. That was when Twyla began revolutionizing "serious" dance in America by breaking all the conventions: working without musical accompaniment, often performing in gymnasiums and outdoors rather than in traditional theater spaces. She was the first American choreographer to create a work specifically for Mikhail Baryshnikov, and when she did finally absorb music into her act, she alternated between classical and jazz, occasionally combining the two. Her work was an unparalleled combination of the discipline associated with ballet and the freedom connected with popular social dancing, qualifying Tharp as the artist who broke down the barriers between the two. Tharp had presaged the hippie movement's values, and when the belated film version of *Hair* created a time capsule for that vanished movement, it was only right that Twyla Tharp would costar as well as choreograph.

DAVID COPPERFIELD

Terror Train (1980)

Illusionist is what David Copperfield likes to be called, since *magician* automatically draws up images of a mustachioed old-timer, stiffly performing routine tricks with cane, cape, and top hat. Single-handedly, Copperfield altered that stereotype, making magic more contemporary via his appearance (blow-dried hair, tight-fitting jeans), approach (dazzling special effects worthy of George Lucas's Industrial Light & Magic), and atmosphere (soft rock music by Peter Gabriel). Copperfield (born David Kotkin in 1956 to Russian-immigrant parents in Metuchen, New Jersey) began performing tricks as a child to overcome an innate shyness, proving to be such a showstopper at an early age that he was invited to join the Society of American Magicians while only twelve, the youngest inductee ever. His phenomenal feats—such as making the Statue of Liberty disappear in 1982—have made him a sensation on TV, though to overcome the public's long-standing prejudice against televised magic, Copperfield always includes a live audience in hopes of setting aside any accusations of trick photography.

Perhaps the possibility of such complaints caused Copperfield to steer clear of motion pictures. To date, he's starred in only one film, an above average slasher flick called *Terror Train*. Directed by the respectable Roger Spottiswoode (*Under Fire*), the movie is considerably less gory and more suspenseful than others of its ilk. A college-graduation costume party takes place on the title vehicle, only to fall prey to a masked killer—a former fraternity member whose life was destroyed by an initiation rite gone sour, causing him to hack his way through the partygoers in revenge. Veteran western star Ben Johnson ran the train, scream

Bill Graham, as Charles "Lucky" Luciano, discusses with Meyer Lansky (Ben Kingsley) their difficult friend Ben Siegel. (courtesy TriStar Pictures)

queen Jamie Lee Curtis played the most beautiful of the damsels in distress, with Copperfield as a mysterious magician providing entertainment along the way, then unmasking the killer at the end—but not making him disappear from sight.

BILL GRAHAM

Bugsy (1991)

As a producer of his own films, Warren Beatty loves to rely on offbeat casting for an interesting edge. After all, who else would have had rock promoter Bill Graham play Charles "Lucky" Luciano in the gangster epic *Bugsy*? It certainly worked: Graham, who died shortly thereafter, cut a striking figure as the hard-edged professional criminal. At a key moment in the film, he breaks with the title character over the antihero's obsession for "actress" Virginia Hall.

Born Wolfgang Grajonca in Berlin, Bill Graham was an orphaned immigrant who drove a taxi, fought in Korea, and managed a mime troupe before opening the Fillmore, where he showcased San Francisco bands. He became an entrepreneur by taking the supposedly anticommercial midsixties sound and turning it into a money-making venture. Ironically, Graham himself closed both the Fillmore West and its New York counterpart in 1971 when he came to believe the purity of the hippie movement, and its concurrent musical scene, had been ruined by acceptance into the mainstream. An intriguing and difficult to grasp man who wrestled all his life with the equally seductive poles of money and art, Graham brought that inner conflict to this film, which effectively dealt with the same issue.

12
ROCK 'N' ROLL IS HERE TO STAY

From the original rockers to today's postmodern performers, they all harbored a hope that movie stardom might be in the offing; it happened for Elvis, David Bowie, and Sting, though others hit that high note only once.

JERRY LEE LEWIS

High School Confidential! (1958)

It's hard to believe, looking back, that Elvis was ever controversial. The easy-going image of his gentle eyes on the cover of early middle-of-the-road recordings such as "Peace in the Valley" make him seem a highly unlikely candidate as the corrupter of youth. On the other hand, the true dark force of early rock was the man they called the Killer. Whatever one thinks of Jerry Lee Lewis personally, this cannot be denied: Chuck Berry provides his only possible competition for the title of most basic hard rocker, steadfastly refusing to move even an inch toward the mainstream, throughout his life remaining true to the purest of early rock sounds. Most everything you ever heard about Jerry Lee is, for better or worse, factual. He abandoned his studies in the ministry to sneak off and sing in honky-tonks, signing with Memphis's Sun label and pioneering (with such numbers as "Great Balls of Fire") the Southern transition from hillbilly to rock 'n' roll, establishing himself as the greatest rockabilly artist ever.

That was the good part; the bad parts included endless addictions and his incestuous marriage to his fourteen-year-old cousin, whom he regularly beat. No wonder big-time Hollywood producers were afraid to try to turn Jerry Lee into the kind of G-rated movie-musical star Elvis had already become. But Hollywood schlockmeisters were more open to Lewis's outlaw ways, so he was cast in what was then considered nothing more than a teen-exploitation flick, but which over the years would gradually achieve camp-classic status: Albert Zugsmith's *High School Confidential!* Russ Tamblyn played the school's new bad boy, living with his sleazy

78

"Touch my guitar, woman, and I'll . . ."; in his only film lead, Roy Orbison protects his instrument from yet another one-shot wonder, pretty Maggie Pierce.

aunt (Mamie Van Doren) and accosting teachers such as Jan Sterling. What nobody realizes is that Russ is actually an undercover cop, out to get the goods on school drug dealer John Drew Barrymore. Jerry Lee performs musically but also acts as the local bandleader who visits the campus with his motorized show. Shortly, all kids are beboppin' to the film's title tune at the outdoor high school hop.

ROY ORBISON

The Fastest Guitar Alive (1968)

In 1956's *Love Me Tender,* Elvis Presley had successfully grafted his rock-'n'-roll performances into a Civil War western by playing up the hillbilly, rather than rhythm-'n'-blues, element of his music. Could the same trick possibly work for Roy Orbison? Filmmaker Michael Moore gave it a try with rock's stoic presence, though unaccountably doing so ten years too late, when popular music had moved on to the acid sound of the hippie era. That only made this appealingly goofy com-

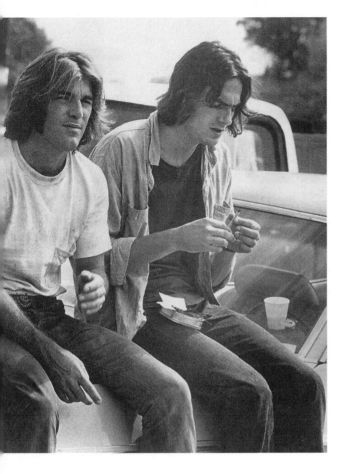

*Dennis Wilson and James Taylor in the best (if least known) of the post–*Easy Rider *road movies,* Two-Lane Blacktop.

bination of dated vocals and timeworn genre clichés all the more likably ludicrous. Orbison and Sammy Jackson played a pair of Johnny Rebs who, like Elvis's kin in *Love Me Tender,* steal a Yankee payroll only to discover that the war is over. Still, one thing made this a must-see: Orbison actually appeared without his trademark dark sunglasses.

With his immobile delivery, Orbison seemed considerably less suited for film stardom than the frenetic Elvis. A Texas native born in 1936, Orbison had early on opted for a traditional country-western career only to shift uncomfortably to rockabilly when Sun signed him in the midfifties. Then came his breakthrough ballad, "Only the Lonely," followed by an endless string of mournfully mellow hits that included the classic "Pretty Woman" in 1964. Though his personal life seemed doomed to endless sadness (Orbison lost his wife and two sons in terrible accidents) and his singing career faded in the midseventies, Orbison finally received the recognition due him in the late eighties, as younger rockers acclaimed the Big O as the equal of the King himself. That honor came none too soon: Orbison died of a heart attack in November 1988.

JAMES TAYLOR AND DENNIS WILSON
Two-Lane Blacktop (1971)

No sooner had *Easy Rider* emerged as a surprise box-office sensation than Hollywood filmmakers began turning out endless imitations, most of them awful: *The Strawberry Statement, Getting Straight, The Revolutionary,* and *Been Down So Long It Looks Like Up to Me* chief among the cycle of "youth-grooving" flicks that opened, then quickly closed over the next two years, proving only that synthetic cinematic rebellion would not sell with the nation's longhairs. *Two-Lane Blacktop* was likewise a box-office bust, yet all similarity to other examples of the brief-lived genre ends there. Directed by Monte Hellman, a protégé of Sam Peckinpah and one of the most intriguing (and tragically wasted) talents of the time, *Two-Lane Blacktop* was as good as a hippie-era road movie could be; understandably, the likably low-key movie eventually became something of a cult item. It concerned an up-tight "suit" (Warren Oates) in a GTO who finds himself locked in a grueling race across the Southwest with two freaks in a '55 Chevy.

The youths were played by James Taylor and Dennis Wilson. Boston-born Taylor had joined Apple Records in 1968, but did not hit his stride until two years later when the soft, countrified folk-rock ballads "Sweet Baby James" and "You've Got a Friend" topped the charts. *Confessional* was the word most music critics seized on to describe Taylor's subtly introspective lyrics, through which he directly tackled his traumatic drug addiction and emotional disturbances, transforming such personal problems into publicly shared art. For a while, he was married to Carly Simon, cutting several notable duet records with her. Dennis Wilson hailed from the opposite end of rock, an original member (in 1961) of Carl and the Passions with brothers Carl and Brian, cousin Mike Love, and longtime pal Al Jardine. Dennis, a devoted surfer, pushed for the creation of a distinct California sound and the changing of the group's name to the Beach Boys. With Brian writing their material, Dennis and his colleagues adapted the fifties pop harmonies of the Four Freshmen to the incessantly driving beat of Chuck Berry's electric guitar. While the other Boys studied transcendental meditation with the Maharishi Yogi, Dennis befriended Charles Manson, beginning a long addiction to booze and drugs. His *Blacktop* appearance marked an attempt to strike out on his own as an actor and musician, but his 1977 solo album, *Pacific Ocean Blue,* made no great impact. His hope for further film roles did not happen. Deeply depressed, he drowned in 1983.

DONOVAN

The Pied Piper (1972)

England's answer to Bob Dylan was how most critics described this hippie-era troubadour. Born Donovan Leitch (the name his son would take when he also became a performer, for the next generation of rock fans) in Glasgow, the eighteen-year-old Donovan came onto the music scene in 1965 looking and sounding precisely the same as Dylan, only with a Brit accent. Songs such as "Catch the Wind" were performed in the same contemporary urban-folksy style that had made Dylan a phenomenon, while even the peaked cap and faded jeans jacket Donovan wore appeared to be borrowed from Dylan. Each performer updated the Depression-era social attitudes of Woody Guthrie, including an idealization of the blue-collar working class, in contemporary blues ballads that optimistically looked forward to an oncoming Age of Aquarius. Indeed, no sooner had Dylan decided to make a major transition and plugged in his guitar, going electric, than Donovan followed suit. Despite all this, Donovan always insisted that he was not a copycat; rather, two similar talents were developing in parallel paths at the same time, though totally separate from one another. Dylan had merely hit it big first.

"Sunshine Superman," "(First) There Is a Mountain," and "Jennifer Juniper" were only a few of Donovan's dozen hits during the late 1960s and early seventies. Then, the bottom fell out of the peace-and-love movement, and Donovan could not adapt; by 1973 he was a dimly remembered relic of a nice but naive period. Donovan did star in a single film, one that intriguingly bridges the gap between the extremes of hippie euphoria and seventies grunge. In this unique and underappreciated retelling of *The Pied Piper,* a European city, menaced by rats and unpleasant adults, serves as perfect corollary to the modern mean streets. Along comes the title character, played by Donovan as the Last Hippie, who leads the children off to form a youth commune. Director Jacques Demy effectively employed an ancient legend to make a contemporary comment. Donovan also provided the musical score, as he did for Franco Zeffirelli's *Brother Sun, Sister Moon*—a hippieish take on the Francis of Assisi legend—in which he did not appear.

ELTON JOHN

Tommy (1975)

When Elton John had his first major hit with "Your Song" in 1969, the short, balding, less than charismatically sexy artist seemed far more likely to be a one-hit wonder than an emerging superstar. But he fooled everyone and soon was the most important influence on rock—as a songwriter and pianist as well as singer—throughout the 1970s. Both his career and abiding influence continued long after that. He'd been born Reginald Kenneth Dwight in Middlesex, En-gland, taking his name from a pair of blues-legend idols, saxophonist Elton Dean and vocalist Long John Baldry. His first major movie work was providing the sound track for a pitiably superficial hippie-era love story called *Friends.* Though his music for that movie has survived, the film itself (John did *not* appear) has understandably been forgotten over the decades. Then, with such diverse megahits as "Crocodile Rock," "Daniel," and "The Bitch Is Back" behind him, Elton was tapped by the erratic auteur Ken Russell for his film version of the Who's rock opera, *Tommy.*

By this time, Elton John had purposefully taken his image into the realm of over-the-top garishness, happily earning himself the epithet the Liberace of

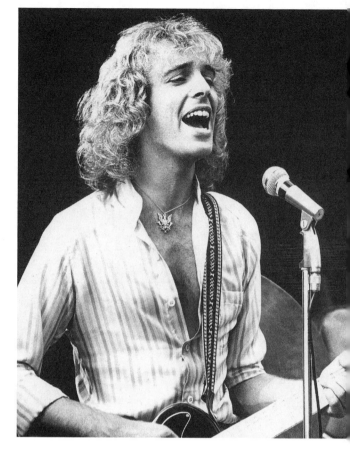

Rock. Naturally enough, he played the Pinball Wizard and, as a living pop nightmare, sang that famous song in the surreal, cartoonish, psychedelic film. Afterward, filmmaker Russell freely admitted that Elton John had not been his first choice for the part, but his only choice; he did not believe that the film could work with any other performer in that role, and most moviegoers (whatever they thought of the film as a whole) agreed wholeheartedly with that assessment. Standing on stilts, Elton John immortalized his image as the most self-satirizing of all rock impresarios. He was also wise enough to realize that, owing to the very uniqueness that made him the perfect person for this part, he was less than qualified for an ongoing acting career.

PETER FRAMPTON

Sgt. Pepper's Lonely Hearts Club Band (1978)

That trendsetting teen magazine of the midsixties, *Rave,* proclaimed Peter Frampton "The Face of '68" owing to the Beckenham (Kent, England) native's traditional pretty-boy good looks, appealingly updated with the requisite long hair for the era of psychedelia. Frampton played guitar with the Herd, Humble Pie, and finally Camel. Unlike most teen-idol pop vocalists, universally scorned by more respected rockers, Frampton was accepted by such luminaries as Billy Preston, Klaus Voorman, even former Beatles George Harrison and Ringo Starr. Perhaps their influence on his music and manner led to Frampton's being cast as a stand-in (along with the Bee Gees) for the Fab Four in Robert Stigwood's *Sgt. Pepper,* the woebegone Tiffany lampshade of a film "inspired" by Beatles tunes from some ten years earlier. The film's failure helped type Frampton as one more of the Bobby

Sherman/David Cassidy youthful has-beens of pop/rock.

Frampton was cast as Billy Shears, one of the many cartoonish characters all "inspired" by various names and references in the Beatles' landmark album. But as is so often the case with films (from *Ode to Billy Joe* to *Red-Headed Stranger*) based on well-regarded narrative recordings, fleshing out the tale in full only makes overobvious what had better been left as richly suggestive. Despite the best efforts of director Michael Schultz (who had recently scored with the likable low-budget ensemble comedy *Car Wash*), the *Sgt. Pepper* movie played to teeny boppers of the 1970s, who had little if any idea what the Beatles had really been about, while turning off serious rock fans, who had regarded the album as a major breakthrough in the history of popular music. By fitting into such a threadbare framework, Frampton put an end to any possible serious rock work in the future.

PAT BENATAR

Union City (1980)

Pat Andrejewski of Brooklyn, born in 1953, studied opera and originally planned to become a concert performer, though fate had other plans. After winning a New York City talent contest in 1975, she signed with Chrysalis. By decade's end, her considerable vocal talent combined with a mainstream feminist attitude allowed the rechristened Pat to emerge as a significant (if incredibly temporary) role model ("the Benatar look" was all the rage for at least fifteen minutes) as well as the pop queen of modified heavy metal, via such hits as "Hit Me With Your Best Shot" and the No. 1 album *Precious Time*. One critic labeled her style "permanent wave music," though her fame proved to be fleeting. But before disappearing from the charts in the mideighties, Benatar slipped into a supporting role in a single film,

Bob Geldof as Pink. (courtesy MGM/UA Entertainment)

Union City, an eerie little thriller from filmmaker Mark Reichert. The Jersey-based drama told a film noir tale in a post-MTV manner. Dennis Lipscomb was the uptight husband, fearing wife Deborah Harry (late of Blondie) was cheating on him, all the while obsessively following (while planning to murder) the man he wrongly held responsible. Benatar played a sex-crazed, newlywed neighbor who befriends Harry and gradually becomes aware of the ever-intensifying situation.

BOB GELDOF

Pink Floyd— The Wall (1982)

Dublin-born Bob Geldof was the vocalist for the Boomtown Rats, Ireland's leading punk-rock band of the mid-1970s. Controversially violent songs such as "I Don't Like Mondays" charted considerably higher in England than they ever did in the United States, where the Rats largely remained a cult phenomenon. Having been referred to more than once as the Mick Jagger of New Wave music, Geldof considered the possibility of following in Mick's footsteps by alternating music with a movie career. He appeared briefly in several lesser known British films of the period, including *No. 1* and *The Secret Policeman's Private Parts,* before winning the lead in Alan Parker's ambitious undertaking *Pink Floyd—The Wall,* expanded from the bestselling and critically acclaimed album of the same name.

Geldof was cast as Pink, a rock star whose emotional anguish and gradual breakdown served as the basis of this nouveau musical, one of the first major films to incorporate the style of rock videos into a feature-length presentation. Geldof's presence was precisely what Parker had needed for his conception, which was to visualize and dramatize the characters and events fleetingly referred to in Pink Floyd's grim lyrics. Geldof's embittered aura of remote, angry, inwardly focused artist/star captured the essence of the project, expressed thusly in Parker's words: "Our story is about a rock-and-roll performer who sits locked in a hotel room . . . a burned-out case. We shuffle in place, reality and nightmare, as we venture into Pink's painful memories, each one a 'brick' in the wall he has gradually built around his feelings." Though Parker rates as a formidable talent at pictorial composition, providing images that were stunning and haunting, his pretentious movie nonetheless made overobvious what had better been left implied, so even die-hard Floyd fans found *The Wall* something of a downer that ran on for way too long. Geldof gave it everything he had, but no other projects have called for a distant, ungiving rock star, helping to explain why he hasn't acted since.

LITTLE RICHARD
Down and Out in Beverly Hills (1986)

Like almost every other early rock-'n'-roll star, Little Richard appeared in early exploitation items including Alan Freed's 1957 minimusical *Don't Knock the Rock* (in which he sang "Tutti Frutti" and "Long Tall Sally") and performed the title song for the more ambitious Frank Tashlin comedy *The Girl Can't Help It* with Jayne Mansfield. He was still at it a decade later, contributing a number to the long-forgotten beach-party flick *Catalina Caper*. But those were singing-only appearances, not one line of dialogue being provided for the musical pioneer born Richard Wayne Penniman in 1932. Then, still looking as youthful as ever though he was well over fifty, Little Richard was approached by writer-director Paul Mazursky to do a full-fledged acting role in his upcoming movie *Down and Out in Beverly Hills,* one of the first adult-oriented movies the Disney company turned out during the Michael Eisner regime, under their new Touchstone Films banner, which allowed Disney to make R-rated pictures without tainting their long-standing image as a purveyor of family films.

Little Richard played Orvis Goodnight, a flamboyant record producer who (like the actor playing him) had been something of a rebel back in the 1950s. Now, though, he likes the quiet life, choosing to live in posh Beverly Hills. The only problem is that Orvis's neighbors (Bette Midler and Richard Dreyfuss) have been in commotion ever since taking in a street person (Nick Nolte) who has convinced them he's a natural-born guru, the source of the spiritual enlightenment that's eluded these financially successful yuppies. Little Richard had a field day with what Mazursky called the "flamboyant" element of his character, for that was the term most critics employed to describe his uniquely satisfying brand of bisexual rock. His hair stretching to the sky in what appeared a mock of the traditional pompadour, his eyes adorned with lavish mascara long before such fey approaches were acceptable, Little Richard took the gospel approach he'd learned during a Pentecostal childhood in Macon, Georgia, and applied it to pop music; in *Down and Out,* he brought it to the movies.

86

13
ALL IN THE FAMILY

T he easiest way to break into movies is to have a relative who has already made it big; the easiest way to become a one-shot wonder is by failing to measure up to mom, dad, or big brother.

CHRISTINA CRAWFORD

Wild in the Country (1961)

When Christina Crawford's now-legendary book, *Mommie Dearest,* was first published in the mid-1970s, Hollywood quickly divided. Half the observers insisted that Christina had told the terrible truth about her mother, superstar Joan Crawford, the other half insisting the book had been pure fantasy by a vindictive monster and unappreciative child. Even within the family, there was no unanimity about Joan: Christina's adopted sister defended their mother while denouncing the book as having been written by "a person born with evil." Christina, then working as L.A. County's commissioner for children's services, defended herself by writing yet another book, *Survivor,* this time chronicling the aftermath of the *Mommie Dearest* scandal.

At that time, Crawford had survived a paralyzing stroke and the breakup of her second marriage. In her younger years, Christina attempted to placate her mother's ambitions for the attractive youth by pursuing a movie career, though there was only one sizable role. She played the spoiled socialite girlfriend of rich bad-boy Gary Lockwood in one of Elvis Presley's few nonmusical (and, commercially speaking, nonsuccessful) movies, *Wild in the Country*. Elvis was cast as a country boy hoping to get a college education and become a writer. He's romanced by seductive counselor Hope Lange, wild-child Tuesday Weld, and nice-girl Millie Perkins. Christina's sultry scene in a bar was one of the film's high spots, though afterward she spent far more time dealing with Mommie Dearest's tirades and tantrums than acting.

Sean Flynn takes the kind of sexy pose his father was so famous for.

SEAN FLYNN
Son of Captain Blood (1962)

"I know it's dangerous," the reckless charmer told friends before leaving Phnom Penh on a motorcycle, "but that's what makes it a good story." Then, the rakish photojournalist zoomed down a dusty highway leading into eastern Cambodia, searching for evidence that North Vietnamese soldiers were operating inside the border. Shortly thereafter, he and a companion were picked up by the Vietcong and marched at gunpoint deep into the jungle. If that sounds like a scene from a fantasy action flick, the ending was all too real. In 1971, as American forces pushed into Cambodia, their captors handed two young men named Flynn and Stone over to the Khmer Rouge.

What followed was an abrupt end for the son of the greatest swashbuckler who ever graced sound movies. Sean Flynn saw his famous father, Errol Flynn, only twice a year during childhood, since the boy lived with his mother, former actress Lili Damita, long since divorced from the gentleman-rogue. Young Flynn flirted with movies early on, playing a bit part in 1960s *Where the Boys Are,* as a college boy frolicking on Florida beaches during spring break. Less than a year later, he was offered his shot at stardom: a fast $10,000 to star in *Son of Captain Blood,* playing the offspring of the dashing pirate his father perfectly incarnated back in 1935. Veteran screenwriter Casey Robinson, who had adapted Rafel Sabatini's novel a quarter century earlier, penned the script. Young Flynn gave it his best shot, but the colorful U.S.-Spanish-Italian coproduction lacked distinction. Afterward, Sean returned to Paris, where he found work in bottom-of-the-barrel B pictures such as *Stop Train 349.* Bored, Flynn seized on the notion of becoming a war correspondent, actually becoming the kind of devil-may-care character his father had played. He was off to Vietnam for *Paris Match,* then was reported missing in 1970, but no body was found. Anyone hoping the story might have a Hollywood-style happy ending was jolted back to reality when Flynn's old colleague Tim Page found the twin graves of Flynn and Stone nearly two decades after they disappeared.

FRANK SINATRA JR.

A Man Called Adam (1966)

Even at the height of his popularity in the mid-1960s, Sammy Davis Jr. rarely played leading roles, more often taking some supporting part in the many movies his best buddy, Frank Sinatra, starred in: *Ocean's Eleven, Sergeants 3, Robin and the Seven Hoods*. A rare exception was this obviously inexpensive, overly melodramatic attempt to dramatize the heart, soul, and mind of a jazz musician. Davis played the title role, a genius with the trumpet (his "performances" were courtesy Nat Adderley) guilt-ridden over the death of his wife and child in a car accident. It only made sense that, in his most personal project, Davis would return the many favors bestowed on him by the Chairman of the Board. Sammy cast Frank junior in the role of Vincent, the young protégé who can learn technique from Adam but must discover music's emotional depth on his own.

A mere twenty-three at the time, Frank junior's second-generation career had already suffered major setbacks. Four years earlier, he'd left the cloister of his home to perform, making the mistake of singing in the same style as his father, thereby inviting uncharitable comparisons. One New York critic derided Junior's show as "mainly mimicry," and that charge, however unfair, would stick. Shortly thereafter, he was kidnapped at gunpoint while performing in Lake Tahoe. Though his father paid the ransom and Junior's vivid recollections of his blindfolded ordeal helped authorities nab the perpetrators, there would always be the stigma, raised by a beleaguered defense lawyer, that Junior staged the whole thing as a publicity stunt. *A Man Called Adam* did not lead to other movie roles, while a stint as cohost (with Joey Heatherton) on *The Golddiggers,* a summer replacement show for Dean Martin, failed to lead to his own series. Junior continued singing until 1977, when the big-band style went totally out of fashion; in 1984, when the big bands came back, so did he. Eventually, Junior would give that up to become conductor for Frank senior's orchestra, attempting to create a cocoon of perfection around his father's aging, ever more imperfect voice. Junior visibly winced as his dad called him "dummy" in front of the audience whenever something went wrong. Years later, Junior made a cameo appearance in Ralph Bakshi's disappointing animated epic *Cool World*. But *A Man Called Adam* remains his only true acting experience.

NEIL CONNERY

Operation Kid Brother (1967)

Operation Kid Brother began as a script called *Operation Casbah,* intended as a minor-league rip-off of the James Bond movies. Then, Italian producer Dario Salsotello mentioned to American writer Mike Stern that he was on the lookout for someone who resembled Sean Connery to play the lead. Stern mentioned that Sean had a younger brother, slaving away as a construction worker in Edinburgh for $10 a day. Stunned, Salsotello determined to hire Neil, then decided to fashion a film that would appear to be an installment in Albert "Cubby" Broccoli's Bond series, concerning the younger brother of the world's greatest secret agent. So the script's working title was changed to *Operation Connery.* For leading ladies, Daniela Bianchi of *From Russia With Love* and Yashiko Yama of *You Only Live Twice* were hired. Adolfo Celi, the villainous head of SPECTRE in *Thunderball,* agreed to appear in a similar role. Both Bernard Lee and Lois Maxwell, scene stealers as Bond's boss "M" and his secretary, Miss Moneypenny, joined the cast in just such parts, though their character names were never uttered for fear of a lawsuit. Everything from the music to the art design was calculated to make the film appear as close to a true Bond as possible, the result being the cinematic equivalent of a knockoff Gucci bag.

At $1,200,000 (considerable at the time), *Operation Kid Brother* (the final release title) rated as the most expensive B movie ever made. Neil, then twenty-eight, bore some resemblance to his brother (Sean was eight years older), but none of the charisma came through, much less acting skill. Neil, who had been living quietly with his wife, Eleanor, and two daughters, was asked if big brother might help out by making a cameo appearance; Neil admitted he and Sean were not particularly close. Sean had given him a Jaguar sports car that the superstar was ready to discard, but, Neil sighed, "I soon discovered the motor was shot." Sean Connery scoffed that the producers should "let Neil go back to plastering." When the film flopped, that's precisely what he did.

SCOTT NEWMAN

Fraternity Row (1977)

"I sometimes feel compelled to dispel a public myth that I get work because of my father," twenty-seven-year-old Scott Newman admitted in 1977 after winning a key role in *Fraternity Row,* writer-producer Charles Gary Allison's graphic study of college hazing in the early 1950s. "No one in his right mind is going to hire somebody to handle a part just because he's somebody's son." Despite the warm relationship Scott had with his father, Paul, being the son of a superstar—however wonderful a person—took its toll. Scott had been battling an alcohol problem for nearly a decade. On another occasion, he complained that "people expect more out of me," and in 1974, he'd been arrested after assaulting a police officer during the breakup of a barroom brawl. He was released to the custody of his father, who immediately brought two psychologists in for full-time therapy. Scott had been involved with motion picture production for some time, though not as an actor. While attending Washington College in Maryland, he and several fraternity brothers tried parachute jumping. Scott was so hooked by the experience that he became a jump instructor, even teaching at Annapolis. When George Roy Hill and Robert Redford, the elder Newman's director and costar for *Butch Cassidy* and *The Sting,* started work on *The Great Waldo Pepper,* young Newman came on board to do stunts, though his father's old friends wouldn't allow him to attempt the most dangerous gag: walking in

Neil Connery, as James Bond's kid brother, romances an endless array of deliciously duplicitous "Bond girls." (courtesy United Artists)

midair from one biplane to another. They knew how devoted their pal was to his boy and couldn't take the chance of putting Scott in such peril.

Scott moved on to small acting roles on TV in *Harry-O* and *Marcus Welby,* then did a brief bit in the Charles Bronson film *Breakheart Pass.* But the role of Chunk Cherry, a sadistic pledgemaster, was clearly his big break. Though he excelled in the part, other offers were not forthcoming. To continue in show business, he sang in a nightclub as "William Scott," determined to be judged for what he could do, not for who he was. Pain from a motorcycle accident caused him to take Darvon and Valium. These, coupled with alcohol, led to his death—ruled accidental, though some believed it to be suicide—on November 28, 1978. Paul Newman got the terrible news at Kenyon College in Ohio; he had returned to his alma mater to direct drama students in a play. He and wife Joanne Woodward dealt with their pain as only the very strong can, finding a positive action to perform rather than surrendering to negativity. They formed the Scott Newman Foundation to combat drug abuse, especially among the young and vulnerable.

As Margo Litzenberger, Kate Burton (far right) joins fellow adventurers Dennis Dun, Donald Li, Kurt Russell, and Kim Cattrall as they stand against a Fu Manchu–type villain in John Carpenter's Big Trouble in Little China. *(courtesy 20th Century–Fox)*

KATE BURTON

Big Trouble in Little China (1986)

When Kate Burton was four years old, she stood in the wings one night while her famous father played King Arthur in the Broadway musical *Camelot*. Supposedly, the little girl understood the difference between theater and real life, yet when she saw her dad mourn the loss of his "wife," Guinevere, after losing her to Lancelot, such distinctions blurred. Before anyone could stop Kate, she rushed out onstage and attempted to assuage his sadness. Ever the pro, Richard pretended that this was part of the planned show, singing the remainder of his song to the child, then took her hand; they walked offstage together. It was, in a manner of speaking, Kate Burton's Broadway debut.

Born in Geneva, Switzerland, but raised in Manhattan, Kate (the product of Burton's marriage to first wife Sybil) initially intended to pursue a career in international diplomacy, studying at the United Nations and Brown University. Yet considering her family heritage, it seemed a foregone conclusion that she'd give the boards a try. At the famed Yale School of Drama, Kate appeared in Shakespeare's *Twelfth Night,* then moved on to the Berkshire Theatre Festival and several Broadway plays, including *Present Laughter*. Her film break came at last when John Carpenter cast her in the pivotal role of Margo Litzenberger, a crusading reporter who chats incessantly as a result of nervousness and abject fear while investigating the nefarious doings of an oriental village. The Fu Manchu clone kidnaps Margo and carries her down to his den of wickedness in the Chinese underworld. Intended as a throwback to thrillers of the 1940s, *Big Trouble in Little China* proved a box-office disaster of the first order. Kate Burton was not offered another film role for seven years, when she would at last play a small supporting role in the minor-league, direct-to-video *Love Matters* with Griffin Dunne and Annette O'Toole. But there have been no other theatrical films to date.

92

14
THE FOURTH ESTATE

Journalists don't spend all their time sitting at their desks, scribing away; here are a handful who made the leap from copy room to movie studio.

LOUELLA PARSONS

Hollywood Hotel (1937)

If Louella Parsons was not America's first film critic, she was certainly *one* of the first and unquestionably the original gossip columnist, turning the private lives of early movie stars into material for her highly influential if often inaccurate column. The daughter of middle-class German-Irish parents in Freeport, Illinois, Parsons (born in 1893) had begun writing as a drama critic for her high-school newspaper. But like most young people of her time, "Lolly" was enthralled with the new medium of motion pictures far more than with traditional live theater. Her column about movies for the *Chicago Record-Herald* was ahead of its time, failing to make much of a stir until 1915, when D. W. Griffith's epic *Birth of a Nation* proved the mettle of movies. As movie critic for New York's *Morning Telegraph,* she praised actress Marion Davis, mistress of William Randolph Hearst; impressed by Lolly's taste, that newspaper mogul hired Parsons for his own team, then syndicated her stories in newspapers worldwide. A bout with tuberculosis sent Parsons packing for the warmer climes of the West Coast; her timing was perfect, as Hollywood had just come into its own.

Though she was always widely read, some secretly complained Parsons couldn't write to save her life, that she enjoyed toying with stars' delicate reputations, and that she was even nastier in person than her only rival, Hedda Hopper. Perhaps intimidated by that pretty newcomer (a former actress), the more mundane Parsons couldn't help but wonder if she might make the opposite odyssey, from invisible columnist to on-screen star. In the midthirties, Lolly was appearing

in a popular radio show, *Hollywood Hotel,* sponsored by Campbell's soups, so she played herself in Busby Berkeley's 1937 film version. The slight story concerned an aspiring star (Dick Powell) who wins a talent contest, then discovers true Hollywood stardom is not easy to achieve, even with Louella Parsons as a guardian angel. Those who knew Lolly scoffed at the idealized self-portrait she here presented: a gentle nurturer of young talent. It was Parsons's single starring role, though she did do a brief cameo near the end of her reign in 1946's *Without Reservations.*

BILL MAULDIN

The Red Badge of Courage (1951)

Growing up as a child in New Mexico, William Henry Mauldin became so frustrated when forced to remain in bed owing to rickets that he took up sketching to escape, creating elaborate visualized fantasies in which he portrayed himself as a knight or cowboy. Bill sensed that cartooning was what he really wanted to do and took a correspondence course, then made a modest living knocking out posters for local companies. During basic training, he casually submitted comic sketches of soldiers to the newspaper of his Oklahoma outfit, the Forty-fifth Division. His work received such acclaim that, when he was shipped out to Europe (Mauldin received the Purple Heart at Salerno), he was assigned to provide comic sketches of bedraggled GIs for the Army's official magazine, *Stars and Stripes.* Mauldin created a comic pair of disgruntled soldiers named Willie and Joe. Their comic misadventures, collected in a 1945 book called *Up Front,* served as the basis for an eventual film in which Tom Ewell and David Wayne were teamed as the Abbott and Costello of the European front.

Indeed, Mauldin was quite active in the film business during the postwar years. In addition to his participation with the *Up Front* movie and its eventual

94

sequel, the cartoonist (then providing newspapers with satiric visions of veterans awkwardly adjusting to civilian life) was hired as the technical adviser for Fred Zinnemann's film *Teresa,* which concerned that very issue. Mauldin also provided a cameo performance in that "lost" film. Then, John Huston announced he was mounting an ambitious version of Stephen Crane's Civil War tale, *The Red Badge of Courage.* While scrupulously authentic to the mid-nineteenth-century milieu, Huston's film would be emotionally informed by the recent World War II experience. To achieve this, Huston cast Audie Murphy (the war's most decorated soldier, already working in Hollywood as a B-western star) as The Youth, tested by battle, and Mauldin as the hero's obnoxious buddy, The Loud Soldier. The excellent movie, now considered a classic, was a commercial disaster. Murphy returned to routine oaters, while Mauldin—after an unsuccessful run for Congress from New York's Twenty-eighth District—concentrated on editorial cartooning, becoming an acclaimed political satirist.

AL CAPP

That Certain Feeling (1956)

When Bob Hope began work on a comedy in which he was to play a neurotic cartoonist, he hoped to cast a real-life incarnation of just such a person as his best pal. Who better, in the mid-1950s, than Al Capp, having achieved cult status via *Li'l Abner.* What was then perceived as the wit and wisdom of Al Capp employed the strip's folksy surface of hillbilly shenanigans to ward off self-anointed censors during the McCarthy era. When cast in *That Certain Feeling,* Capp was at the height of his popularity. *Abner* had been transformed into a hit Broadway musical, and a lavish film version was already being planned. The term Dogpatch had entered the English language, designating any backward community; Sadie Hawkins Day, a rube role-reversal celebration in which girls pursue

Al Capp as the comic-strip writer who becomes Bob Hope's sidekick in That Certain Feeling.

boys, was adopted by high schools across the country as a popular spring ritual. John Steinbeck referred to Capp as "the best writer in the world today," insisting his work legitimized the comic strip as a true art form. Pundits pondered why liberal-minded Capp would choose to team up with a longtime conservative Republican like Hope.

Ten years later, Capp was vilified by the same Old Left loyalists, who were now backing Joan Baez, targeted for vicious attacks in Capp's strip, his once-ripe humor curdling at the sight of antiwar demonstrators. What once seemed an uncompromising attitude now appeared a ruthless mean streak. When old friends begged him to back off, Capp merely smiled knowingly and went on to attack Baez and other counterculture heroes with sledgehammer subtlety. Overnight, his syndicated strip—once carried in nearly a thousand papers nationwide—lost half of its spots. He was said to have verbally abused and sexually harassed a young woman sent to interview him; his daughter Catherine died, an apparent suicide. Capp, crushed by the realization that a once adoring public had turned against him, retired in 1977, swiftly slipping into oblivion, then passing away, heartbroken, two years later.

REX REED

Myra Breckinridge (1970)

Growing up in rural Texas, Louisiana, and Mississippi, Rex Taylor Reed found himself changing towns and schools every couple of months, owing to his itinerant father's work as an oil-field supervisor. Unable to adjust to the endless new situations, Reed instead withdrew, hiding out in movie theaters, eventually preferring life as depicted on-screen to anything around him. Not surprisingly, at Louisiana State University, the journalism major wrote about movies, as well as other components of pop culture. Following graduation, he knocked about as everything from a pancake cook in the Gulf of Mexico to a record salesman at Bloomingdale's in New York. Then came the breakthrough: in 1965, then twenty-seven-year-old freelancer Reed scored interviews with Buster Keaton and Jean-Paul Belmondo at a film festival and sold the stories to the *New York Times* and an early incarnation of *New York* magazine. Thanks to the double-barreled exposure, Reed was shortly penning columns for *Cosmopolitan* and *Women's Wear Daily*. Though his reviews of young stars often sounded like poison-pen letters, Reed was always more charitable to actresses from Hollywood's golden era, once claiming that "the old broads are the ones who interest me the most."

Perhaps that explains why he joined the cast of *Myra Breckinridge*, living legend Mae West being a headliner. Based on the controversial novel by Gore Vidal, *Myra* cast the overtly effeminate Reed as Myron, who in the opening scene requests a sex-change operation. "If I cut it off," his kindly doctor explains, "it won't grow

Jimmy Breslin, playing the role of a contractor of musicians, with Joe Brooks in If Ever I See You Again. *(courtesy Columbia Pictures)*

back." Following the operation, his alter ego and the title character is played by Raquel Welch, whose career somehow survived this catastrophic film that was savaged by critics (including Reed himself, who picked *Myra* as the worst film of the year) and ignored by the public. When asked if he feared attacks by fellow critics, Reed blithely replied, "What can they do? Wreck my acting career?"

JIMMY BRESLIN

If Ever I See You Again (1978)

If Columbo had been a journalist instead of a police detective, he'd have been Jimmy Breslin: an ever-rumpled tough guy with a big soft spot in his heart, a man of old-fashioned values yet with a liberal's conscience, Breslin proved himself the prose poet of Broadway's back alleys for our modern mean streets, a Damon Runyon redux for the era of Martin Scorsese and *Taxi Driver.* Shortly after his birth in Jamaica (Borough of Queens) in 1930, this son of a man who worked with his hands and a cultivated English-teacher mother immediately began balancing his love for the coarse men's world of contact sports and aromatic cigars with a strong sense of colorful idiom in describing just such surroundings. Attending an occasional class at Long Island University while knocking around from one area newspaper to another, Breslin finally ended up at the old *New York Herald Tribune,* where his no-nonsense sports reporting eventually led to a column that allowed him to invariably take the cause of the common man as universal underdog, fighting against monolithic systems.

Such a colorful character was a natural for the movies. The reporters played by Paul Sorvino in *Slow Dancing in the Big City* and John Belushi in *Continental Divide* were, to understate the case, Breslinesque. For years, though, Breslin turned down film offers. Perhaps that stemmed from his disappointment with his presence on WNBC-TV, which he considered a mere shadow of his print persona. "The Breslin in the television studio is fat, uncomfortable, with a terrible speaking voice," was how Jimmy critically dismissed his video work. Eventually, though, Breslin gave in and tried a single film role; surprisingly, it was in the kind of sentimental dreck Breslin the journalist always warned his readers against, Joe Brooks's *If Ever I See You Again.* The Oscar-winning songwriter cast himself as a composer of Madison Avenue jingles, with Breslin as his best pal, a contractor of musicians for the ads they collaborated on. Leonard Maltin spoke for most critics when he insisted, "Breslin should stick to his typewriter." Wisely, Breslin took that sage advice.

STUDS TERKEL
Eight Men Out (1988)

John Sayles's version of the famed White Sox scandal, which grew out of the 1919 World Series fix, asserted the players had been justified in throwing the big game owing to unfair treatment by their team owner. Sayles portrayed a working-class rebellion against an authoritarian capitalist elite, and to convey this essentially socialist message he related his tale through the point of view of two jaded, world-weary sportswriters, Ring Lardner and Hugh Fullerton. Sayles cast himself as the younger man, while for the role of Lardner's mentor he tapped Studs Terkel, the Chicago-based journalist who had written about everything from sports to jazz, also proving during the early days of television (1949–53) that, at its best, the live talk show could be a viable artistic medium.

A sometimes stage and radio actor who had been born in the Bronx but grew up in the Windy City, Terkel had developed his penchant for what he tagged "guerrilla journalism" early on in life. His widowed mother supported the family by running the Wells-Grand Hotel on Chicago's North Side, just off the Loop, allowing the impressionable young Louis Terkel to meet and observe the blue-collar workers who lived there, as well as the gangster element that lorded over the nearby street turf. After briefly flirting with a career in the law, Terkel backed off such pursuits and took the pen name Studs after James T. Farrell's Chicago-based literary hero, Studs Lonigan. Terkel joined the Federal Writers Project during the darkest days of the Great Depression. He wrote one play, *Amazing Grace,* which received mixed reviews at best. He will always be remembered for his triptych of books (all transcriptions of tape-recorded interviews with diverse people) on basic American issues: *Division Street* (race relations), *Hard Times* (the legacy of the thirties), and *Working* (studying our nation's changing view of its essential ethic), as well as his award-winning TV series *Studs Place.* In each, he developed and perfected the twentieth-century art form known as oral history.

15
SIGNIFICANT OTHERS

Wives and husbands of significant people often land a key movie role, though the status of Mr. or Ms. Celebrity can in the long run be a damning indictment.

DOROTHY COONAN

Wild Boys of the Road (1933)

Dark-haired, pug-nosed, and freckle-faced Dorothy Coonan won work as a chorus dancer in such early sound films as *The Show of Shows* and Busby Berkeley's *Whoopee!* before reaching the age of eighteen. Born in Minneapolis on Thanksgiving, 1914, she'd come to Hollywood and covered her freckles with makeup, hoping to make herself look more glamorous, having no idea that those very freckles would be her claim to one-shot-wonder fame. William Wellman was planning a sociological study of the young people taking to the open road during those dark early days of the Great Depression. In his story, a teenage girl would disguise herself as a boy, Shakespeare style, traveling with Frankie Darrow and the other tough kids. Problem was, all the women he tested were either too womanly or not womanly enough. One look at Dorothy Coonan's freckled face and Wellman knew he had the perfect person. In a floppy hat and overalls, she'd be the ideal tomboy, yet, when the time came, she could slip out of her disguise and look gorgeous.

The film, released by Warner Bros. in 1933, was significant even beyond its unsparing portrayal of disenfranchised young people in search of their place in the sun. Though the first half depicts the heartlessness with which local authorities treat such lost and lonely youth, *Wild Boys* suggested in its second portion that things were about to change. A judge, who bears a striking resemblance to the recently elected president Franklin Roosevelt, insists to the depressed youths that a new deal is on the way. Whether the film reflected or affected politics is difficult to say, but shortly after its release, the American political situation had changed to liberalism. Wellman was satisfied that he'd at last been able to make an important statement. He was so impressed by his leading lady's charms that, when the production was completed, he asked for Dorothy's hand in marriage. She happily agreed to leave films to become Mrs. William Wellman.

NEILE ADAMS (McQUEEN)

This Could Be the Night (1957)

Despite plenty of competition, dancer Neile Adams as Gladys all but stole the show when *The Pajama Gang* threatened to run forever at Broadway's St. James Theatre during the midfifties. She was swept off her feet, though, when on their first date a young actor named Steven McQueen (he'd replaced Ben Gazzara onstage in *A Hatful of Rain*) rode up on a motorcycle after one night's show. Still wearing her crinolines, she hopped up behind him and roared off into the night. They were married a few months later in Mexico, so when McQueen headed west to star in *The Blob,* Neile made the difficult decision to leave her beloved Great White Way and follow her man. One glance at her exotic good looks (born in Manila, she was of Eurasian ancestry) had bigwigs predicting imminent stardom. It might just have happened: Neile won a showy role as a club dancer in *This Could Be the Night* with Jean Simmons, Paul Douglas, and Tony Franciosa. Her sexy "Extra! Extra!" routine was the talk of the town.

But her success only made

Neile Adams in the sensational "Extra! Extra!" specialty number that briefly made her the toast of Hollywood. (courtesy Metro-Goldwyn-Mayer)

Steve angry and jealous. For the sake of their relationship (Steve "did not allow," in her later words, his wife to work) Neile agreed to spend the next fifteen years as his wife and mother of son Chad and daughter Terry. Her reward for this was to suffer the indignities of his affairs with Lee Remick and other glamorous women. When in the early 1970s Steve's highly publicized romance with model-turned-actress Ali MacGraw became serious, Neile shortly found herself living as a single mom, if an upscale one. Through all this, she did manage to maintain an ongoing friendship with Steve. But it was time to enjoy the career she'd denied herself. Neile returned to her first great love, dancing, first by performing in a 1977 L.A. production of *Paint Your Wagon,* then guesting as master teacher for gifted California students. She remarried, this time to businessman Alvin Toffel, and after Steve's long, painful death from cancer, she penned a book about their tempestuous relationship. *My Husband My Friend: A Memoir,* published by Atheneum Publishers, dealt squarely with his cocaine habit and physical abusiveness, also detailing their many happy moments.

TARITA

Mutiny on the Bounty (1962)

No sooner had Marlon Brando divorced his first wife, the gorgeous but ill-tempered Anna Kashfi, then he rushed into a second marriage with Movita, the considerably older actress best remembered as a beautiful native girl whom Fletcher Christian (Clark Gable) becomes involved with in the 1935 Oscar winner *Mutiny on the Bounty.* Brando may actually have been in love with the character Movita had enacted in her most famous film, and perhaps the relationship didn't work because the real woman couldn't compete with Brando's fiction-inspired mental image of what she ought to be like. Intriguingly enough, Brando shortly agreed to play Fletcher in the remake of *Mutiny* then being planned at MGM. On location in Tahiti, he first met Tarita, the young woman who would portray Movita's former role opposite him. She was of Chinese and Tahitian origin, and Brando fell head over heels in love; perhaps she could incarnate his romantic image of her screen character in a way that Movita had apparently been unable to do.

Before being cast, Tarita had been waitressing and working as a part-time cook at a little hash house. She was seriously involved with the Danish chef there, but one glance at the charismatic American actor and the naive young woman was overwhelmed. The filming proved disastrous, with endless rewrites, arguments over the film's intent, a change of directors (from Carol Reed to Lewis Milestone) in midmovie, and endless weather problems sending what was to have been a fairly conventional remake out of control. Initially budgeted at under $10 million but coming in at well over $20 million, *Mutiny* briefly rated as the most

Fletcher Christian falls under the spell of native girl Maimiti, just as Marlon Brando fell under the spell of the first-time actress, Tarita. (courtesy Arcola Prod./MGM)

expensive movie ever made, though less than a year later the debacle of *Cleopatra* would dwarf this film's problems. But Brando had found the woman with whom he would share his life. Fearful of the darkening world situation and hoping to create some separate peace, Brando bought the South Sea island of Teti'aroa, where he and Tarita lived with their children. As he tragically learned, it's impossible to run away from encroaching ugliness, since it will follow you. One by one, his beloved offspring experienced unhappy fates. Always, though, Tarita was there to share the little joys and huge sorrows with him.

CLAUDINE LONGET
The Party (1968)

Blake Edwards's *The Party* was both a revival of old-fashioned sight-gag-a-second comedies from the silent days and a satire on the superficiality of contemporary Hollywood's social scene. Peter Sellers played a wide-eyed Indian actor imported for a remake of *Gunga Din,* visiting a snobby party and, by evening's end, literally destroying it, however unintentionally.

The only other nonphony at the affair, a vivacious young Frenchwoman, was portrayed by Andy Williams's wife, Claudine Longet, just then enjoying a brief bout with stardom. Longet first met Williams when, in 1960, the popular singer visited the City of Lights to record an album called *Under Paris Skies*. Claudine, one of seven children born to a manufacturer of electronic hospital equipment, was then dancing with the Delia Scalia Ballet Company. Her fleeting contact with Williams convinced Claudine that she wanted to work in America, but there were few invitations for a ballet dancer. When Claudine learned that a cancan company was rehearsing a U.S. version of the Folies-Bergère, she quickly signed up and later

Claudine Longet and Peter Sellers, as the only two unpretentious people at a snooty Hollywood party, encounter a pompous cowboy star. (Denny Miller).

that year met Williams again when he played Vegas.

Something clicked, he invited her to Hollywood to appear on his upcoming special, and shortly thereafter the two were married. They had three children and much success; she cohosted his Christmas specials, did a small role in the *McHale's Navy* film, and cut a pop album, *Claudine,* singing (if that's the term) cover versions of other people's hits in a sexy whisp of a voice. Surprisingly, it went gold. But though *The Party* was a huge hit, there were no other film roles, and frustrated and anxious, Longet split from Williams, moving to Aspen, Colorado, where she shared a home with former ski champion Vladimir "Spider" Sabich. In 1976, she shot him in the stomach with his .22-caliber pistol, later claiming in court that it was an accident, though his family remained convinced she'd killed him following an argument. Longet was found guilty of "criminally negligent homicide," a misdemeanor, and sentenced to thirty days in jail, at a time of her own choosing. It was an unaccountably light sentence that outraged many Aspen residents. Afterward, Longet—clearly grateful to her defense lawyer Ron Austin—married him. Her last words to the reporters who'd covered the criminal case had been, "I hope I never have to see any of you ever again." Claudine Longet got that wish. Other than in vulgar gags about her final moments with Spider Sabich, the once ambitious Frenchwoman never surfaced again.

SHAKIRA CAINE
The Man Who Would Be King (1975)

Shakira Caine as the silent, sensuous princess who captivates Sean Connery and real-life husband Michael Caine in John Huston's The Man Who Would Be King. *(courtesy Columbia Pictures)*

She was born Shakira Baksh, a Kashmiri Indian from British Guiana (now called Guyana) who as a teenage girl carefully considered the quality of life around her and determined to leave as quickly as possible. Sensing that her striking beauty could be her ticket out, Shakira entered the Miss Guiana contest, easily won, then flew to England for the 1967 Miss World contest, being named third runner-up. Winning or losing was considerably less important than making her exit; shortly, she was employed as a popular London model. One night, actor Michael Caine was relaxing in front of his telly and caught the most breath-taking woman he'd ever seen, decked out as a Brazilian peasant in a commercial for Maxwell House coffee, and immediately determined to learn her identity. A mutual friend in the advertising business arranged their first date. Though he invited Shakira to join his life's adventure, Caine was at the time a bit Alfie-ish, resisting marriage until Shakira announced she was pregnant. They were immediately wed; she gave birth to their daughter, Natasha.

Then, in 1975, Shakira accompanied her husband, his costar Sean Connery, and director John Huston on location for the shooting of *The Man Who Would Be King,* a handsome epic based on Kipling's classic adventure yarn about two louts who temporarily become gods of a lost tribe. Almost immediately, Huston sensed his leading lady, Patricia Neal's daughter Tessa Dahl, was not working out, since she could not be made up to look exotic enough. While sharing his problems with Caine, Huston glanced over his star's shoulder and realized Shakira was precisely the right person to play the princess; a mystical persona was more significant than acting ability considering the character's lack of dialogue. But the experience, which "terrified" Shakira, didn't create in her any burning ambition to be a star. "This is her first and last movie," Michael declared. "She's going to stay home and have kids." That's precisely what she did, along with running a successful sideline career as a fashion designer.

16
STRANGE INTERLUDES

These people played parts that were so strange, a follow-up seemed all but impossible; how could you equal, much less top, their strange stuff?

JEAN ARLISS

Homicidal (1961)

No sooner had William Castle seen Alfred Hitchcock's *Psycho* and read the record-breaking box-office returns in *Variety,* than he set to work on his own B-movie rip-off of the screen's first violent psychosexual thriller. Shortly, he had *Homicidal* ready to go, concerning a beautiful, mysterious young nurse who appears guilty of a murder that could only have been committed by a man. In the film's then-shocking denouement, the nurse reveals she is indeed an effeminate man in disguise. Budding starlet Victoria Shaw, offered the part, was offended by the perversity and turned the script down flat. Castle then recast, though for that surprise ending to work, the schlockmeister had to keep the gender of the unknown top-billed star shrouded in secrecy, explaining why he chose to bill the performer as "Jean Arliss," which could have gone either way. Indeed, audiences walked out of the theater trying to decide if the dual roles had been played by a male or female performer.

Jean Arliss was, in fact, the actress who had previously been billed as Joan Marshall and who, in later years, would work as a producer under the name Joan Ashby, following her marriage to director Hal Ashby. Raised in Evanston, Illinois, Joan Schrepfermann had always wanted to be an actress, though a childhood bout with polio convinced her family that this was not to be. Nonetheless, she persevered, taking up dancing for exercise, eventually recovering so completely that she performed at Chicago's Chez Paree at night while attending drama school at the Goodman Theatre by day. She found work as a photographer's model and local TV actress as Joan Sanders, taking her first husband's last name. Two husbands later, the five-foot-six-inch brunette arrived in Hollywood, landing her-

Jean Arliss (right) *as the strange, and slightly effeminate, young man who menaces Glenn Corbett and Patricia Breslin in* Homicidal, *William Castle's low-budget answer to Hitchcock's* Psycho. *(courtesy Columbia Pictures)*

self a spot as a dancer on TV's *The Red Skelton Show*. In 1958, she landed the role of Sailor Duval, attractive ward to Dane Clark's Slate Shannon in the Caribbean-based adventure show *Bold Venture*. After *Homicidal* hit it big in theaters, "Jean" was offered numerous roles—as a man! As it turned out, Hollywood producers had, like viewers, been confused by Joan's convincing performance. No one in the movie business was willing to believe Jean Arliss didn't really exist; this was Hollywood's real-life Victor/Victoria tale. So Joan gave up acting and began working behind the cameras; she died in 1992 of lung cancer.

JOHN HANSEN

The Christine Jorgensen Story (1970)

John Hansen was an eighteen-year-old high school athlete living in Downey, California, in 1970, one of five children born to an insurance salesman and his wife. He was performing in family-oriented shows when he was snatched from oblivion to star in this exploitation flick about a real-life 1950s man who under-

106

went the world's first successful sex-change operation to become a woman. Originally, Christine had wanted to play the role him/herself, but when producer Ed Small nixed that idea, he/she then insisted that a girl be cast. But director Irving Rapper nixed that idea, too, going on to explain his thinking at the time: "A female impersonator was exactly what I didn't want. John was with that all-American group at Disneyland, singing and dancing. Much to his surprise, I cast him after he read only four lines."

Rapper saw something in John Hansen that struck him as precisely right for what would clearly be a daring part to play: "In person, John reflects no glamour at all, but has an incandescent quality on-screen. [Producer] Small kept after me to make John more and more effeminate, but I resisted that. I always had him speak as softly as possible and gave him a few discrete effeminate gestures. He has such burly shoulders [that] we had to place the camera [in positions that were] the least favorable to them after George becomes Christine." His mother had a more immediate reaction to hearing that her son had been cast in the role: "I may throw up." At least she didn't have to worry about ever going to see John in another movie.

PALOMA PICASSO

Immoral Tales (1975)

Growing up with a famous parent is difficult enough, but being a love child proves even more precarious to one's psyche. Paloma Picasso, born in 1949 to the master of modern art and Françoise Gilot (Picasso was still legally married to Olga Koklova at the time), found herself in such a position, yet it apparently did not dent her self-esteem. Shortly after befriending Paloma in the late 1970s, Lauren Bacall noted in amazement, "She's so open, sweet, disarming, and plain normal that it's a shock to the system." Perhaps, though, the "open" part is debatable, since more than one of Paloma's old pals have described her as sphinxlike. There was always the sense that something deep, perhaps dark, lurked just beneath that placid surface, hinted at in the humorous edges of her smile and the piercing solemnity of her eyes. Which might help us understand her choice for the single film Paloma appeared in: Borowcyk's *Immoral Tales,* a quartet of strange stories ranging from contemporary comedy to period horror.

Paloma chose the latter, a retelling of the Erzebeth Bathory legend. Real-life aristocratic cousin to Count Dracula, Bathory maintained her fabled beauty by traveling about the Middle Eastern European countryside, taking up temporary residence in various castles, then sending her minions out to kidnap virginal local girls so she could bathe in their pure blood. Bathory was eventually walled up in a room, left to grow old staring at her aging image in a mirror. That is presented in the film with a graphicness that originally won the movie an X rating. When asked why she chose to act in such a picture, this living Mona Lisa merely smiled and said, "Because I liked the character." Like Bathory, Paloma enjoyed creating shocks, showing up at fashionable parties in extravagant outfits to turn herself into a fashion statement, expressing through her presence a sharp wit for the absurd not unlike the one found in her father's paintings. Paloma created set designs for plays and designed jewelry, from Saint Laurent accessories to 22k-gold bracelets for Zolotas. After living for four years with Argentinian playwright Rafael Lopez Sanchez, Paloma married him in 1978, moving into an apartment on the Seine. That same year, she and her brother Claude oversaw the creation of Paris's now rightly famous Picasso Museum.

Paloma Picasso starred as the legendary vampiress Erzebeth Bathory in Immoral Tales, *her only film. (courtesy Photofest)*

ANNE CARLISLE
Liquid Sky (1983)

Liquid Sky was *the* cult movie of 1983; after being quietly slipped into the Waverly Twin theater in New York's Greenwich Village, the independent film, shot on a minuscule $500,000 budget, garnered rave reviews (*New York* magazine hailed it as "the funniest, craziest, dirtiest, most perversely beautiful science-fiction movie ever made") and became a phenomenon amid members of the New Wave scene. One year later, it was still playing. *Liquid Sky* told the story, in a dreamlike post-MTV manner, of Margaret, a bisexual punk model, and Jimmy, a misogynistic druggie. Both the woman and the man were played by actress Anne Carlisle. A native of New Milford, Connecticut, she had moved to Manhattan to study painting, sculpture, and holography at the School of Visual Art. For the fun of it, she also took acting lessons at the Robert Brady Studios, discovering that this was what she really wanted to do.

For a while, Anne modeled for La Rocka, the city's "first New Wave modeling agency," and appeared in a

Anne Carlisle as Jimmy, one of the two roles she played in Liquid Sky. *(photo by Yuri Neyman, courtesy Z-Films)*

super-8 experimental film, *Fish.* She met Russian-born director Slava Tsukerman and his wife, Nina Kerova, though a low-budget film they discussed doing together with Anne as the star fell through. Tsukerman, who had become somewhat obsessed with the emerging New Wave scene around him, encouraged Carlisle to work on a script about a diminutive alien who visits Earth, hoping to locate the magical chemical released during orgasm and heroin injection. The scenes of Margaret's lovers dissolving into a green mist as they reach climax were filmed in Carlisle's loft apartment. She was a total collaborator with Tsukerman and his producer/casting-director wife. Afterward, Carlisle dressed in conservative tweeds, hoping to convince more mainstream casting directors that she was not the oddball (or, more correctly, *either* of the oddballs) she'd played in the film. The hope was to surprise everyone with how straight she really was and springboard from cult appeal to mainstream stardom. But only low-budget movie maven Larry Cohen (*It's Alive!*) was willing to give her a shot, though the minor thriller they filmed together (*Blind Alley,* a.k.a. *Perfect Strangers*) proved to be a disappointment and went direct to video. Though there were no other starring vehicles for Carlisle, *Liquid Sky* remains one of the great "midnight movies" of all time.

GARY KEMP AND MARTIN KEMP

The Krays (1990)

Peter Medak's oppressively violent but effectively realistic variation on the gangster film told the true story of slum-born twins, Martin and Reginald Kray, who reacted to their harsh environment by assuming a survival-of-the-fittest attitude, rising in power by any means possible to control London's underworld during the 1960s. One was straight and one was gay; both were hard, cold, and Machiavellian, making this emotionally aloof movie fascinating though frightening to watch. As cold-blooded and calculated as the two brothers could be toward their adversaries, they were also (if the film is to be believed) dedicated to each other, and even more so toward their mother, Violet Kray (played in the film by Billie Whitelaw), who was treated as the adored queen of their blood-based personal empire. The film, though too depressing to become a mainstream hit, has since become a cult classic and is among the strangest of strange interludes in movie history.

Equally strange was the casting. The stars, Gary and Martin Kemp, were in fact brothers but most definitely were *not* twins. Guitarist/songwriter Gary had formed the U.K. group Spandau Ballet in 1979 as a furious reaction against the emerging punk scene. Referring to his group as "the new romantics," Gary idolized the charmingly funky soul music (mostly black) from America and wanted to introduce his countrymen to a revised Brit version. Brother Martin, born in 1961 and a year younger than Gary, played the bass. In England, their music became hugely popular with people in their late twenties and early thirties who longed for old-fashioned style and technique in popular entertainment. Their fans were stunned when such gushing romantics made their screen debut not in a nice family film but in this grotesque study of decadence. Other than the film *The Krays,* the Kemps are best known to American audiences for their appearance in 1985's Live Aid, though they have appeared separately in obscure British films.

17
IT'S A GREAT ACT, BUT—

T hey weren't chosen for acting ability; they were chosen because they were precisely right for one role, and one role only.

J. SCOTT SMART

The Fat Man (1951)

The moment that *The Thin Man* hit theater screens in 1934, the public fell in love with the suave sleuths played by William Powell and Myrna Loy. As they continued their upscale snooping in a succession of appealing films lasting until 1947, most people had the impression that the title referred to Powell, though in fact "the thin man" had been one of the suspects in the very first series entry, based on a novel by noted crime-fiction writer Dashiell Hammett. But in another of his books, *The Fat Man,* Hammett had indeed employed that moniker to describe a most unique detective, a corpulent gourmet who balanced stints in the kitchen with time for solving crimes. When the Powell-Loy series had at last ground to a halt, Hollywood producers began thinking about starting up a series of films about that other Hammett sleuth.

The Fat Man had been popular on the radio for some time, and the unseen man who provided the voice for the title character was in fact physically perfect for the role. J. Scott Smart weighed in at 255 pounds. The five-foot-nine-inch Scotch-Irish actor, descended from *Mayflower* pilgrims, had been born on November 27, 1902. Early on, he'd decided to become an actor and began working in Buffalo, New York, in local stock companies. His rich, resonant voice helped him win radio roles; before long, the big fellow was hired by the famed "March of Time" crew to imitate actual voices, ranging from Hitler to the pope, for docudrama re-creations that many people took to be the real thing.

Naturally, he tried his hand at films, winding up at Universal, where he had minor parts in long-forgotten films such as *Top of the Town.* At thirty-six, discouraged with Hollywood, Smart returned to the East Coast where he was

111

tapped for solid roles in such Broadway plays as *The Pirate*. It was then that Smart was approached for radio's *The Fat Man* show; he began doing the voice in 1946, the series successfully running for four and a half years. Not so, unfortunately, the film. When Smart returned to his old studio, Universal, he was informed that rather than a classy production in the *Thin Man* tradition, *The Fat Man* would be produced as what used to be called a programmer: a respectable but at best medium-budget studio film allowing contract players to earn their keep. A pre-stardom Rock Hudson was featured, along with singer Julie London, Jayne Meadows (future wife of Steve Allen), and circus clown Emmett Kelly in one of his rare film roles, appearing in the finale that brought Smart to a circus for the unmasking of the villain. The results were solid though notably uninspired, and the lukewarm public response did not merit a follow-up. Smart returned to the radio, his medium of choice; he died in 1960.

FRIEDRICH LEDEBUR

Moby Dick (1956)

Born in upper Austria, son of a count who reigned as master of a great country estate, Friedrich Ledebur might seem an odd choice to play Herman Melville's cannibal harpooner, Queequeg from the South Seas. But an odd series of circumstances conspired to bring the six-foot-six continental sophisticate together with filmmaker John Huston and led to an inspired bit of casting. Early on in his life, Ledebur discovered two great loves: horses, which his father raised and bred, and the live theater. Before long, young Friedrich was training the horses on the family estate, becoming a first-rate polo player as well. After a stint at the University of Vienna where he majored in chemistry but also studied agricultural engineering, Ledebur made it a point to seek out the legendary impresario of expressionist theater Max Reinhardt in Vienna, studying with the master and engaging in live theater work.

Ledebur hunted big game around the world; while in England, he met and married actress Iris Tree, daughter of the famed Sir Herbert Beerbohm Tree. His deep feeling for horses eventually brought Ledebur to America; where better for a fan of equestrian accomplishment to journey than to the Far West? There, he worked on ranches, breaking horses and riding in rodeos. Then, filmmaker Robert Rossen, in preproduction to film his epic *Alexander the Great* with Richard Burton, met Ledebur and convinced him to join the film company in Spain, where Ledebur was put in charge of the production's two thousand horses. Noticing his employee's unique look, Rossen awarded him a bit part as well. Upon returning to the States, Rossen listened to old friend Huston complain about his need to find a large, taciturn, quietly fascinating presence for the part of Ishmael's companion in *Moby Dick*. Rossen's eyes lit up as he made the recommendation that Huston would happily follow.

112

HAROLD SAKATA

Goldfinger (1964)

Every supervillain in an early 1960s James Bond film was accompanied by a colorful henchman who ruthlessly if uniquely dispatched enemies. Auric Goldfinger was no exception: Gert Frobe had Harold Sakata around as Oddjob, a mustachioed, tuxedo-bedecked Korean killer wearing a lethal, razor-sharp bowler hat, which he sent flying off like a boomerang to murder anyone in their way. Oddjob was the heavy who painted Shirley Eaton gold, removing that beautiful British blonde from the story way too early in the proceedings.

Hard to believe that, as a young man growing up in Hawaii, Sakata had been a skinny weakling of 105 pounds, but that was the case; he built himself up through rigorous training programs and became an Olympic weight lifter. As Tosh Togo, a comically villainous pro wrestler on London TV, Sakata was spotted by producer Harry Saltzman and cast in the film. On the set, he mistakenly hit Sean Connery when director Guy Hamilton called out for "more realism"; Connery was out cold for three days. Sakata later played Oddjoblike characters on such TV shows as *Batman* and occasionally made a brief cameo appearance, always evoking his unforgettable Oddjob role, in such films as *Impulse* and *The Jaws of Death* before his death in 1982.

NICK APOLLO FORTE

Broadway Danny Rose (1984)

When Woody Allen began work on this Runyonesque tale of a low-level agent and the semitalented Italian singer he manages, casting agents were sent searching for an overweight, over-the-hill singer. One had the bright idea to step into a record store on the corner of Manhattan's Forty-ninth Street and flip through the items in the bargain bin. Staring up at him was the face of Nick Apollo Forte, looking like a combination of Tony Bennett on a bad day and Buddy Hackett on a good one. Later listening to cuts on the album, *Images,* Allen sensed that if Nick Apollo Forte had not been born, someone would have had to create him if the role of Lou Canova (whose only "hit" single had been on the charts for fifteen minutes) was to be perfectly cast.

Born Nicola Antonio Forte, Nick changed his middle name when, at eighteen, he'd been booked to play with Della Reese at the Apollo Theatre in Harlem. Forte had visited a fortune-teller who insisted that if he adopted the theater's name for his own, godlike stardom would follow. That never happened; a year later, Nick took a day job managing a shoe store, married his pretty clerk Rosalie Trapasso, then began fathering seven children between gigs as a late-night lounge singer. Nick lived in Waterbury, Connecticut, serving as his own

Small-time agent Danny Rose (Woody Allen, left) gives his all for his only remaining client, Lou Canova (Nick Apollo Forte). (photo by Brian Hamill, courtesy Orion Pictures)

booking agent; he didn't even have a résumé to send when Woody contacted him about the film. Nonetheless, he got the job, though only after promising to dye his strawberry-blond hair jet-black. Forte, who had never even seen a Woody Allen film, suggested that one of his own compositions, "Agita" (Italian for indigestion), might be right for the sound track; Woody made it the theme song. When filming was completed, its "star" quietly returned to the Northeast lounge circuit. The only impact his critically acclaimed film performance had was to allow him to up his asking price from $100 to $150 per night.

ANDRE THE GIANT

The Princess Bride (1987)

Though he actually had bit parts and walk-ons in a half dozen films including *Micki + Maude,* Andre the Giant will always be remembered as the one-shot wonder whose persona as a professional wrestler helped him win a key role in *The Princess Bride,* Rob

Reiner's warmly regarded film of novelist William Goldman's sweet-spirited spoof of old-fashioned adventure tales. Indeed, Andre held his own against the competition of Mandy Patinkin, Wallace Shawn, Robin Wright, Peter Falk, and Billy Crystal (among others), playing the role of Fezzik, a dull-witted but good-natured giant who helps to kidnap Princess Buttercup but later sees the error of his ways, then helps the heroes save her. Who else could have played that part (without resorting to special effects) but this massive (seven feet five inches, 525 pounds) French national who'd left his small village east of Paris at age fifteen to learn the wrestling trade?

Born Andre Rene Roussimoff, he had soon developed acromegaly, an excessive secretion of the growth hormones, which caused his head, face, hands, feet, and chest to progressively enlarge year by year. That certainly didn't stop Andre from carving out a unique career for himself. His wrestling skills took him far from Paris, first to Manchester, England, for further training, then the big move to America. Andre—as gentle a giant in real life as in the film—insisted the *Princess Bride* role had given him great satisfaction: "I love kids and I like to make them happy." He died five years later, at age forty-six, after suffering a heart attack while visiting his native France to attend his father's funeral.

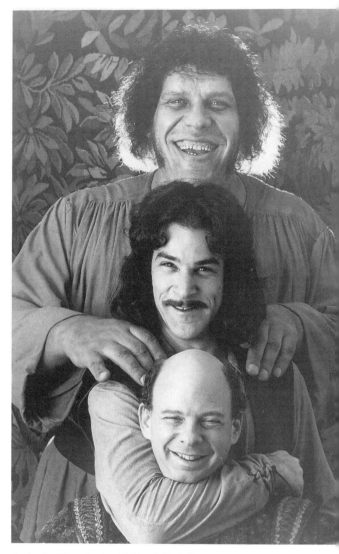

Andre the Giant (top) *with Mandy Patinkin as Montoya, and Wallace Shawn as Vizzini, in* The Princess Bride. *(courtesy 20th Century–Fox)*

18
ALL THE WRITE STUFF

Major authors sometimes get bitten by the acting bug; here are some who tried translating the written word to celluloid, and not just behind the scenes.

JOHN O'HARA

The General Died at Dawn (1936)

When John O'Hara's first novel, *Appointment in Samarra,* was released in 1934, the tall writer with the big ears and penetrating eyes, then just short of thirty, was already something of a celebrity, thanks to his noted work as a journalist. This son of a Pennsylvania doctor had left his family's cushy upper-middle-class surroundings to burn the midnight oil along New York's Fifty-second Street, covering the back alleys of the theater district, particularly those shady dives where Tin Pan Alley songs were invested with the proper saloon spin by worn, weary men standing at some halfway beacon between fading entertainer and full-fledged derelict. For the *Herald Tribune,* the *Daily Mirror,* and the *Morning Telegraph,* O'Hara had built himself a reputation as hard-boiled reporter who washed down his words with straight gin. Anyone looking for another Ernest Hemingway or the next Ring Lardner need search no further.

O'Hara was always genuinely interested in movies, working as a press agent for motion pictures for a while, then heading out to California, where he wrote for numerous studios: Paramount in 1924, Sam Goldwyn in 1937, RKO-Radio Pictures in 1939, and 20th Century–Fox in 1940. Shortly thereafter, he would pen *Newsweek*'s "Entertainment Week" column. This love of film, combined with his notoriety, helps explain why O'Hara took an acting job in *The General Died at Dawn,* Paramount's 1936 version of the much-discussed novel by Charles G. Booth. Though on the surface a tale of romance and adventure set in China's northern districts, the book had, beneath its patina of melodrama, dealt realistical-

116

Richard Wright, playing his own creation Bigger Thomas, peers in at family and friends, from whom he has become alienated owing to his crime. (courtesy Walter Gould Presentation)

ly with the oppression of the common people by petty tyrants and local war-lords in those difficult days just before the outbreak of World War II. Rugged Gary Cooper and elegant Madeleine Carroll were cast as the attractive couple thrown together when confronted by devious, brilliant, power-mad General Wang (Akim Tamiroff). One scene featured several reporters interviewing the hero (intriguingly enough, named O'Hara!) aboard the Orient Express. Two were played by the film's screenwriter and director, Clifford Odets and Lewis Milestone; the other, the big, good-looking guy with the large ears and penetrating eyes, was John O'Hara.

RICHARD WRIGHT

Native Son (1950)

Little in Richard Wright's childhood suggested he would emerge as an esteemed author; his own grandmother insisted he'd end up on the gallows someday owing to her ward's troublemaking in rural Mississippi. But while working menial jobs in Memphis at age fifteen, Wright noticed a newspaper story attacking someone named H. L. Mencken. Convinced that anyone who offended the Southern ruling class had to be worth reading, Wright talked a white pal into taking out anything by or about Mencken from the local library. Devouring all the works that Mencken recommended in his *Book of Prefaces,* Wright hit on the idea of trying his own hand as a scribe. While in Chicago, he became aware of the Robert Nixon case: a young black had been executed in 1938 for killing a white woman. Fashioning a fictional character based partly on what Wright had learned about Nixon and partly on his own experiences, Wright came up with Bigger Thomas.

An arrogant bully befriended by the pretty white debutante for whom he's employed as a chauffeur, Bigger accidentally kills the young woman, then compounds his problem with further crimes while attempting to cover up his initial action for fear that a black man cannot get a fair trial in America. Proceeding from the revolutionary if debatable premise that environmental influences and racial prejudice are responsible for black crime, rather than perceiving violent acts as the individual responsibility of the person who perpetrates them, the book— first published in 1940—created a stir, establishing Wright as the first significant twentieth-century black author. An inveterate movie fan, Wright starred in a Hollywood version of his book in 1950. Unfortunately, the project was too watered down to capture much of the novel's angry essence, and Wright's performance as Bigger is more interesting than successful. Ironically, though, the experience allowed him to artistically live out his grandmother's prophecy: as Bigger, Wright goes to the gallows in the final scene.

ERICH MARIA REMARQUE
A Time to Love and a Time to Die (1958)

In his youth, German-born Remarque worked as everything from a stonecutter to a salesman for a tombstone company; at one point, he was employed as an organist at an insane asylum. But the most significant event in his life would be the Great War: when political leaders insisted it was an honor to fight and die for one's country, young Remarque had no reason to question their integrity. After several years of brutal battles, he had transformed into a pacifist who despised all such patriotic jargon. So he struck back by the most effective means a writer can, by penning a novel that devastated readers with its antiwar message. Though *All Quiet on the Western Front* portrayed young German soldiers, the 1929 book so successfully cut across national differences that even American veterans could read and love this tribute to the common fighting man, which praised every unknown soldier's courage while damning the forces that throw men of any nation into war.

By 1939, Remarque was living in the United States, so he was an American when World War II broke out. But his novel about that conflict, *A Time to Love and a Time to Die*, followed the pattern of his first book in telling the tale of a German youth who finds romance during a brief leave, then must return to the front to fight and die in a war he no longer supports. The movie version never caught on quite the same way that the early talkie version of *All Quiet* had, perhaps because the producers were unable to land Paul Newman or Rock Hudson for the lead, and their third choice, newcomer John Gavin, had the looks but not the talent. Still, one scene stands out: the hero's meeting with the wisest man he has ever met, a noble professor played by author Erich Maria Remarque. In that year, 1958, Remarque was overwhelmed by Hollywood; he married actress Paulette Goddard then.

118

Truman Capote (far left) as the epicene host to Elsa Lanchester, Estelle Winwood, Peter Falk, David Niven, Maggie Smith, and James Coco, playing the world's greatest fictional detectives or reasonable facsimiles thereof. (courtesy Columbia Pictures)

TRUMAN CAPOTE

Murder by Death (1976)

Though as a writer Truman Capote enjoyed a long and happy connection to motion pictures, he appeared in only one, *Murder by Death,* a spoof of all the old detective movies that another writer, Neil Simon, had adored in his youth. But those movies weren't being made anymore, since the demise of the studio system and the emergence of screen realism, so Simon concocted a loving spoof that served as an apotheosis of the genre. His script brought together such disparate types as the hard-boiled gumshoe (Peter Falk), the suave husband-and-wife sleuths (David Niven and Maggie Smith), the oriental problem solver (Peter Sel-lers), the Belgian intellectual (James Coco), and England's dotty old grande-dame detective (Elsa Lanchester). All were invited to an isolated mansion where their epicene host (Capote) challenged them to solve a perplexing murder. "I have a sassy voice," Capote once said of himself, "and a changeling face." Moviegoers were treated to both in *Murder by Death.*

Capote's campy portrayal revealed a silly side to his personality that occasionally surfaced in his writing. Born Truman Streckfus Persons in New Orleans, later taking the surname of his foster father, young Truman was a lonely child who shuffled back and forth from his family in the South to boarding schools in New York City. His only happy memories were of Miss Sook Faulk, the elderly cousin he later immortalized in such stories as "A Christmas Memory." Capote began to write "prose poems"—*Other Voices, Other Rooms, The Grass Harp*—which conveyed his deep belief that in writing, as in life, style was everything, substance nothing. His first flirtation with Hollywood happened when he was picked to pen the screenplay for the John Huston–Humphrey Bogart black comedy *Beat the Devil,* in which Capote kidded *The Maltese Falcon* in much the way Simon would later burlesque the genre in *Murder by Death.* Capote's popular novella *Breakfast at Tiffany's* was adapted into a beloved Audrey Hepburn–Blake Edwards vehicle, though by the early 1960s, Capote—like other writers, including Tom Wolfe and Norman Mailer—came to believe the once certain lines between fiction and journalism were fast disappearing. So Capote spent six years writing a detailed study of the unmotivated murder of a Kansas family, the Clutters, by two crazed rednecks, employing the devices of fiction but applying them to fact. *In Cold Blood,* a bestseller, was turned into a landmark film in 1967.

JERZY KOSINSKI

Reds (1981)

No producer has ever enjoyed casting nonactors in character roles quite as much as Warren Beatty, who knows that every truly fascinating person is capable of delivering a great performance if only he or she can be matched with precisely the right part. For the role of Grigory Zinoviev, the intense Soviet bureaucrat in *Reds,* Beatty wanted no one other than Jerzy Kosinski, the noted author who not only looked precisely right for this role but also had, in his book *The Future Is Ours, Comrade: Conversations with the Russians,* verbally captured and morally commented on the very same dehumanization that occurs under a totalitarian regime (be it communist or otherwise) that Beatty's motion picture focused on. Beatty played the leading role and also directed this melodrama about American activist/author John Reed (*Ten Days That Shook the World*) and his involvement with the initially idealistic, all-too-soon corrupted Russian Revolution.

Kosinski was born on June 14, 1933, in Lodz, Poland, the only child of well-to-do Jewish intellectuals. But the boy's briefly sheltered childhood was shattered the moment that Hitler invaded Poland. Separated from his parents, the disoriented child was briefly cared for by strangers, then found himself wandering the European countryside (much like the fictional boy in the 1948 film *The Search*), eventually becoming so traumatized by the experience that he was struck mute. Reunited with his parents after the war, Jerzy slowly regained his voice and became a student at the Polish Academy of Sciences, then carefully planned his escape to America. On arrival, Jerzy worked as everything from a paint scraper on excursion-line boats to a projectionist at a movie theater. All the while, he honed his writing skills and eventually turned out *The Painted Bird,* a 1965 autobiographical novel based on his frightening early experiences. *Being There* and *Steps* followed, cementing his reputation as a literary artist of the first order. In *Reds,* he also proved his considerable abilities as an actor. He committed suicide in 1991.

NORMAN MAILER
Ragtime (1981)

No contemporary novelist has had more to do with the movies—or, for that matter, developed a literary style so clearly influenced by cinematic storytelling—than Norman Mailer. Two of his bestselling novels—*The Naked and the Dead* (1948) and *An American*

Norman Mailer as architect Stanford White takes on a Dionysian look shortly before being done in by his rival. (courtesy Paramount Pictures)

Dream (1965)—were made into Hollywood films, the former successfully, the latter less so. His "nonfiction novel" about convicted killer Gary Gilmore served as the source of one of the best TV movies ever made, with Mailer himself contributing the screenplay. And he has written extensively about Marilyn Monroe, doing his part to insure her status as the most durable of movie stars. Throughout the 1960s, before Hollywood began absorbing elements of underground filmmaking into the mainstream, Mailer wrote, directed, produced, and even appeared in a trio of home movies shown only on the avant-garde art-house circuit: *Wild 90, Maidstone,* and *Beyond the Law.* In 1994, he directed the Hollywood version of his book *Tough Guys Don't Dance.* But the enfant terrible of post–World War II letters—the bravura writer who had carefully styled himself into a Jewish Hemingway, self-consciously living a macho lifestyle of hard drinking and public brawling while ostensibly engaged on a spiritual search for existential truth—was called upon to act only once.

    It was in *Ragtime,* Milos Forman's nobly ambitious if ultimately awkward attempt to whittle down the E. L. Doctorow bestseller of the same name into a conventional motion picture. The book, described by critics as a "mosaic," combined fact and fiction (an approach Mailer himself gravitated toward in later works such as *Armies of the Night*), offering a panoramic portrait of America in transition during that golden age just before World War I forever darkened the new century. Forman's whittling down of the work destroyed the epic quality. One plot element Forman did include was the fact-based story of Evelyn Nesbit, mistress of wealthy architect Stanford White. He was murdered in 1906 by her off-balance admirer, millionaire Harry K. Thaw. Elizabeth McGovern played Nesbit, with Mailer effectively cast as her sugar daddy. Mailer delivered his lines acceptably, though his great moment is also his last: the look in his eyes when Harry Thaw approaches him in a restaurant, draws out a gun, and pulls the trigger is priceless in a way that Mailer's best prose always is.

WILLIAM S. BURROUGHS

Drugstore Cowboy (1989)

No one would have guessed from William Seward Burroughs's posh St. Louis upbringing that the wealthy grandson/namesake of the man who'd invented the adding machine would in time become the prime voice of America's underground. Yet even as a child, young Burroughs recoiled against the oppressive conventions of everyday life, eventually escaping the suffocating ennui by becoming a social and literary outlaw. First, though, came a respectable Harvard education, followed by a search for self in New York City that led to odd jobs as everything from a factory worker to private eye. Following a brief stint in the Army Air Force during World War II, the terminally bored Burroughs dabbled in heroin, becoming addicted, eventually realizing the habit was a life-threatening disaster. After moving to Mexico to escape prosecution, Burroughs wrote about his addiction, documentary style. *Junkie* was published in 1953 (under the pseudonym William Lee) when Burroughs was thirty-nine. Controversy would never completely forsake him; Burroughs shot his second wife to death, presumably by accident, while fumbling with a pistol, an incident that would later find its way into his hallucinatory 1959 novel, *Naked Lunch*. That book—in style, influenced by Franz Kafka's paranoid visions of modern man stifled by cold bureaucracies and James Joyce's experiments with nonlinear prose—earned Burroughs a place of honor amongst such beat-generation writers as Jack Kerouac, Allen Ginsberg, and Lawrence Ferlinghetti, all friends and admirers.

Yet Burroughs's books—from *The Yage Letters* to *The Soft Machine*—were as moral in purpose as they were anarchic in attitude. His work insists that drug addiction should be considered a diagnosable disease, since the stigma of criminality pushes addicts out of the mainstream, forcing them into crime to feed their

William S. Burroughs (left) *as the defrocked, drug-addicted priest who threatens to lure the hero, Bob Hughes (Matt Dillon), back into addiction in* Drugstore Cowboy. *(courtesy Avenue Pictures)*

habits. It made sense, then, that when Gus Van Sant filmed *Drugstore Cowboy,* prison inmate James Fogle's unpublished autobiography about addicts committing violent crimes to finance habits, Burroughs made his dramatic debut (alongside Matt Dillon and Kelly Lynch) as one of the older addicts. On-screen, Burroughs looked like a Kafka character come to life: a hollow man, blandly conventional in thick glasses and drab business suit, a living cog in the world's soulless mechanism. Burroughs can also be glimpsed in *Heavy Petting,* a 1988 documentary about the fifties, as well as in David Blair's experimental work *Wax,* a shot-on-video counterculture piece that, in its portrait of inhuman systems gobbling up all individuality, is indeed Burroughs-like in conception.

PAUL BOWLES

The Sheltering Sky (1990)

When Paul Bowles's controversial first novel *The Sheltering Sky* appeared in 1949, critics referred to the book as everything from "visionary" and "puzzling" to "decadent" and "corrupting." One reviewer noted it was "essentially unfilmable," perhaps the ultimate compliment. The finest works of fiction are so perfectly realized as literature that they can only be diminished by screen adaptation. *Sky* begins in the real world—specifically, northern Africa—though gradually the reader senses that Bowles has transformed his detailed portraits of teaming cities

123

and empty deserts into an internalized, existential landscape of the psyche, not unlike a Salvador Dalí painting. The story concerns a civilized, conventional married couple, Port and Kit Moresby, who escape their ennui by traveling to the very edge of the Sahara. Deeply attracted to the exotic culture they encounter, each gives in to decadent desires. Port is thrilled by late-night homosexual encounters in forbidden alleyways, while the seemingly modern woman Kit willingly becomes the slave of a bedouin warrior. But the thrill of liberation from traditional codes leads to their destruction, their dark fate rendered in a perversely polite prose.

For more than forty years following the book's ten-week run on the *New York Times* bestseller list, and continual cult-novel status thereafter, no one figured out a way to bring this book to the screen. Yet Bernardo Bertolucci (*The Last Emperor*) was attracted by the challenge, as well as to the sexual confusion of Bowles's characters. Casting John Malkovich and Debra Winger as Port and Kit, Bertolucci also persuaded Bowles to costar as the mystery man first encountered in a dimly lit bar. He directly addresses the audience watching the film, explaining the deeper meaning of all the bizarre doings on-screen. Bowles's legendary appearance—at once "craggy, austere, and laconic"—added weight to the film, though hardly enough to qualify the movie as successful. What was best about the book remained its elusive qualities of suggestion, so Bertolucci's vivid visualizations of the places and events only cut away the novel's greatest strength. While this marked Bowles's first and only screen appearance, it's worth noting that he had previously been employed as creator of incidental music and full scores for several movies during the 1950s, including the famed production of *Cyrano de Bergerac*, Jose Ferrer's Academy Award winner.

19
THEY DIED TOO SOON

The title is self-explanatory; here are stars who might have gone the limit had death not taken them far too early in their careers.

PEG ENTWISTLE

Thirteen Women (1932)

From Jean Harlow to Mae West, platinum blondes dominated the big screen during the early 1930s; none appeared to have a better chance of making the big time than this strikingly classic beauty. Born Lillian Millicent Entwistle in England in 1908, she was the daughter of popular stage actors. Her father, Robert, brought the entire family with him to America when he won a major Broadway role, though the man died shortly thereafter. Peg never considered any career but acting. She was Ophelia in a production of *Hamlet* in 1925, and after a succession of small roles won rave reviews for the lead in a show called *Tommy* two years later. She married, then divorced, actor Robert Keith. When sound came to movies, she joined the throng of Broadway performers rushing out to Hollywood.

People who knew Peg insisted she quickly became obsessed with the famed HOLLYWOOD (then, HOLLYWOODLAND) sign on Mt. Lee, staring up at it constantly, considering this to be the ultimate symbol of Tinseltown success. But though Peg was compared to fast-rising Bette Davis in terms of looks and talent, the good roles were not forthcoming. She won a single important part: Hazel Cousins, one of a group of prissy former school chums who are, one by one, murdered by the half-caste girl (Myrna Loy) they once rejected. Peg delivered an outstanding performance, but in the editing room, her role was whittled down to a minor part. Though briefly touted as an upcoming glamour queen, her flavor-of-the-month status passed before anything happened; RKO dropped her contract, and her meager savings were running out. On the evening of September 18, 1932,

Peg borrowed a pretty, flowery silk dress from actress Effie Shannon, calmly strolled up Beachwood Drive in the direction of the Hollywood Hills, climbed up the fifty-foot letter *H*, and after leaving a cryptic suicide note ("If I could have done this long ago, I could have saved a lot of pain"), leaped to her death. As Eve Golden commented years later, it was the way she'd died rather than anything she'd done in life "which resulted in banner headlines. The sheer outrageous style, the almost witty symbolism, of Peg's suicide was too delicious to ignore. Indeed, modern urban legends tell of scores of leapers from the HOLLYWOOD sign . . . but the only documented suicide was starlet Peg Entwistle."

JUDY TYLER

Jailhouse Rock (1957)

Judy Tyler was a mere twenty-four years old when she was killed instantly in a car accident near a southern-Wyoming roadside hamlet called, of all things, Billy the Kid—certainly an out-of-the-way place for a talented Hollywood newcomer, who was being hailed as the next great musical star, to meet her untimely end. Also fatally injured in the crash was her young husband, a TV actor named Gregory Lafayette, whom Tyler had married four months earlier. Lafayette was rushed to a Laramie hospital, but he died a few hours afterward. The driver of the other car was also killed. Tyler had just completed work on Elvis Presley's third feature film, *Jailhouse Rock,* in which she played the music-business insider who helps the country boy get started on a recording career. When informed of the accident, a stunned and numbed Presley announced that he would probably be unable to watch the film when editing had been completed and it was ready for release.

The daughter of Julian S. Hess of Nutmeg Ridge, Connecticut, Tyler had grown up in and around Teaneck, New Jersey. Show biz was in Judy's blood: her father had been a onetime jazz trumpet player, while her mother, Lorelei, was a former Ziegfeld Follies girl. In a nationwide beauty contest, the Miss Stardust 1949 competition, Tyler had easily won the title, then gone on to play the lead in the Rodgers and Hammerstein stage musical *Pipe Dream*. She had also appeared as a featured singer/dancer at New York's Copacabana, portrayed Princess Summer-Fall-Winter-Spring on TV's beloved *Howdy Doody* show, even done a low-budget movie called *Bop Girl Goes Calypso,* an exploitation flick designed to cash in on the supposed craze for Jamaican music that Harry Belafonte's recordings were expected to usher in. At the time of her death, Judy Tyler was vacationing before returning to New York to join the regular cast of CBS-TV's popular *Pantomime Quiz*.

126

PINA PELLICER
One Eyed-Jacks (1961)

Marlon Brando is not an actor one ordinarily associates with the western, but he did star in and direct one of the most bizarre oaters ever made: *One Eyed-Jacks,* based on Charles Neider's novel *The Authentic Death of Hendry Jones.* The movie (originally to have been directed by Stanley Kubrick) featured Brando in a serape a full five years before Clint Eastwood would don one for his spaghetti westerns. The breathtaking photography of California's Monterey coast, with its splendid vistas of slowly crashing surf, provided a marvelously incongruous contrast to the shoot-outs one would expect to see played out in Monument Valley. Brando played Rio, the young outlaw who cannot forgive his onetime partner (Karl Malden) for betraying him and, worse still, becoming a detested lawman. For revenge, he pretends to pay a friendly visit, all the

Pina Pellicer as the aristocratic beauty who loses her heart to an American gunfighter (Marlon Brando), while in the background, Karl Malden, as her protective father, looks on. In the film, as in real life, her father could not protect her.

while planning to seduce and "spoil" the lawman's daughter. Things get sticky, however, when Rio realizes that he's in love with young Louisa.

She was played by Pina Pellicer, born twenty-two years earlier as Josefina Pellicer Lopez Uergo in Mexico City. The reed-thin, sad-eyed, sensitive beauty, daughter of a prominent attorney, had attended the University of Mexico with hopes of becoming a history teacher. There, she became fascinated with drama, learning the fabled Stanislavski method from a Japanese drama coach. She appeared onstage and on TV in the Mexican production of *Diary of Anne Frank.* Brando picked her out of a hundred hopefuls who wanted to costar with him, but like her character in the script, Pina came from a highly traditional family, headed by a strong father figure, who insisted on temporarily shutting down his law firm to accompany his daughter and "protect" her from the evils she might encounter. Apparently, he was not able to completely protect her from Brando. Pina fell under the spell of the magnetic actor and became intimately involved with him.

But when the film was finished, so, too, was their affair, leaving her confused and depressed. Pellicer made her way home; shortly thereafter, she was named Best International Actress at the San Sebastian Film Festival awards for her work. In Madrid, she did a little film called *Rogelia* and, in Mexico, another called *Macaria*, though neither was ever widely distributed out of their native lands. Still waters, apparently, really do run deep; on December 10, 1964, Pina Pellicer lost her long-time bout with depression and took her life.

LENNY BAKER
Next Stop, Greenwich Village (1976)

Paul Mazursky's most unabashedly autobiographical film told the story of a nice Jewish boy from Brooklyn who in 1953 shocks his family by announcing plans to move to Manhattan's most bohemian community and pursue an acting career. A nostalgic, personal blend of comedy and drama, the film worked in large part owing to the performance of Lenny Baker as the thinly disguised young Mazursky. Baker was nominated for a Golden Globe Award after *Next Stop* opened to rave reviews if modest business. Before the big break the Boston University graduate, trained as a stage actor, had spent summers working at the O'Neill Center's National Playwrights Conference in Waterford, Connecticut, as well as with the Phoenix Theatre repertory company. Before *Next Stop,* he'd appeared briefly in two films, *The Hospital* (1971) and *The Paper Chase* (1973), in nominal roles.

The great hope was that Lenny's star turn would do for him what *The Graduate* had done for another nice Jewish boy, Dustin Hoffman, one decade earlier. That never happened in Baker's case; too much of a character actor for traditional leads but now too big a star for smaller scene-stealing roles, he accepted that awkward situation without complaint and headed back to Broadway, where he was barraged with offers. Prime among them was *I Love My Wife,* a contemporary musical about wife-swapping. Walter Kerr of the *Times* called him "a total joy—as an actor, he has always been one of a kind." Dozens of other stage offers, including one to do Shakespeare in the Park, poured in. But before long, Baker was too sick to act. He'd been diagnosed with cancer; he died in 1982 in a Hallandale, Florida, hospital at age thirty-seven.

DOMINIQUE DUNNE
Poltergeist (1982)

In *Poltergeist,* an average American family finds itself menaced by ghosts that rise up out of an ancient Indian burial ground in their backyard. The upscale horror film, presented by Steven Spielberg, focuses mainly on the problems of the dis-

Lenny Baker as the young Paul Mazursky in the autobiographical memory movie Next Stop, Greenwich Village. *(courtesy 20th Century–Fox)*

traught parents (Craig T. Nelson and JoBeth Williams) and their little boy (Oliver Robins) and girl (Heather O'Rourke), but there was also a third child: Dana, a lovely, soft-spoken teenager played by Dominique Dunne, who brightened her several scenes, holding out the promise of an important career. Instead, the twenty-two-year-old died on November 4, 1982, at Cedars-Sinai Medical Center, where she had been kept alive on life-support systems for six days following her strangulation by John Sweeney, Dunne's twenty-six-year-old former boyfriend. A night-shift chef at Ma Maison restaurant for the previous seven years, Sweeney had shared Dunne's home on Rangley Avenue in West Hollywood until the actress informed him that the relationship was over. He moved out but showed up on that fateful Saturday morning begging Dunne to allow him to return. When she refused, Sweeney strangled her, then waited nearby for the police, telling deputies, "I killed my girlfriend."

What might seem a clear case of confessed murder turned into a heated battle over the concept of individual responsibility. Sweeney's lawyers argued that since their client had not arrived at the home with plans of killing the girl but rather hoping to revive their relationship, he should therefore be convicted on a lesser charge of involuntary manslaughter. Dunne was the niece of noted author-screenwriter John Gregory Dunne (*True Confessions*) and sister of actor Griffin Dunne (*After Hours*). Dominique had earlier played roles in made-for-TV movies including *The Day the Loving Stopped* and *Diary of a Teenage Hitchhiker*. She'd been a regular in the brief TV series based on the hit movie *Breaking Away* and was noticed by many critics for her standout performance in *The Haunting of Harrington House,* a CBS after-school special. That role brought her to the attention of Spielberg, who promptly cast her in *Poltergeist.*

REBECCA SCHAEFFER
Scenes From the Class Struggle in Beverly Hills (1989)

Hollywood's fear of obsessed fans reached its frightfully logical conclusion on the morning of July 18, 1989, when nineteen-year-old John Bardo of Tucson, Arizona, rang the doorbell of an apartment at 120 N. Sweetzer Avenue in West Los Angeles. When actress Rebecca Schaeffer answered, Bardo shot her dead. Bardo had begun writing to Schaeffer two years earlier, at first appearing to be merely one more member of the public charmed by the actress when she played Patti Russell, younger sister to Pam Dawber's title character, on the *My Sister Sam* TV series from 1986 to 1988. Though the show was less than distinguished, it had just launched what appeared to be an exciting movie career. In Paul Bartel's empty satire *Scenes,* Schaeffer plays Zandra, the daughter of Jacqueline Bisset's character, Clare Lipkin. Schaeffer had also completed a part in Dyan Cannon's directorial debut, *One Point of View,* though that film was never released. Later on the very day that she was killed, Schaeffer had been set to talk with Francis Coppola about playing Michael Corleone's daughter in the third *Godfather* film, a role that would have put her in the same league as Winona Ryder.

Dr. Stuart Fischoff, a psychologist who also writes film scripts, explained that Bardo "probably had fantasized an intimate relationship with her. What happens with TV is even the people who are too psychologically weak to go outside and relate to [others or catch a movie] can relate to [characters they see on] television. Security consultant Gavin de Becker worried about "a blurring of the line" in the public's behavior toward celebrities "that we come to feel intimately involved with [but] really don't know." Twenty-one at the time of her death, Schaeffer had grown up in Portland, Oregon, the daughter of a child-psychologist father who had also studied Yiddish theater in New York, and a writer mother. After briefly considering a career as a rabbi, Rebecca dropped out of high school to head for New York, searching for elusive modeling jobs (at five feet seven inches she was too short to succeed as a mannequin) and studying acting. Though she had felt at home in Manhattan, Schaeffer had come to California when the *Sam* role beckoned. It would lead to her brush with movie stardom in *Scenes* and, tragically, her premature death.

20
STAGEBOUND

T hey were the superstars of Broadway's Great White Way and regional theaters around the country; they tried, and failed, to transfer that status to
movies.

CLAIRE LUCE

Up the River (1930)

As an actress, Claire Luce had a unique cross to bear: all her life, she was confused
with Claire Boothe Luce, a sometimes stage actress (*Candida*), playwright (*The
Women*), magazine editor (*Vanity Fair*), politician (elected to the House of
Representatives from Connecticut), and U.S. ambassador to Italy (first woman ever
to serve in that capacity for any major world power), as well as wife of *Time* magazine's president, Henry Robinson Luce. Though Claire Luce never did anything
quite so spectacular, she was revered in a quieter way as one of the finest live-the-
ater actresses working in America throughout the thirties, forties, and fifties. Also,
Claire Luce had at least one up on Claire Boothe Luce: the latter never appeared in
a single motion picture, though the former did do one. It was *Up the River,* an early
talkie that paired the actress (born in Syracuse, New York) with two talented, sexy
newcomers, Humphrey Bogart and Spencer Tracy.

She played Judy, an innocent young woman of the Great Depression who,
after being framed for a crime she didn't commit, serves time in the women's section of the same prison in which her boyfriend Steve (Bogart) is also incarcerated.
When he's released and appears ready to return to a life of crime, Judy convinces
another prisoner, Saint Louis (Tracy) to escape, set Steve on the right path, then
return to his life behind bars. John Ford, who directed the Fox project, personally
picked Luce for her role, predicting the film would make her a reigning queen of
the silver screen. But pretty Claire Luce didn't think much of movies, preferring
the stage, where she could react to a live audience. Originally setting her sights on

becoming a dancer, Claire had toured with the troupe run by that incendiary blonde Texas Guinan, then headed for France, where she became one of the glamour girls at the Casino de Paris, then returned home to become a Ziegfeld girl. Before long, Claire was winning top roles in important plays, creating the part of Curley's wife in John Steinbeck's *Of Mice and Men*. After that, she enacted most of Shakespeare's women, as well as female roles by Eugene O'Neill, George Bernard Shaw, and Tennessee Williams. She worked constantly during the golden age of live TV, taught drama at New York University, and proved her prowess as a painter with numerous one-woman exhibitions. Nonetheless, Claire Luce would constantly find herself explaining to someone, "No, I am *not* Claire Boothe Luce!"

Lynn Fontanne

The Guardsmen (1931)

Alfred Lunt was a would-be architect from Wisconsin's Lake Country who headed for Harvard but was waylaid by a Boston theater group that noticed his elegant elocution and offered him a job. Lillie Louise "Lynn" Fontanne was the daughter of an Essex, England, brass-type founder who studied acting with Dame Ellen Terry, then toured America doing everything from Shakespeare to vaudeville. When the two met in New York during the summer of 1919, they were young hopefuls, intent on landing acting jobs at the Hudson Theatre. Shortly, he was starring in *Clarence,* she in *Dulcy;* when the two wed on May 26, 1922, they had metamorphosed into the bright lights of live theater. Their first joint outing was *The Guardsmen* for the Theatre Guild, one critic insisting he'd witnessed "a moment in theatrical history." During the next two decades, the first couple of the legitimate stage appeared in two dozen prestigious plays, though their dialogue-driven approach caused them to avoid then-silent films. They were persuaded to appear fleetingly in a single silent, *Second Youth* (1922), the unhappy experience convincing Lynn that the cinema was not their medium, though Alfred did do several pictures, including D. W. Griffith's *Sally of the Sawdust* with W. C. Fields.

Then came sound and, with it, Hollywood's wooing of people with tried-and-true voices. Noted director Sidney Franklin guided the couple through a handsome filmization of the play that had started it all nearly a decade earlier, maintaining the charm of Molnar's confection about an overly jealous husband who devises a complex test of his attractive wife's faithfulness: he pretends to be another man and woos her in disguise. Even during production, however, the stars feared that the early crude microphones would not do justice to their voices. According to legend, Lunt was so upset that he insisted his wife go see the finished film first, then report back. Neither was satisfied with the results, so the couple beat a hasty retreat back to the boards. Despite the rapid rise in quality of voice recording, they could not be convinced to try film again. Still, they continued appearing in several plays a year, most significantly Robert Sherwood's *There Shall Be No Night,* a Pulitzer Prize winner that took little Finland's point of view during its late-1930s war with Russia.

DORETTA MORROW
Because You're Mine (1952)

In one of his most popular vehicles, Mario Lanza played an arrogant opera star not unlike himself. Drafted, he falls in love with the sister of his tough top sergeant (James Whitmore). She was played by Doretta Morrow (born Marano), musical veteran of such Broadway shows as *The Chocolate Soldier* and *Where's Charley?* As the tragic Tuptim in *The King and I,* she performed the now-classic "I Have Dreamed" and won ecstatic reviews. MGM lured the lovely, talented

Doretta Morrow as the sergeant's sister beloved by drafted opera star Mario Lanza in Because You're Mine. *(courtesy MGM)*

Morrow to Hollywood; Joe Pasternak took one look at her and signed her without even bothering to do the usual screen test. But after *Because You're Mine,* Lanza, famed for his gargantuan appetites, let himself go, becoming too out of shape for any further films. Plans to team the two regularly were scrapped. MGM knew Doretta was a special talent, yet they couldn't quite decide what to do with her.

Undaunted, Morrow, a cousin of pop singer Vic Damone, sang on the supper-club circuit, wowing audiences at New York's posh St. Regis hotel. Then it was back to her roots in legitimate theater, always her first great love. Morrow traveled to London where she starred in a production of *Kismet* that ran for over a thousand performances. When the show closed, she did British pantomime with the popular comic Bob Monkhouse. Doretta married Lloyds of London underwriter Albert Hardman (her third husband). A long struggle with cancer took her life in 1960; she was forty-one.

TODD DUNCAN

Unchained (1955)

Thanks to its inclusion in the film *Ghost* and a prominent place in the heart of Kirstie Alley's character on TV's *Cheers,* the Righteous Brothers' rendition of "Unchained Melody" has entered the popular imagination as the definitive recording of that tune. Few people today recall that a generation earlier, the song provided hits for Roy Hamilton, Les Baxter, and Al Hibbler, all of whom recorded it after the haunting piece of music first made its debut in the 1955 film *Unchained,* an ultrarealistic look at life in California's Chino, the experimental prison without bars. Fewer still remember that the first person to sing the song was in fact Todd Duncan, the actor who mournfully performs it in the all-but-forgotten film. The producer of *Unchained* was Walter Wanger, one of the few Hollywood VIPs ever to serve time, incarcerated for beating the man he suspected of being the lover of his wife, actress Joan Bennett. The experience made Wanger sensitive to the issues of prisoners, so writer-director Hall Bartlett was assigned to research the then-novel notion of a minimum-security prison, where the key stipulation was that any prisoner who made a run for the outside would, when and if recaptured, be assigned to a sterner, more orthodox prison.

In the film's climactic sequence, Duncan fights a white prisoner (Elroy "Crazylegs" Hirsch, football player turned Burt Lancaster wanna-be) about to go over the wall. Though he loses the fight, Duncan's brutal resistance convinces his opponent to remain in Chino. Earlier, Duncan had performed "The Unchained Melody" one long, lonely night, and his rendition remains the single most memorable performance. Bartlett wrote this role with Duncan in mind; Todd Duncan had, in real life, served eleven years in jail for a robbery and killing, bringing a sense of authenticity, as well as acting skill, to the part. Duncan was then concentrating on Broadway roles that made the most of his considerable talents. He was the original Porgy in *Porgy and Bess* and was performing in *Lost in the Stars* when offered the key role in *Unchained.* He performed beautifully in the film, but expressed no real interest in remaining in Hollywood, where few projects struck him as boasting such integrity of purpose. Duncan headed back to the East Coast where for years he continued his highly successful stage career.

JOHN RAITT

The Pajama Game (1957)

Anyone who ever wondered why Hollywood steadfastly refuses to recast the successful star of a Broadway play in the film version need look no further than this integrity-plus rendering of the hit 1950s musical *Pajama Game.* The story con-

134

cerns a factory working woman who grieves for labor and the handsome new foreman with whom she falls in love. Doris Day, playing the role Mary Martin had created onstage, exuded movie-star charisma, but John Raitt— so acclaimed for his performance in New York—looked lost and awkward, so the kind of chemistry Day would later enjoy with such bona fide screen personalities as Rock Hudson, James Garner, and Rod Taylor was sadly lacking. Raitt was forty at the time that he played what would prove to be his first and last starring film role.

The Santa Ana, California, native had been shooting for a career in serious music with the Los Angeles Civic Light Opera Company, then briefly tried for a film career, doing bit parts in the films *Flight Command* and *Ziegfeld Girl*. Then he was tapped for the Billy Bigelow role in the Broadway-bound *Carousel*, for which he won the New York Drama Critics' Award. From then on, he was a staple of the American musical theater, his return bout to Hollywood proving to be but a momentary detour. In addition to Sid Sorokin in both the live and filmed renditions of *Pajama Game,* Raitt played the male leads in *Annie Get Your Gun, Kismet,* and *Zorba* (among others) onstage, in varied cities, to universal acclaim.

John Raitt, a fine stage performer, clearly had no movie-star charisma to match that of his costar Doris Day in The Pajama Game. *(courtesy Movie Star News)*

PETER PALMER

Li'l Abner (1959)

While planning their lavish Broadway musical based on the beloved Dogpatch characters, producers Norman Panama and Melvin Frank realized they faced a major problem. None of the actors who looked right for the part could sing, while

The Dogpatch characters, including Leslie Parrish as Daisy Mae (right), *gather around Peter Palmer in* Li'l Abner. *(courtesy Paramount Pictures)*

none of the talented singers they interviewed even remotely resembled Al Capp's mythical hero. One Sunday evening, the frustrated duo tried to relax by watching TV; when the program was interrupted by an annoying commercial, Panama reached for the dial and spun the channel over to *The Ed Sullivan Show.* There they saw an answer to their dream: a six-foot-four, ruggedly handsome young man—the spitting image of Abner—launching into a vivid rendition of "Grenada." The man was Peter Palmer, a Milwaukee-born, Missouri-raised all-state football tackle who had won a sports scholarship to the University of Illinois, where he uniquely combined his athletic abilities with his love of song: before home games, he would sing the national anthem in full football regalia.

Growing ever more interested in music, Peter spent the summer of 1952 performing with the St. Louis Municipal Opera. His combination of good looks and natural abilities allowed him to easily win talent contests, one of which brought him to Los Angeles, where Paramount considered signing him as a contract player. Such plans fell apart when Palmer received his draft notice, Paramount fearing his shot at stardom would quickly fade. Undaunted, Palmer made the best of that bad situation; during his first year of service, he won the All-Army Entertainment Contest while competing against five thousand other singers. As the winner, he was awarded that spot on the *Sullivan* show and was "discovered" by Panama and Frank, proving that second chances do

136

sometimes happen. Palmer played Abner on Broadway for two years and repeated the role in the movie version. Turned off by Hollywood's subsequent attempt to typecast him as a hillbilly, Palmer refused offers to do Abnerish roles in bad films and returned to stage work, playing the leads in *Carousel, Oklahoma!* and *The Unsinkable Molly Brown*. In 1967, he had a supporting role as a tough Army sergeant on the brief-lived *Custer* TV western, then organized USO tours, headlining troupes of performers entertaining in Vietnam.

CAROL LAWRENCE

A View From the Bridge (1962)

Sidney Lumet's film version of Arthur Miller's play *A View From the Bridge* updated the intense sexual emotions within a single family, so associated with Greek tragedy, for a modern context. An immigrant obsessively attempts to protect the virginity of his young niece from a handsome suitor, never realizing until a final epiphany that he wants the girl for himself. Lumet picked a cast of fine stage actors for what was essentially a one-set movie, most everything happening in the shabby apartment of the protagonists. Raf Vallone was the tortured longshoreman, Maureen Stapleton his neglected wife, and twenty-eight-year-old stage actress Carol Lawrence the innocent but seductive niece.

Carol Lawrence as the sweet, naive immigrant girl who inadvertently comes between her uncle (Raf Vallone) and his wife (Maureen Stapleton). (courtesy Continental Distributing)

A native of Melrose Park, Illinois, Carol Maria Laraia had planned on a show business career from childhood, early on changing her name so television announcers would have an easier time pronouncing it. Dancing lessons, high school choir, and amateur theatrics made clear this was a budding talent, so she attended Northwestern on scholarship. But after a successful first year, Lawrence, visiting

New York with her parents, was invited to audition for Leonard Sillman's *New Faces of 1952;* she got the job and dropped out of college. A role in *South Pacific* followed, and after several flop musicals came the once-in-a-lifetime part of Maria in the Jerome Robbins/Arthur Laurents production, *West Side Story.* Lawrence's dazzling dancing, singing, and acting propelled her to major stardom, so far as Broadway was concerned. In the words of Garry Moore, Carol was an "enchanting" stage personality. Unfortunately, that enchantment did not come across on-screen. Warner Brothers executives who saw her in *A View From the Bridge* decided they'd be better off with Natalie Wood as Hollywood's Maria, though Marni Nixon had to dub in the singing voice. Lawrence found work on TV, appearing in such golden-age dramatic anthologies as *U.S. Steel Hour.* And she became a staple on *The Tonight Show,* singing Broadway show tunes and chatting with Johnny Carson. Yet while she remained a popular celebrity for many years, Lawrence never made that elusive transition to motion picture star.

CHITA RIVERA

Sweet Charity (1969)

On Broadway, Chita Rivera played the two best roles written for a Latin actress: Anita, the sexy, streetwise gang girl in *West Side Story* (1957), and Rose, sophisticated career woman who realizes her Spanish heritage stands in the way of her marrying fiancé Albert in *Bye Bye Birdie* (1960). But in the screen version of *West Side,* the part of Anita went to Rita Moreno, another fine Hispanic performer; in the disappointing screen version of *Birdie,* Janet Leigh strained unconvincingly to be "Spanish Rosa." If movie stardom failed to materialize, Chita's status as contemporary queen of the Broadway musical promises to run on forever, from *Chicago* to *Kiss of the Spider Woman.* Perhaps that's for the best; Rivera always considered her work on her single film a less than pleasant experience. In the midsixties, she'd been touring in *Sweet Charity* (Gwen Verdon had created the role on Broadway), though superstar Shirley MacLaine was already set for the film. Nonetheless, Rivera was persuaded by director Bob Fosse to take on the supporting role of Nickie, Charity's cheap tart of a roommate. Fans of Rivera's dancing can be thankful that a number in which she, MacLaine, and Paula Kelly hoof together atop the roof of their shabby apartment building forever immortalized Chita's talents.

Despite that, Rivera confessed that she was glad to return to the more ephemeral world of live theater as soon as the production was wrapped. "The Hollywood mentality," the woman born Dolores Conchita Figuero del Rivera later explained, is one that looks at a production as "really a job out of which sometimes comes fame." In her mind, the highly preferable "Broadway mentality" is based on "dedication, hard work, and the development of a craft."

21
POLITICS AS (UN)USUAL

Politicos, statesmen, and lawyers who had one shining screen hour.

HELEN GAHAGAN (DOUGLAS)

She (1935)

In 1935, Helen Gahagan played the title character in *She,* an elaborate film version of H. Rider Haggard's adventure classic about a lost city and Ayesha, its cruel, seductive, enigmatic queen. Critics and public alike found Gahagan aloof and off-putting. Badly burned, she spurned all future film offers, returning to her first love, live theater. In truth, if ever there was a case of screen image conflicting with reality, this was it. Born in 1900 to a successful East Coast civil engineer, Gahagan was raised in a conservative Republican household of considerable means. While a student at Barnard College of Columbia University, she discovered the theater and coauthored a play, *Shadows on the Moon.* This, and her already renowned aristocratic beauty, brought her to the attention of the Broadway theater crowd. Shortly, she was appearing in such important plays as *Manhattan, Dreams for Sale,* and *The Enchanted Cottage* between 1920 and 1926.

 Since acting came so easily, Gahagan decided to press herself and fulfill her mother's dream that her daughter become an opera star. Helen studied in Rimini, Italy, then made an impressive debut in Czechoslovakia, later touring throughout Europe. Returning to the New York theater scene in 1930, she starred in David Belasco's last big production, *Tonight or Never,* falling head over heels in love at first sight with costar Melvyn Douglas. When they married, she was moved by his progressive beliefs to reconsider her politics. A car trip across America allowed Helen to see the Okies firsthand; she was as touched by the poverty and desolation as John Steinbeck had been when moved to write *The*

139

Grapes of Wrath. Shortly, Gahagan began turning down plumb theater roles to try to help, becoming a dyed-in-the-wool liberal Democrat and supporter of presidential candidate Franklin D. Roosevelt. With his election, Gahagan's gradual shift from actress to career politician accelerated. Soon she was on the National Advisory Committee for the WPA, then was the first woman ever elected as a Democrat to Congress from California's Fourteenth District, a largely low-income area. Gahagan used her position to fight against racial discrimination and in favor of small farmers, a grassroots populist who nevertheless remained one of the most glamorous women in the country. Naturally, she was a prime target of witch-hunters during the McCarthy era. Though Helen Gahagan may have failed on film because there she appeared icy, she was anything but in real life and never failed in any arena that she entered except the unique world of movies.

JUDGE JOSEPH WELCH
Anatomy of a Murder (1959)

Long before the world heard of Wapner or Ito, there was Joseph Nye Welch, the first judge to become a national celebrity via television. At the time, Welch was still a lawyer: in April 1954, he was named special counsel to handle the Army's case during the televised hearings between seemingly all-powerful Sen. Joseph McCarthy and then–Secretary of the Army Robert Stevens. A petty thug who had exploited the country's rabid fear of communism during the post–World War II years, McCarthy and others of his ilk had already initiated the infamous Hollywood blacklist, destroying the careers of talented and mostly innocent people. Now, McCarthy believed, he'd do much the same kind of damage to the armed forces. Thankfully, he was wrong. Welch entered the televised courtroom and for the next two months won the hearts and minds of the public, in part through the penetrating things he had to say, in part owing to his marvelous on-camera presence. His elderly face (Welch was sixty-three at the time) beamed with amazement at McCarthy's shamelessly bludgeoning tactics, while his bemused eyes revealed a sharp insight that clearly saw through any jingoistic sham. When the hearings ended in June, McCarthy had been destroyed by the medium that had transformed Welch into a star.

Newspaper reporters turned out "serious journalism" that sounded more like theater reviews. The *New York Times* praised Welch as "a gentleman viewing bedlam with calm. . . . A dubious smile often creeps across his face when testimony is not to his liking." *Life* liked the fact that "his elaborate politeness and gentility mask a highly active, well-disciplined, bear-trap mind." When director Otto Preminger began work on a major courtroom drama about a murky murder case, he sensed that while actors might well play lawyers for the defense (James Stewart) and prosecution (George C. Scott), such an approach would not work in casting the judge, whose facial reactions must always reveal to the film's viewer whether the arguments and testimony are to be believed or not. While reading Wendell Mayes's script, Preminger pictured Welch (long since appointed judge) reacting to everything that took place, much as he had done on live TV. Typecasting paid off; though this turned out to be Welch's only stab at the movies, he proved that sometimes the real thing is far more convincing than even the most powerful acting.

JOHN V. LINDSAY
Rosebud (1975)

Yes, Virginia, there really was such a thing as a liberal Republican once upon a time, and John Lindsay was foremost among them. First he was United States representative of the Seventeenth Congressional District of New York, and finally New York City's mayor throughout the latter part of the sixties. This third-generation American excelled at sports

A pensive John V. Lindsay as the government official caught in the crossfire in Otto Preminger's Rosebud. *(courtesy United Artists Corp.)*

(particularly rowing) while at Yale, then joined the Naval Reserve, serving in World War II. As an Ivy League man of decisive action and eloquent words, the ruggedly classy Lindsay was the Grand Old Party's answer to Jack Kennedy, whom Lindsay openly admired. Though initially elected as an Eisenhower Republican, he consistently supported Kennedy on such issues as civil rights legislation and the Peace Corps. There was much talk of the governorship, or possibly a run for the presidency, but Lindsay's timing was off.

First, the mounting (some would say insurmountable) problems of garbage and crime in New York, compounded by his apparent inability to solve them, typed him as a man of style rather than substance. Meanwhile, the Republican Party's continuous shift to the right ruled Lindsay out as a significant

141

Russell (Julian Bond) and Mary (Pam Grier) cheer their pal Wendell Scott on in Greased Lightning. *(courtesy Warner Bros.)*

national leader. Since he'd always been movie-star handsome, filmmaker Otto Preminger decided to try to make a Paul Newman–type actor out of Lindsay, casting the former mayor as a clean-cut government executive attempting to stop Arab terrorists from kidnapping five young beauties aboard a luxury yacht. Though his costars included such luminaries as Peter O'Toole, Richard Attenborough, and Raf Vallone, *Rosebud* was clearly no *Citizen Kane,* so Lindsay wisely left Hollywood behind and returned to his lucrative law career.

JULIAN BOND
Greased Lightning (1977)

The whole world is watching. That's what the kids in the streets screamed out during the Democratic National Convention in Chicago during the summer of 1968, when police swooped down on the longhairs as they attempted to influence decisions being made inside the convention hall, where Hubert Humphrey was receiving the party's nomination over objections of antiwar demonstrators. One of the few good things to come out of that ugly moment was the lingering memory of Julian Bond, handsome young Georgia state senator who spoke softly but conveyed great substance; some of the attendees even attempted to place his name in nomination as a possible candidate for vice president. Afterward, most people who

142

had watched the bitter event on television concurred that Bond did indeed have a good shot at becoming our first black vice president and waited to see what would happen. Surprisingly, little did: though Julian Bond remained a voice of intelligent moderation in national politics, he never achieved (or perhaps even aspired to) the higher levels of office that so many admirers expected of him.

He did, however, take a surprising interest in acting. Richard Pryor, a supporter of Bond's, persuaded the young politician to appear in *Greased Lightning,* one of the better vehicles Pryor found for himself during his brief period as a superstar during the mid-1970s. Pryor played real-life stock-car racer Wendell Scott, the first black man to break the color barrier and become an acknowledged champion at that sport. Scott had honed his driving skills first as a taxi driver, then while running moonshine whiskey on Virginia's back roads. Deciding to go professional, he made himself felt on the stock-car circuit throughout the 1960s and won his deserved place in sports history. Pryor nicely enacted the role of Wendell, with Beau Bridges cast as the white boy who initially opposes him and then becomes a great pal. Pryor's then girlfriend Pam Grier was around as Scott's girlfriend Mary, and as Russell, chief among those family members and friends who cheer Scott on at the big race, was none other than politico Julian Bond.

DANIEL BERRIGAN

The Mission (1986)

Roland Joffe's thoughtful historical epic concerned the exploitation of Brazil's natives in the late eighteenth century by greed-driven merchants out to enslave the Indian population and exploit their natural treasures. Standing against such forces was an idealistic group of Jesuits, dedicated to protecting the simple people they had converted to Christianity. The role of one of those priests, the quiet but intense Father Sebastian, was a natural for Daniel Berrigan, whose entire life had been based on the heartfelt belief that the Catholic Church ought to be an agent of radical, nonviolent activism for the underclass rather than an arm of the political and capitalistic Establishment. Daniel had been jailed for those antiwar activities he and his brother, Philip, involved themselves in during the darkest days of Vietnam, though in fact ever since his harsh boyhood in Depression-era Minnesota, he'd learned from his labor-organizer father Thomas the need to work with and for those who were without power or money.

Daniel's 1971 off-Broadway play, *The Trial of the Catonsville Nine,* detailed the experiences of the brothers and their fellow antiwar conspirators, who on May 17, 1968, had marched into Maryland's Selective Service Board 33. Housed in a Knights of Columbus Hall, the Catonsville location symbolized the Church's acquiescence to the powers that be rather than to their God-given duty to defending the downtrodden, in the Berrigans' eyes. They then destroyed the records of boys about to be drafted, Daniel having prepared a meditation that read in part: "Our apologies, good friends, for the fracture of good order. The burning of paper, instead of children . . . The violence stops here." After becoming a fugitive from the law, the pacifist priest was transformed into a counterculture hero—one of the few people over the age of thirty who could be "trusted" by the nation's temporarily activist youth—eventually vindicated when the entire country tired of the war and turned on it. He continued to write and speak about the need for a Church that was in tune with its true obligations to take a stand and portrayed just such a passive-resistance position on film when he costarred with Robert De Niro and Jeremy Irons in 1986's *The Mission.*

JIM GARRISON

The Big Easy (1987)

This 1987 Jim McBride thriller, set in New Orleans, starred Dennis Quaid as a local Cajun police detective, steeped in the city's widely accepted milieu of rampant corruption. Ellen Barkin played the idealistic new assistant DA he runs afoul of during the investigation of a particularly gruesome murder case. Her boss, the local lawyer who runs the show, was played by Jim Garrison, himself no stranger to the scene herein depicted. Back in February of 1967, Garrison had stunned the nation by announcing that he was opening investigations into "the role of New Orleans in the assassination of President John Fitzgerald Kennedy," accusing one David Ferrie of being the appointed getaway pilot in the scheme. Four days later, Ferrie was found dead under mysterious circumstances.

On March 1, Garrison arrested local businessman and real-estate developer Clay Shaw, insisting this bastion of society had been living a double life in the homosexual underworld as Clay Bertrand, though Garrison was never able to prove his case. During the following years, supporters insisted Garrison had uncovered the true plot to kill Kennedy but was hampered by lack of proof. Detractors, including other Kennedy-conspiracy theorists, countered that Garrison's theory was the least likely of all possibilities, and that he had convinced himself of New Orleans' primary role in the crime of the century simply because that was where he, Jim Garrison, happened to reside and wield power. Discredited and, in the eyes of many, disgraced, Garrison never backed off his theory. When Oliver Stone set to work on his pro-Garrison film, 1991's *JFK,* with Kevin Costner cast more as an old-fashioned Capraesque hero than was the actual man, Stone puckishly cast Garrison in a nonspeaking cameo as his own nemesis, Chief Justice of the Supreme Court Earl Warren. Garrison died shortly after that film's release; *The Big Easy* was his only true acting role.

22

THE EXOTICS

The exquisite beauties who failed to find a screen niche.

ELIZABETH THREATT

The Big Sky (1952)

Based on a novel by A. B. Guthrie, Howard Hawks's epic *The Big Sky* told of the earliest mountain men, journeying by keelboat deep into Indian country to trade for furs. Kirk Douglas and Dewey Martin were the young heroes; Teal Eye, the breathtaking Indian princess who guides them, was played by Elizabeth "Coyote" Threatt. Though her name sounded like the outrageous fantasy of some Tinseltown press agent, it was real. Born in Kershaw, South Carolina, on April 12, 1926, she was the child of William Threatt (a Cherokee Indian) and his wife, Bess (of English descent). Her father being an Army man, they moved shortly after their daughter's birth; Elizabeth attended both grammar and high school in Pensacola, Florida. She expressed no interest in acting, despite being the local beauty. Shy and living in horror of having her picture taken, Elizabeth quietly went to work as a civilian employee for the Army Air Corps in Charlotte. One of her roommates, amazed that such a gorgeous woman could be so lacking in vanity, secretly took a photo and sent it off to a model search. Harry Conover contacted her, though Elizabeth continued to resist. Finally, in 1945, she agreed to go to New York City for an interview; agents took one look at the tall, green-eyed, ravishing brunette and hired her on the spot.

She worked regularly as a New York runway model, eventually specializing as a photographic mannequin after joining the John Powers organization. Powers suggested Elizabeth might be right for *The Big Sky* when his friend Hawks mentioned that he was looking for a striking unknown. Owing to an accident, she was on crutches when she met the legendary producer, yet he was certain that she

145

was just what he wanted. By the time that she made the movie, Elizabeth had divorced her husband of five years, businessman Louis Chused, and was living as a single mother near the RKO studios with her daughter, Rona. The pat studio biography presented her as a demure, well-adjusted woman, though Kirk Douglas recalled a very different personality in his 1988 biography, *The Ragman's Son:* "We'd go walking in the woods, skinny-dipping. She'd lie naked on the riverbank, look at me with big beautiful eyes, and in a soft voice with just a hint of a Southern drawl, ask me to beat her with my belt. I thought it was a joke. She pleaded. I had never run into a masochist before. She really wanted to be beaten. I hit her with my belt. She just stared at me. 'You're holding back.' It was almost as if she wanted to be punished for something. I hit her. There was never any impression of pain on her part."

EIKO ANDO
The Barbarian and the Geisha (1958)

For years, director John Huston and star John Wayne discussed doing a film biography of Townsend Harris, first accredited U.S. diplomatic representative to Japan, who, in 1856, entered "the forbidden empire," ending two hundred years of isolation. The two Johns believed that, arriving on theater screens more than a decade following World War II, the movie might usher in a new, happier postwar stage in U.S.-Japanese understanding. But politics and biography can only take a film so far; in Old Hollywood thinking, the public must have a pretty face. So a fictional subplot, allowing for the film's exploitive-sounding title, was added. A woman named Okichi, who historically had served as the stiff-upper-lipped Harris's laundress, was here transformed into his geisha lover. For the role, Huston picked Eiko Ando, a breathtaking burlesque queen from Tokyo. Huston had met and rejected some 150 Asian actresses, all eager for the part, when he recalled Ando, having been introduced to the dazzling beauty by mutual friends.

At twenty-four, Eiko was highly athletic and had studied English. The Manchurian-born actress was the offspring of a once-prosperous banker, whose world had come crashing down around him when, during the war years, the family's property was confiscated; the man died three years before his daughter's fleeting moment of international fame. Eiko had early on set her sights for a career as a performer. As a teenager, she sang in Tokyo clubs, then took a job as a seminude dancer in the Nichi Geiki Music Hall. Though not bothered by the necessity of doing nude specialty numbers, Eiko set her sights higher, traveling to Paris and Rome to study with voice coaches, developing a strong contralto style. In the film, she looked lovely in period costumes and did her best to heat up the scenes with Wayne. Sadly, "hot" was not the way anyone would describe the film's box-office

Chana Eden, as the Jewish European woman who has emigrated to early twentieth-century Florida, comforts a downtrodden Christopher Plummer in Nicholas Ray's forgotten masterpiece Wind Across the Everglades. *(courtesy Warner Bros.)*

reception. Despite a title that promised a lot, word quickly spread that this was a lukewarm historical film rather than the kind of western or World War II epic Wayne's fans enjoyed watching him in. The durable actor survived this, a rare flop for him; Eiko, however, was soon back in Tokyo's nightclubs, stripping once more.

CHANA EDEN

Wind Across the Everglades (1958)

One of the great forgotten films of all time, this eccentric Nicholas Ray opus spins an early-twentieth-century tale of an environmentalist (Christopher Plummer) who journeys deep into Florida's swamps, where he confronts a poacher (Burl Ives) to save the wildlife. Thirty years ahead of its time, *Wind* not only offered an ecological statement but featured the most oddball supporting cast ever assembled: former stripper Gypsy Rose Lee, novelist MacKinlay Kantor, circus clown Emmett Kelly, and young Peter Falk, making his movie debut. The lead female character, a Jewish woman whose family had transplanted their Eastern European culture to the Florida Keys, was played by Israeli-born beauty Chana Eden. Her last name was the invention of Hollywood's glamour machine; she'd been born Chana (pronounced "Hahna" with a guttural *H*) Messinger in Haifa, serving for two years as machine gunner in the Israeli Army.

Show business was even then in her heart: she volunteered to entertain the Navy by singing in the Israeli equivalent of USO shows. Afterward, the five-foot-six-inch, brown-haired beauty went to work as an El Al stewardess, allowing her to leave Israeli, finally settling in Hollywood with hopes of becoming a director. "Everything seemed to fall in my lap," she later reflected. "I was new and different. Two studios offered me contracts. It all came so easily that it scared me." The expression "flavor of the month" did not yet exist, other than in the ice-cream

147

business, but that's what Chana Eden was. She appeared in some thirty-five TV shows, including *Have Gun Will Travel,* and was offered (but turned down) a recurring role in the *Adventures in Paradise* series. Chana quickly tired of being Tinseltown's all-purpose ethnic, playing everything from Cuban to Arab to Native American. She agreed to do a 1957 singing gig at a New York nightclub; one night, writer Budd Schulberg (*On the Waterfront, What Makes Sammy Run?*) caught her act. He was celebrating the completion of his latest screenplay; one look at the exotic beauty onstage and Schulberg knew he'd found his leading lady for *Wind.* When the film flopped, so did her hope of becoming Israel's answer to Sophia Loren. Chana never again starred in a Hollywood film. However, in 1982, when Kirk Douglas needed an actress to play a middle-aged Israeli woman opposite him in the made-for-TV film *Remembrance of Love,* Chana Eden—now older, but no less lovely—filled the bill perfectly.

ELANA EDEN

The Story of Ruth (1960)

When 20th Century–Fox set out to film the biblical story of Ruth, they decided to hire an unknown Israeli actress for authenticity. The irony is that the historical Ruth was not born Hebrew, but renounced her multitude of gods after discovering the Torah. During the talent search, someone at the studio recalled that only a year earlier, an Israeli woman named Elana (means "tree") Lani Cooper had been tested for the lead in *The Diary of Anne Frank* and was pretty much set for the part until Millie Perkins had been discovered. After hearing this disappointing news, Elana had assumed fame had passed her by forever and so went back to work on a kibbutz, then planned on entering the Israeli Army.

She was the daughter of Zvi Cooper, born in Russia, and Judith Sokolovski Cooper, of Poland. Both had come to Israel shortly after World War II, living in near-poverty by the Jordan River in a small village called Bat-Yam, just beyond Jaffa. Elana's father worked as a landscape gardener; there was an older brother and sister. When not studying or working in the fields, Elana practiced drama at the Habima Theater, then played Jessica in *The Merchant of Venice* in Tel Aviv. Flown to Hollywood, she was quickly put on a weight-reduction plan (from a chunky 114 pounds to a svelte 100 in two weeks) and given a last name that sounded properly Hebraic. Ironically, most ethnic actors were, at the time, assigned nonethnic-sounding names like Cooper, though in Elana's case, the opposite occurred, seeing as she would debut in a Bible story. The studio signed her to a seven-year contract, but following the lukewarm response to *Ruth,* the then nineteen-year-old received no other film roles.

148

CORINNA TSOPEI

A Man Called Horse (1970)

The Old Hollywood never did right by Native Americans, until recently preferring to put white people in swarthy makeup, then pretend they look like Indians and hope the audience would buy it. Elliot Silverstein's version of *A Man Called Horse,* intended as a breakthrough in the depiction of Native Americans, was in fact a case in point. Though the film promised the first honest screen image of Plains Indians, seen through the eyes of a white male captive, the twelve-year-old heroine of Dorothy Johnson's original story was here enacted by a mature Greek woman who in 1964 had won the Miss Universe crown in Miami. At that event, Jackie Gleason had taken one look at Corinna Tsopei, smiled, and muttered his famous "How sweet it is!" She, just then learn-

John Morgan, a.k.a. Horse (Richard Harris), looking like a holdover from the British Invasion of 1964, falls in love with his "Indian" captor, Little Freedom (Corinna Tsopei) in A Man Called Horse. *(courtesy Cinema Center Films)*

ing English, picked up that expression and used it in every situation that arose. Corinna was swiftly transplanted to Hollywood, playing showy bits in such fluffy studio films as *Caprice* with Doris Day and *A Guide for the Married Man* with Walter Matthau.

Then she was cast as Little Freedom, the striking but unrealistically glamorous Indian woman who falls madly in love with her white slave and assigned "horse," played by Richard Harris, in this vigorous but compromised nouveau western. As they exchanged flowers in the wilderness, the two actually looked more like aging hippies than frontier denizens. After that, no other roles were forthcoming. In 1981, Tsopei—who had once threatened to return to Europe if she failed to become a major movie star—instead married director Freddie Fields on the deck of the Malibu house they'd been sharing for some time. David Begelman, a studio power broker who achieved mainstream notoriety by forging actor Cliff Robertson's name on a check, was best man.

As Shaman, Princess Elizabeth of Toro
courageously looks on as an evil dictator
(Trevor Thomas) orders her to be killed. One
reason why the role was such a natural for
Elizabeth is that in real life she had faced
just such a situation with Uganda's Idi
Amin. (courtesy Columbia Pictures)

ELIZABETH OF TORO
Sheena (1984)

Talk of a major *Sheena* movie began in the
mid-1970s when producers searched for
compromises between jiggle-jiggle vehicles to display the era's glamorous female
stars with stories about strong women that
female audiences would feel comfortable
with in the postfeminist era. *Sheena* seemed
made to order: a campy, old-fashioned
comic-book story (the new *Superman*
movies were highly popular in Reagan's
retro-eighties) featuring a statuesque,
scantily clothed blonde. Farrah Fawcett
and Priscilla Presley campaigned for the
role by posing in leopardskin sarongs,
though the part eventually went to Tanya
Roberts, last and least of *Charlie's Angels*.
Looking more like a misplaced Valley girl
than a sensuous savage, Roberts failed to
convey the charisma that thirty years earlier
established Irish McCalla as TV's first sex symbol.

Making matters worse for Roberts was the on-screen competition. Early in
the film, the orphaned Sheena is raised in the wilds by Shaman, an earth mother who
teaches the child everything she needs to know about survival while endowing Sheena
with a deep sense of natural wisdom. In the Shaman role, a black actress billed as
Elizabeth of Toro conveyed all those key qualities—strength, smartness, style, sexi-
ness, and substance—so obviously missing from Roberts's Sheena. Though lacking
acting experience, Elizabeth of Toro was able to play this remarkable woman because
she was one herself. The former foreign minister of Uganda, Elizabeth had been born
into the royal court of Toro, at that time an independent state eventually annexed by
neighboring Uganda. The brilliant young woman was educated at Cambridge and
admitted to the bar in England, proving she could balance brains with beauty by
dividing her time between the bar and a second career as high-fashion model.
Returning to her homeland, she attracted the eye of Idi Amin, who appointed her
first as roving ambassador, then in 1974 as foreign minister. But when he proposed
marriage and she flatly refused, Amin angrily dismissed her from the prestigious post.
Fearful for her life, Elizabeth slipped into self-imposed exile in Kenya, where she
caught the notice of filmmakers and won her role in *Sheena*.

23
COMEDIANS NOT MEANT
FOR MOVIES

L enny Bruce and some others.

LENNY BRUCE

Dance Hall Racket (1953)

"I learned the truth from Lenny Bruce," Paul Simon wailed in a heartfelt ballad about the counterculture icon who transformed stand-up comedy from garish Vegas entertainment into a legitimate (if hardly respectable) art form. The man born Leonard Alfred Schneider in 1926 to a Long Island businessman and an iconoclastic, free-spirited woman spent his early years (following the divorce of Lenny's incompatible parents) bouncing back and forth between his father's conventional, conservative home and his mother's bohemian digs. Often, he accompanied her to burlesque shows, where the brilliant but terribly confused youth cultivated his taste for living on the edge. Following a World War II Navy stint, Lenny plugged into the New York arts scene. Prodded by his mother, Sally Marr, Lenny studied acting and discovered his natural skills at comedy. He appeared ready to hit the big time when, on April 18, 1949, he tied for first place on *Arthur Godfrey's Talent Scouts*.

But legitimate jobs still eluded Lenny, who had by this time changed his last name. Shortly, he was practicing his craft in strip clubs, where he met and married dancer Honey Harlowe. Hoping to land a Hollywood contract as his politically oriented colleague Mort Sahl had done, Lenny couldn't get cast in a major studio film. Miffed, he wrote an exploitation flick for himself and the two women in his life, Honey and his mom. In *Dance Hall Racket,* Lenny cast himself as a nasty hood who beats up bums in a cheesy joint and seduces all the bimbos, the best-endowed played by Honey. The film was directed by Phil Tucker, whose level of incompetence made Ed Wood Jr. look like Orson Welles. Tucker is best remembered for his

Lenny Bruce is a nasty punk in Dance Hall Racket, *which he wrote himself; wife Honey Harlowe and mother Sally Marr costarred. (courtesy Photofest)*

trash masterpiece *Robot Monster,* which rivals *Plan 9 from Outer Space* as "worst movie ever made." *Dance Hall Racket* was so bad that wide theatrical release could not be arranged, being too sordid and sleazy for booking on late-night TV. Indeed, many people—even Bruce aficionados—are amazed to learn Lenny starred in a film, so lost has *Dance Hall Racket* been over the years. Even in the early 1970s, when Julian Barry's play and Bob Fosse's film resurrected Lenny (who died of an overdose in 1966 after being hounded by authorities on obscenity charges), lifting him to legendary status, *Dance Hall Racket* did not resurface. Only recently has the film—intended as drama, though so shoddy it can only be watched as an unintentional comedy—been released on home video. Lenny would have appreciated the situation; after all, he once wrote that "satire is tragedy plus time."

WOODY WOODBURY

For Those Who Think Young (1964)

Back in the early sixties, two comics named Woody were hitting it big on the college circuit. In the Northeast, Woody Allen wowed Ivy Leaguers with his intellectual wit; in warmer climes, Woody Woodbury knocked the surf set dead with considerably less subtle gags. Allen would go on to become a world-class filmmaker; Woodbury would star in only one film, an upscale beach-party flick by way of a Pepsi commercial that cast Woodbury as a reasonable facsimile of himself, a comical college professor with a big heart, eager to straighten out the problems of such delectable beach bunnies as Pamela Tiffin, Nancy Sinatra, and Claudia Martin.

Woodbury, a former Marine from St. Paul, Minnesota, had always entertained his leatherneck buddies with silly songs and stories. When in 1947 they threw a "getting out" party for him at the Peacock Club in Jacksonville, Florida, the owner was so impressed by Woody's impromptu monologue that he offered Woody a permanent job. Later, Woody ran his own club, the Chart Room in the Bahama Hotel, on the beach near Fort Lauderdale, where he caught on with visiting kids during the annual spring break. The rest of the year, he entertained vacationers from the North, always dressed in a red Ban-Lon golf shirt and well-worn Marine fatigue cap. Hunched over the small piano (he invented "sit down" rather than stand-up comedy) that he kept onstage, Woodbury delivered slightly off-color gags. He hosted TV's *Who Do You Trust* after Johnny Carson left for *The Tonight Show* and, in 1967, headlined a ninety-minute syndicated talk show, though it lasted only one year, the field being crowded then with Mike Douglas, Merv Griffin, and several others competing for station slots. After that, Woody performed occasionally at Caesars Palace, then quietly faded from sight.

JACK E. LEONARD

The Fat Spy (1965)

Long before Don Rickles came on the scene, the uncontested master of the cruel insult was Jack E. Leonard, a rotund, belligerent, mean-spirited (at least when "on") comedian who insulted everyone mercilessly. Incredibly enough, those who knew him best insist that, the moment Jack E. Leonard walked offstage, he was in fact the sweetest, gentlest of human beings. If true, that would qualify him as the opposite of so many show business personalities, who carefully hide their true nasty natures behind a façade of friendliness. Leonard was heavily in demand as toastmaster at testimonial Friars Club dinners. Though his put-downs were legendary, Leonard—a Chicago native who had attended Northwest University—scrupulously avoided "bad" language, so his highly quotable gag lines (importantly, along with his name) won more space in columns than those from other speakers at such engagements, helping to transform him from a cult favorite into a national figure.

Between flights, Soupy Sales flirted with glamour girl Beverly Adams. (courtesy Columbia Pictures)

Leonard, who also sang well and (like W. C. Fields before him) was a graceful dancer, made the TV rounds in the midsixties, including countless performances on the popular *Mike Douglas Show*. There were cameo appearances in several minor films, but only one lead, in *The Fat Spy,* a spoof of the then-flourishing superagent flicks as well as TV's *Man from U.N.C.L.E.* Leonard played dual roles, as both hero and bad guy; his romantic lead was Jayne Mansfield, then at the end of her tether, while comedy relief was supplied by Phyllis Diller, and old-time movie heavy Brian Donlevy did the honors in the tough-guy department. The film, shot in Florida, was a bust, so Leonard retreated to his popular Vegas act. He died in 1973, at age sixty-one, after heart surgery failed to revive him following his collapse during an opening-night act at New York's Rainbow Grill.

SOUPY SALES

Birds Do It (1966)

Before there was Pee-wee Herman, adults and children alike crowded around the TV to watch Soupy Sales, the first performer to tread a delicate balance between actually doing and openly spoofing a kiddie show. Beginning in Detroit in 1953, then moving on to Los Angeles and finally New York, Sales (born Milton Hines in North Carolina, nicknamed Soupy since his last name sounded like a popular brand) brought pie-in-the-face slapstick to the afternoon hours when more traditional hosts were simply showing cartoons. He carried on tongue-in-cheek conversations with a dog named Fang, suggested by pretend paws. Soupy was considered an avant-garde hipster artist by grown-ups who "dug" his act, a talentless, out-of-control jerk by those who didn't. In 1962, he briefly headlined an ABC nighttime network show and was so beloved by celebrities that the likes of Frank Sinatra, Burt Lancaster, and Tony Curtis would stop by for cameo appearances—and the obligatory pie in the face.

Shortly before they took to writing film scripts such as *Bonnie and Clyde,* the team of David Newman and Robert Benton penned a profile on Sales for a New York newspaper, insisting that "Soupy *is* television. Put him in another medium and he'd vanish. He belongs on that little screen, live." Their words proved prophetic. In 1966, Sales—exhausted from doing a record 5,370 TV appearances—announced he'd signed a contract with Columbia Pictures that would transform him into a combination Jerry Lewis/Harry Ritz. The flimsy plot of

Popular comic Joan Rivers has done only one film acting role to date, playing a complacent suburbanite who can't understand why Burt Lancaster wants to dive into her backyard pool in The Swimmer. *(courtesy Photofest)*

his first (and only) project had Soupy discovering how to fly, with an old Army officer (Arthur O'Connell) trying to harness that power for the country's good. But *Birds Do It* opened and closed quickly, ending further Hollywood dreams. Another one-shot wonder was in the cast: Frank Nastasi, who had provided off-camera voices on Soupy's TV series, played his best pal.

JOAN RIVERS

The Swimmer (1968)

Sarcastic, stylishly outfitted Joan Rivers has become such an icon of talk TV and the Home Shopping Network that it surprises some fans to learn she once hoped to become a serious actress. The daughter of a Brooklyn doctor and his doting wife, Joan Molinsky moved early on with her family to suburban Larchmont where, despite a teenager's endless insecurities, Joan seized on the notion of a show business career, studying drama at Adelphi. She even found extra work in a grade-

Z comedy called *Mr. Universe,* with Jack Carson as a con man trying to pawn off Vincent Edwards as a wrestling star. Then Joan studied English and social anthropology at Barnard College, briefly opting for a steady job as fashion coordinator for the Bond clothing stores.

But show business was in her blood; Joan started working small Greenwich Village clubs, joined Second City's improv troupe, even toured with the USO until she was booked on *The Tonight Show* in 1965 and became a huge favorite with Johnny Carson's audience, thanks to a kafkaesque ability to render memories of suburban angst in surrealistically comic terms. Joan then played her only dramatic role: she's one of the affluent, ennui-ridden residents of an upscale Connecticut development who try to grasp why one of their ilk (Burt Lancaster) is swimming his way across the area via backyard pools. Then, Joan's TV career took off so successfully that there was little time for character acting. She later did a brief cameo in her own writing-directing debut film, *Rabbit Test* with Billy Crystal, and provided the voice for the female robot in pal Mel Brooks's *Spaceballs.* But *The Swimmer* remains her only acting role to date.

ANDY KAUFMAN

Heartbeeps (1981)

On May 16, 1984, nonsmoker Andy Kaufman died of lung cancer at age thirty-five, bringing a shocking, swift end to the strange, confusing career of this young comic. He had performed cameos in several films but had a leading role in only one, *Heartbeeps,* a sincere and ambitious if ultimately ineffectual attempt to make a sweet-spirited romantic comedy about two robots (Kaufman and Bernadette Peters) who fall in love and run away together. If handled delicately, this might have been a minor classic, but owing to Allan Arkush's slapdash treatment, *Heartbeeps* was, at best, a diamond in the rough, though Kaufman did project (even under Stan Winston's heavy makeup) the image of a big little boy that had been his hallmark on TV's *Taxi* (where he played Latka from 1978 to 1983).

Onstage, as a stand-up, he would alternately confound, amaze, and infuriate audiences by setting out to read the entire text of *The Great Gatsby* or encouraging everyone to sing along to endless verses of "Old MacDonald Had a Farm" rather than delivering funny lines. As a guest on *Saturday Night Live,* Kaufman challenged women to come on the show and wrestle with him for "intergender champion of the world"; the problem was, nobody could decide if this was intended as sexist or antisexist humor. His approach was nothing if not offbeat, eccentric, and iconoclastic. His single film lead suggested his talent had depths that would unfortunately never be tapped.

156

24
THE BEAUTIFUL BLONDES . . .
BUT NOT A MARILYN
AMONG THEM

T here's a lyric in the very successful Broadway musical comedy *A Funny Thing Happened on the Way to the Forum*. The song's title is *All I Am Is Lovely*. Alas, that was practically the only claim to fame of these beauties.

JOY HARMON

Cool Hand Luke (1967)

Cool Hand Luke is full of memorable scenes, yet one stands out for its plentiful pulchritude in this essentially all-male movie. The title character, played by Paul Newman, and fellow chain-gang members slave away in the afternoon sun, repairing a road, under the ever-watchful eyes of guards. Suddenly, a girlish blonde drives near, steps out of her car, and proceeds to wash the automobile, her slight dress becoming drenched.

"She doesn't know what she's doing to us," a prisoner sighs.

"She knows *just* what she's doing," Luke cynically counters.

The teen-tease was played by Joy Harmon, who was in fact twenty-seven at the time. Born in Jackson Heights, Long Island, Joy learned about the movies from her father, who once worked for the Roxy Theatre in New York City and still had important connections. He helped his pretty daughter begin a modeling career at age three, when she appeared in Vyvyann Donner's fashion segments for the then-popular 20th Century–Fox theatrical newsreels. The family moved to Hartford, Connecticut, where in 1955 locals turned out to watch a Gregory Peck vehicle, *Man in the Gray Flannel Suit,* being filmed on location. A talent scout pulled Joy from the throng and put the radiant girl in a crowd scene. She was bitten by the show biz bug, though all she could find was occasional extra work as a dancer in teen-oriented films such as *Let's Rock!* (1958) with Julius La Rosa and *Village of the Giants* (1965)

157

Ewa Aulin as Candy.

with Tommy Kirk. She also appeared as the obligatory dumb blonde in TV-sketch comedy, working with the likes of Steve Allen, Jonathan Winters, Garry Moore, and Dave Garroway. Newspapers, in those prefeminist times, regularly featured photographs of leggy starlets, so Harmon supplied them with endless shots of her filling out a bathing suit. At one point, the press dubbed her "Cheesecake Queen of America." Such limited fame, however, does not necessarily translate into movie stardom. After *Luke,* it became clear that younger women were stealing Harmon's thunder; she retired from show business at age thirty.

EWA AULIN
Candy (1968)

During the holiday season of 1968, the era when Americans lined up to see something like *White Christmas* with Bing Crosby seemed but a distant memory. Instead, immense highway billboards now hyped the film version of the Terry Southern–Mason Hoffenberg novel *Candy,* a cult fave during the quieter Kennedy era just a few years earlier. Now, though, in an age of cultural upheaval, social protest, and sexual revolution, *Candy* was considered perfect for a major movie. So little kids accompanying their moms to the mall peered out the car window and, instead of Santa, glimpsed larger-than-life images of a naked blonde, bound to a wall by chains, awaiting her latest lover. In the film, those men included top stars Richard Burton, Marlon Brando, and Walter Matthau. The girl of the hour was seventeen-year-old Ewa Aulin, a Swedish teenager signed by Robert Haggiag after he tested and rejected such other international beauties as Pia Degermark (*Elvira Madigan*), England's Sue George, and Sidney Rome. Aulin, boasting a picture-perfect 36-24-35 figure, was hyped as a "new find," though she had actually appeared in two inconsequential European-lensed films and won the Miss International Teen title at age fifteen.

Aulin left the Stockholm home she shared with her divorcée mother (she never met her biological father) and secretly married English actor and aspiring author John Shadow, thirty-two, in Tijuana, Mexico, keeping their union a secret during the filmmaking and subsequent publicity tour. In those days of tighter budgets, Aulin was reportedly paid a mere $20,000 for her work, though she and Shadow were somehow able to acquire a Rome villa, to which they retreated after the horrid reviews for *Candy*—the film and, particularly, her performance—swiftly ended any hope for a Hollywood career. One year later, Ewa was playing bit parts in international coproductions such as *Start the Revolution Without Me*. "My only ambition," she announced on the eve of *Candy*'s release, "is to make the world a more beautiful place." For two hours of screen time, her blonde good looks achieved that aim.

JANET LANDGARD

The Swimmer (1968)

In his oblique short story "The Swimmer," John Cheever offered a subtle suburban satire in which a lone man, standing on a hill overlooking his Connecticut neighborhood, seizes upon the notion of swimming rather than walking home by stripping to his shorts and diving into one after another of his neighbors' successive pools. At first, the idea seems appealingly eccentric until it gradually becomes clear the hero is deranged. All that's waiting for him at home is the empty house that his wife and children—for reasons we never learn—have vacated. In narrative fiction, an author can slip in and out of such a character's mind; for their film, Frank and Eleanor Perry decided to add a companion for the hero (Burt Lancaster) to talk with, automatically destroying the basic concept, that being the man's loneliness. Worse, to make the movie commercial, the Perrys opted to give Lancaster a beautiful blonde in a bikini, supposedly his family's onetime baby-sitter, allowing Lancaster to grin in admiration while delivering such dreadful (and clearly non-Cheeverian) lines as "That belly's as firm as a sheaf of golden wheat!"

For that girl, Janet Landgard—clearly California born and bred, looking hopelessly out of place in the New England setting—was cast. At fourteen, Landgard had aspired to be a veterinarian, though she tried modeling when her grandmother suggested she had precisely the right look. Within four months, Landgard had graced the covers of twenty-five national magazines, then picked up a continuing role as an idealized girl-next-door type on TV's *The Donna Reed Show*, appearing in more than forty episodes. After *The Swimmer*, she did summer stock on Long Island and studied with L.A.'s ANTA Theatre group. All for naught; following dismal critical reaction to *The Swimmer*, Landgard headed for Europe, where the best she could do was a small role in the spaghetti western *Arizona Land Raiders* with George Maharis.

159

25
UNTENABLE IMPORTS

Superstars in their native lands, they were brought to Hollywood where—like Garbo and Dietrich—it was assumed they would likewise appeal to American audiences; in these cases, it didn't happen.

FRANCISKA GAAL

The Buccaneer (1938)

For Cecil B. DeMille's appealingly artificial epic about swashbuckler Jean Lafitte and his role in the Battle of New Orleans, the operatic filmmaker invented a lively love triangle involving "the good pirate" (Fredric March) with a New Orleans socialite (Margot Grahame) as well as with Gretchen, a little Dutch child-woman whom he has rescued from an abandoned ship. The legendary showman C.B. decided to introduce an exciting new star in the latter role; after a lengthy search, he decided on Hungarian actress Franciska Gaal, claiming that she blended the best qualities of Helen Hayes, Elisabeth Bergner, and Mary Pickford.

Born in Budapest, Gaal had always been superstitious: she was the thirteenth child in her family and so feared throughout her life that she was living under a curse. Certainly, the curse of one-shot wonder would haunt her, at least so far as Hollywood was concerned. Gaal, who had attended but been dropped from the Stage Academy of Hungary, had doggedly hung around a Budapest theater where the play *The Stupid Man* was in rehearsal, learning all the roles just in case her big break ever came; when the ingenue took sick, she got the part by default. There were several German-language pictures with titles like *Miss Paprika* and *Love and Kisses, Veronica,* which caught the attention of Paramount's talent scouts. Signed to a contract, she received full star buildup for *The Buccaneer.* But audiences, who enjoyed such cloying little-girl types when DeMille first began making movies, had by the late thirties come to prefer such

160

tough-talking Depression-era dollies as Joan Blondell and Ginger Rogers, or bona fide glamour girls such as Marlene Dietrich and Greta Garbo. Gaal might have hit big had she come to America a generation earlier; now, audiences found her whiny approach to be silly and off-putting, spelling a quick end to her hopes for Hollywood stardom.

BRIGITTE AUBER

To Catch a Thief (1955)

In Alfred Hitchcock's most sophisticated comedy-thriller, Cary Grant was cast as Robie, a former jewel thief presently living on the French Riviera who discovers someone is framing him for the kind of cat burglaries he was once famous for. Grace Kelly played the American heiress who falls in love with him, simultaneously attracted and repelled by the possibility of being his next victim. In the film's unforgettable denouement, high atop a Monaco mansion, Robie realizes the impersonator is none other than the pretty daughter of an old Resistance friend who has been hiding him. Pert, pouty Danielle is jealous since, during the war, he playfully seduced and then callously abandoned her. Danielle was played by Brigitte Auber, a petite "brownette" (as they used to say) with striking blue eyes and legs to die for, a fact not lost on Hitch, who made the most of her sultry, catlike features.

Born in Paris in 1929 on the Left Bank of the old quarter of St-Germain-des-Prés, Brigitte grew up in a household headed by a writer father and milliner mother. There were two older sisters, all living together in a unique atmosphere halfway between the bohemian and bourgeois worlds surrounding them. Brigitte's first great interest was music and dance; she concentrated her studies on piano and ballet. Then, a chance visit to a friend's drama class convinced her that she wanted to act. There were appearances in half a dozen minor French films, including *Vendetta de Camargue* and *Femmes de Paris,* though none were exported to America. As an equestrian, she appeared in several Parisian circuses, performing dangerous routines on the trapeze at the annual Grand Gala des Artistes de Paris. It was this unique skill, beyond her obvious beauty and acting talent, that convinced Hitchcock Brigitte Auber was precisely whom he needed for his film's final vertigo-inducing sequence.

MIJANOU BARDOT

Sex Kittens Go to College (1960)

After the 1957 release of *And God Created Woman,* Bardolatry swept America. Marilyn Monroe at last had serious competition as the world's great sex symbol from a petite French blonde named Brigitte. Hollywood wooed her; surprisingly, B.B.

Mijanou Bardot shows off her sexy smile and considerable assets in the gym. (courtesy Allied Artists)

proved unresponsive. Then, American producers learned there was another, younger Bardot. If they could just bring her here, lightning might strike twice. So it was that Mijanou Bardot, Brigitte's then twenty-one-year-old sister and fresh from the convent school she'd been attending, flew over from Paris late in 1959. Her initial project was Albert Zugsmith's latest grade-Z production, originally to be titled *Sexpot Goes to College,* years later released to television as *The Beauty and the Robot,* but circulated to teen-oriented double-bill grindhouses and déclassé drive-ins in 1960 as *Sex Kittens Go to College.* Zugsmith put the legendary Ed Wood to shame with his shabby sets, incoherent plots, and a direction of actors that alternated between over-the-top histrionics and deadening monotone, creating a strange cinematic netherworld between total incompetence and unintended surrealism.

The five-foot-six-inch, red-headed Mijanou was cast as a foreign-exchange student picking her way through the maze of romantic shenanigans occurring between fellow students and sex-starved teachers. A virginal coed (Tuesday Weld) fears she may be losing her boyfriend (Martin Milner) to his nymphomaniac professor (Mamie Van Doren). The eclectic supporting cast includes Pamela (wife of James) Mason, comic Louis Nye, horror-film veteran John Carradine, and former child star Jackie Coogan. Mijanou, admittedly the more demure of the Bardot sisters, was stunned by what she experienced. "I was not too happy here," she admitted just before leaving in January 1960, never to return. "It was not like I dreamed it would be. Not glamour, just the hardest kind of work. In Paris, we report to the studio about ten o'clock in the morning and prepare leisurely for work in the early forenoon. Here, I am up at six, in makeup department at seven, wardrobe at eight—and so I am tired all the time." Besides, "it was most lonely sitting in a hotel room night after night studying a script—and fearful to go on a date because I could not converse easily. I did not even see southern California, or any scenery. Just that hotel room."

BEKIM FEHMIU
The Adventurers (1970)

Variety once referred to Bekim Fehmiu as "the one authentic superstar Yugoslavia has ever produced." He appeared in countless Eastern European films, none released in the United States. Fehmiu picked up the lead in one early film, *I Even Met Some Happy Gypsies,* when the actual Gypsy slated to play the part dropped out days before filming commenced. Fehmiu stepped in, the movie was completed, and it shared the Grand Prix at the Cannes Film Festival in 1968, insuring that it would be shown at art houses in America. The wife and son of director Lewis Gilbert (just then basking in the success of the James Bond extravaganza *You Only Live Twice* and readying for his next project, an adaptation of Harold Robbins's bestseller *The Adventurers*) caught the little movie. When Gilbert later mentioned to the family

Bekim Fehmiu, rugged star of countless regional movies that have never played mainstream America. (courtesy Paramount Pictures)

that he was having a hard time casting the role of international playboy/diplomat Dax Xenos, both wife and son nominated Fehmiu.

The rest, as they say, is history, though there's no record as to whether their suggestion, and its unhappy outcome, had a lasting effect on the Gilberts' family life. Shot at a cost of $15 million (now a trifle, then qualifying it as one of the most expensive movies ever made), *The Adventurers* rated as a bomb of the first order. Paramount had hoped it might be one of those critic-proof films, such as *The Carpetbaggers* or *Valley of the Dolls* from the previous decade. But this was the early 1970s, and in the post–*Easy Rider* era, such a slick, empty epic suddenly seemed anachronistic. Someone had to be blamed, so the old Hollywood hands salvaged their reputations by pointing their collective finger at the new kid on the block. Fehmiu returned home, appearing in some regional film and theater productions, though a car accident in 1978 curtailed such activity. An Albanian living in the Serbian capital of Belgrade with his wife and two sons, he found himself, in 1993 at age fifty-seven, menaced by the outbreak of violence. When the war caused schools to be shut down, Fehmiu took it upon himself to supervise the education of his young relatives. One son, Uliks, has chosen to pursue an acting career. Whether *Son of Dax* will someday be on his slate remains to be seen.

JORGE RIVERO

Rio Lobo (1970)

When is a one-shot wonder not a one-shot wonder? When he's starred in more than fifty movies, though even die-hard film buffs are absolutely certain he made only one. That's the case with Jorge Rivero, brought to Hollywood for one major production, then sent packing for his home in Mexico City where Rivero would appear, for the next quarter century, in cheaply made action flicks that failed to receive wide theatrical release stateside, though some did appear briefly in L.A.'s barrio moviehouses. Rivero originally intended to choose between careers as a professional athlete or chemical engineer. While in college, his good looks got him an offer of a role in the inexpensive Mexican production of *The Invisible Man,* which led to parts in the popular telenovelas, those serialized soap operas that inspire fanatic loyalty on Latino TV. In 1969, Howard Hawks set to work on *Rio Lobo,* a follow-up to *Rio Bravo* and *El Dorado,* which would serve as the filmmaker's swan song. Hoping this movie might cross over and catch on big in the third-world market, the wily producer-director decided that America's John Wayne would share top billing with some highly popular Latino film personality.

So it was that Rivero was cast as Pierre Cardona, a Confederate officer who leads his guerrilla outfit on a raid of a Union gold train. When Yankee colonel Cord McNally (Wayne) learns of the attack, he determines to track down the raiders, though the war has since ended. McNally is not interested in vengeance against Cardona, whom he considers a worthy adversary, but is after the traitor in his own company who leaked word of the shipment, believing Cardona can help him locate and then kill this man. Despite generally kind reviews, Rivero afterward was unable to find another high-status vehicle. Small supporting parts in unsuccessful and barely released westerns such as *Soldier Blue* and *The Last Hard Men* were all he could get. Rivero tried everything he could think of, eventually Anglicizing his first name to George for several cheap European productions. In 1984, he received a work permit and bought a house in Hollywood, flying back and forth from Mexico City, where he was always mobbed on the streets by adoring fans, to Los Angeles, where he would walk unrecognized to the open casting lines where he'd join the other unknowns.

26
SCENE STEALERS

Major stars found themselves being upstaged by these incredible talents who came along, stole a motion picture, oftentimes won an Oscar nomination in a Best Supporting category, and then disappeared.

DORIS DAVENPORT

The Westerner (1940)

William Wyler didn't make many westerns, but his two stabs at the genre—*The Westerner* and 1958's *The Big Country*—are generally considered classics of their kind. Wyler's first concerned Cole Hardin (Gary Cooper), a lone gunfighter who wanders into a range war between cattlemen and their ally, Judge Roy Bean (Walter Brennan), and the community of dirt farmers pouring into the area, who inadvertently threaten the lifestyle based on the open range and the philosophy of rugged individualism. Cooper's lanky hero changes sides the moment he meets a pretty farmer's daughter, played to perfection by Doris Davenport, who holds her own against the experienced actor-star in every scene. Her attractiveness and natural talent suggested that a bright new light of the silver screen had arrived, though that was not to be the case.

The Moline, Illinois, native had grown up in Hollywood and, like so many other glamour girls making the rounds of the studio lots, had played minor, decorative parts—in MGM's *Kid Millions* with Eddie Cantor and RKO's *Sorority House* (under the name Doris Jordan, which she had adopted while briefly working as a Powers model in New York City)—without making any major waves. Then David O. Selznick—unable to choose between Bette Davis and Joan Crawford, either of whom would have killed for the role—was definitely leaning Doris's way for the role of Scarlett O'Hara in *Gone With the Wind*. Though the least known of the many women who were up for the part, Doris would probably have had it but for the fact that Doris's then mentor, Sam Goldwyn, slotted her in the Wyler film, shooting at

165

roughly the same time, so Selznick instead settled for Vivien Leigh. Davenport and Wyler didn't get along (he was miffed that his wife, Margaret Tallichet, was not allowed to play the role). Generally disgusted with the way in which the movie business worked, and never particularly ambitious, Doris married and moved to Monterey, where for many years thereafter she worked as a photo-lab assistant. She died on June 18, 1980, at age sixty-three.

DOROTHY COMINGORE

Citizen Kane (1941)

"I don't wanna be an opera singer, Charlie!" Dorothy Comingore and Orson Welles in Citizen Kane. *(courtesy RKO Radio Pictures)*

Born in L.A. in 1918, Dorothy Comingore did bit parts in early films under the name Linda Winters after being discovered by Charlie Chaplin. She can fleetingly be glimpsed in comedy shorts with the Three Stooges, in several low-grade westerns, and in a party scene in Frank Capra's 1939 classic *Mr. Smith Goes to Washington*. Orson Welles was impressed enough by what he saw to cast Dorothy as Susan Alexander, the second Mrs. Kane, a simple music-shop salesperson transformed into a bogus opera star by the megalomaniac title character. Though she was mesmerizing in the role and did briefly appear in *The Hairy Ape* three years later, other major roles were not forthcoming, owing to her lifelong addiction to alcohol and leftish political leanings. Called before the infamous House Un-American Activities Committee, Dorothy refused to state whether she was or had ever been a member of the Communist Party and was swiftly blacklisted. There was a bitter court fight with her former first husband, screenwriter Richard Collins, for the custody of their children, which she lost; after that, her already heavy drinking increased noticeably.

She was arrested in 1953 on "commercial vice" charges when, at age forty, she offered to trade sex for $10 to two men she had met in a bar, reportedly saying, "I'm a little short of cash just now," unaware they were plainclothes police detectives. In time, she was committed to Camarillo State Mental Hospital following a psychopathic court hearing at General Hospital. Her former husband novelist Theodore Strauss had appeared as the petitioning witness for her commitment, which she calmly accepted. She remained there for many years. The woman who had played Susan Alexander Kane in what is generally considered the greatest movie ever made died in obscurity in 1971.

SUSAN HARRISON
Sweet Smell of Success (1957)

Sweet Smell of Success, a thinly disguised exposé of newspaper columnist Walter Winchell (Burt Lancaster) and his most fawning sycophant (Tony Curtis), still stands as one of the landmark dramas of the 1950s. Stunning newcomer Susan Harrison made a dynamic debut as Lancaster's younger sister, a young woman in love with a jazz musician (Martin Milner). Rave reviews suggested that the five-foot-seven-inch, eighteen-year-old beauty was headed for superstardom, though other than a bit part in a B biker flick, she would never again appear on film. Harrison (real name, Susan Colin), a Boston University dropout, had been discovered by producer Harold Hecht, who spotted her modeling in Greenwich Village and was impressed by the youth's poise and presence. She brought her beat-generation ways with her to Hollywood, including a penchant for long hair, black stockings, and oversize sweaters. Also along for the bumpy ride was a bearded nightclub singer, whom she married just before starting the film, then divorced the moment it was completed. Cast and crew members recall dubbing her the ding-a-ling girl of the year, a term reserved for gorgeous, talented, but incurably flaky

Susan Harrison, as the demure younger sister of the nasty Walter Winchell–type columnist played by Burt Lancaster. (courtesy United Artists)

women. On the set, Susan often grew moody, refusing to chat with costar Curtis between scenes, secretly burning with the suspicion that no one liked her.

Susan soon married an aspiring writer, Joel Cohen, whom she had met at the divorce party that she and former husband Phillipe together hosted. Harrison retreated to Broadway, where she appeared in William Saroyan's *The Cave Dwellers,* then spent two years in Tucson with her husband and little boy. She returned to Los Angeles and did *Playhouse 90.* Then Susan sued Hecht for $25,000, claiming her contract with him had guaranteed her three pictures, though she was the one who had deserted him and Hollywood. Unemployable, Susan hit the headlines one final time before her premature death. In 1965, the newly divorced single mother, living in a shabby apartment, was arrested for child neglect. Her little boy, Daniel, had badly bruised himself (some insisted he'd been abused by his mother), though the former actress did not get around to taking him to a hospital for over a month, during which time Daniel lapsed into semiparalysis and, according to deputy district attorney John Miner, sustained permanent brain damage. Harrison received a suspended ninety-day jail sentence, then drifted out of the limelight forever.

MAURA MCGIVENEY

Do Not Disturb (1965)

The sad fate of this hazel-eyed blonde proved that good looks, acting skill, and considerable charisma do not necessarily guarantee success in show business. Born in London in 1935 to parents of Irish descent, McGiveney's father was the fabled Owen "Quick Change" McGiveney, who toured the Continent in Dickens's *Oliver Twist,* playing all the characters. Young Maura, exposed to the ecstatic reactions of the audience, vowed to be an actress and studied at the Royal Academy of Dramatic Arts, then moved to Hollywood. As a child, she had appeared briefly in the film *The Secret Garden* (Margaret O'Brien played the lead) and in 1959 won a bit part in Alfred Hitchcock's classic *North by Northwest.* When major movie roles were not immediately forthcoming, McGiveney survived by becoming president of the Freeway Circuit, a theater troupe that staged plays in the L.A. suburbs. There were occasional acting assignments on TV shows such as *Dr. Kildare* and *Perry Mason,* then at last the big break: a role in *Do Not Disturb* as the beautiful British secretary who tries to seduce boss Rod Taylor over the objections of his wife, Doris Day. Though McGiveney was called upon to dye her naturally blond hair a drab brown, she managed to shine through, winning a nomination for the Golden Globe Award as Most Promising Newcomer. Still, producers didn't know precisely what to do with her. Maura was too pretty for character parts, not quite gorgeous enough for romantic leads.

After four years without a film, Maura hoped TV might make her the star that she clearly deserved to be. ABC thought they could simultaneously rip off two popular NBC shows, the news satire *That Was the Week That Was* and the slapsticky *Laugh-In,* by creating *Turn-On.* McGiveney hired on as a counterpart to Nancy Ames on *TW3,* "The Body Politic," a curvaceous blonde who caustically comments on the state of affairs. After a single telecast on February 5, 1969, ABC and sponsor Bristol-Myers pulled the plug on the singularly unfunny but distressingly vulgar show, qualifying *Turn-On* as one of only four in the history of television to last a single week. McGiveney rarely worked after that and developed a serious drinking problem, dying of cirrhosis of the liver at age fifty-five in 1990.

MICHAEL MEYERS

Goodbye, Columbus (1969)

Even as *The Graduate* of two years earlier had transformed Dustin Hoffman and Katharine Ross from virtual unknowns into overnight celebrities, so, too, did this late-1960s youth-grooving film (based on Philip Roth's far more serious-minded novel) have the same impact for Broadway actor Richard Benjamin and supermod-

Michael Meyers as Ali MacGraw's Jewish-jock brother in Goodbye, Columbus. *(courtesy Paramount Pictures)*

el Ali MacGraw. But critics and public agreed that the greatest performance by a young newcomer in the popular film was delivered by Michael Meyers, as MacGraw's goofy, Jewish-jock brother. The young man had never even considered a career in the movies before landing the role. Arriving at New York's Plaza Hotel where Meyers was to be an usher at a friend's wedding, he was spotted by director Larry Peerce, who was just then casting the upcoming film and knew that this genial young man was precisely what he wanted.

Meyers displayed a delightful lack of self-consciousness in front of the camera. "I wasn't affected by it," he would recall years later. "I just did it." The results were magical, and another person might have been bitten by the acting bug, giving up the life he'd planned to pursue stardom. Fortunately, Meyers (whose name has caused him to be confused with both the *Saturday Night Live* alum Mike Myers and the fictional "thing" in the *Halloween* horror films) was far too smart for that. He had planned to attend medical school and used his entire $4,000 salary to help finance that goal. "It was all gravy, fun, ego-gratifying," Meyers later reflected about his brief bout with stardom, "and it paid for my education. But I always knew my priorities." He did eventually appear in several TV commercials, guested on some talk shows, and was a four-time loser on TV's *The Dating Game*. But the focus was on more serious matters, including a three-year residency at Santa Monica hospital. Uncomfortable with his work as a psychiatric resident in New York and a job in the emergency room of a Jersey hospital, Meyers discovered his true calling. Hungry for a deep commitment with patients who would become lifelong friends, he opted for family practice as an old-fashioned all-purpose family doctor, rather than following the current rage for specialization. Meyers and his artist wife, Patti, moved into a small Santa Monica home where, while she was painting, he turned scribe and wrote *Goodbye, Columbus, Hello Medicine,* a humorous overview of his intriguing, special, worthwhile life.

27
THAT'S COUNTRY!

From rockabilly to gentrified bluegrass, here are the C&W performers who briefly left Nashville for Tinseltown.

FARON YOUNG

Daniel Boone, Trail Blazer (1956)

Mexico seems like a pretty strange place to film a movie set in Kentucky, but that's where this low-budget yet surprisingly accurate version of the Boone legend from Republic Pictures was shot, in their TruColor process shortly before that financially strapped company threw in the towel. Bruce Bennett played the title hero, with Lon Chaney Jr. (then specializing in Indian roles, ranging from the feature *Battles of Chief Pontiac* to TV's *Hawkeye and the Last of the Mohicans*) as Chief Black Fish, the man who started out as Boone's archenemy, then became foster father to the famed woodsman. Also in the cast, playing a young scout (here called simply Faron, though presumably based on the real-life pioneer and Boone friend Flanders Colloway) who courts Daniel's daughter, was country singer Faron Young. To satisfy his fans, the people at Republic Pictures even allowed the popular performer to sing one song ("Long Green Valley") while standing astride the mighty walls of old Fort Boonsborough.

Born in Shreveport, Louisiana, in 1932, Faron Young had dropped out of college to join the local *Louisiana Hayride* TV program, sometimes performing as a duo with fellow country performer and close friend Webb Pierce. After an early-fifties stint in the Army interrupted his Capitol recording career, Young—much like Elvis—managed to bounce back with several honky-tonk hits including "I've Got Five Dollars and It's Saturday Night." In those pre–*Hee Haw* days, numerous country-western movies were made specifically for distribution in the South, so Young sang (but didn't act) in a minor item called *Country Music Holiday,* then hoped and trusted that his dramatic part in *Boone* would set him off on a film

171

Hank Williams Jr.—long before donning country-grunge duds and growing a thick beard—was pawned off as a combination of his father and Elvis Presley in the rural musical drama A Time to Sing.

career. When that didn't happen, he left his youthful honky-tonk roots behind and eased into more middle-of-the-road country crooning. Moreover, Young became an extremely important Nashville personality when he also started up the trade paper *Music City News,* which for many years was considered the journalistic bible of that branch of the music industry.

HANK WILLIAMS JR.

A Time to Sing (1968)

"I just can't call Hank Williams Jr. 'Junior' anymore," a country contemporary warbled in the midseventies. At about that time, Hank finally stepped out from the shadows of his legendary honky-tonk writer-performer father and forged his own identity as a gruff good ol' boy who liked beer, broads, and football, singing their praises in a far rougher, brawling manner than his gentle, croakyvoiced daddy would have approved of. "All My Rowdy Friends" in 1981 made clear Junior had forever distanced himself from the Williams Sr. clone his mother, Audrey, had attempted to mold him into during his formative years, a most difficult time for the young man who was told he ought to idolize his father, yet deep down inside wanted to emerge as a country-western artist with his own singular style.

Hank's only sustained dramatic film role occurred during that awkward period. In *A Time to Sing,* Junior was cast as a sweet but confused country boy, not unlike the ones Elvis played in such films as *Wild in the Country,* and it seems safe to say that the filmmakers hoped they might just come up with another such movie star. The film's plot had Hank desperate to sing but always repressing that desire for the sake of his authoritative uncle/guardian (Ed Begley), who didn't approve of such stuff. Shelley Fabares, who enjoyed the distinction of starring opposite Elvis in three films, played Junior's lady love, thereby cinching the connection to the King. But the film did not have the kind of impact that Elvis's minimusicals did, not even at rural, all-family drive-in theaters located in the Bible Belt, where it had been hoped that *A Time to Sing* would score big. Later, the beer-bellied, bearded "transformed" Hank contributed singing-only performances to such films as *Roadie* and *Willa,* though thankfully he was never again called upon to act as he had in *A Time to Sing.*

KENNY ROGERS

Six Pack (1982)

If the word *crossover* didn't already exist, it would have had to be created to describe the approach of Kenny Rogers. He flirted with a half dozen musical styles during his long and durable music career. As compared to many of the more traditional Nashville performers, who were always locked into their country roots and derived their sense of integrity from that total commitment, Rogers—who, as a Texas native, always featured an element of country in his vocals—latched onto any musical trend that was popular, hoping to have a hit with it and often doing just that. Only in the mid-1970s, when his success as a mainstream performer seemed to be behind him, did Rogers establish himself as a country performer, and even then, his records were so uncannily mainstream that they immediately began to climb on the pop charts as well. A child of the Great Depression (Rogers was born in 1937) and the offspring of an alcoholic father, Rogers turned to music as his escape when he and young pal Mickey Gilley played together in Houston. Embarking on a career as a performer and recording artist, Rogers first tried rockabilly with the Scholars, then opted for jazz with Bobby Doyle, pop with Kirby Stone, folk with the New Christy Minstrels, and finally soft rock with the First Edition. When that group hit

Reba McEntire and Michael Gross as the well-armed country couple who can't wait to get a good shot at those pesky giant earthworms. (courtesy Universal Pictures)

it big with "Reuben James," he stuck with it. When a few years later he was reduced to hawking tapes that could teach people guitar lessons at home, he opted for gentrified hillbilly and, beginning with "Lucille," turned out hits that put him back on top.

Naturally, he and his famous promoter Ken Kragen hoped that a movie career might be forthcoming. Rogers was top-billed in *Six Pack,* which cast him as Brewster Baker, a good ol' country boy who likes to race cars but finds himself saddled with a half dozen little orphan kids. The movie was supposed to be heartwarming, but with its uneven blend of hick humor and melodramatic plotting, *Six Pack* offered only the worst sort of schlock sentimentality. It failed to score a hit even on the rural drive-in circuit that caters to fans of country music. Badly bruised by the rejection, Rogers never again tried a major theatrical film. However, he became a huge success in *The Gambler* made-for-TV movies, based on his hit recording.

REBA MCENTIRE

Tremors (1990)

One critic tagged this 1990 release "the best film of 1958," a retro monster movie made with a purposely tacky edge for modern fans of fifties creature-features. Kevin Bacon, Fred Ward, and Michael Gross headed a cast of likable misfits who find themselves surrounded in the Nevada desert by giant underground worms that threaten to overrun their little sanctuary. Country-western singer Reba McEntire played the pistol-packin' momma who shoots the predators down with an acumen the men can only marvel at. Her on-screen presence was all that her many fans could hope for. Like many a country star before her, Reba here made clear that the kind of naturalness the country music audience loves best is as easy to project in front of a camera as it is in concert. However, other than a cameo appearance in *North*, she has not—at this writing—again ventured into any serious movie work.

A true cowgirl from Oklahoma, Reba and her relatives began singing on the rodeo circuit (where they also performed in various events) until recording star Red Steagall caught her rendition of the national anthem and arranged for Reba to make a demo tape in Nashville. Lending just a hint of hillbilly twirl to intense tearjerker ballads, Reba had a string of hits beginning with "Can't Even Get the Blues" in 1983. Her feisty image in music videos naturally led Reba into motion picture work, though unlike Dolly Parton, she appears uninterested in being a movie star. Perhaps if another part as juicy as the one in *Tremors* comes along, she'll go for it and end her status as a one-shot wonder.

JOHN COUGAR MELLENCAMP

Falling From Grace (1992)

Born in Indiana in 1951, John Mellencamp was inspired by the black music he heard on Detroit radio stations. Envisioning himself as just such a performer, he headed for New York, where producer Tony DeFries decided that the hard-edged youngster could be a rebel-rock star, but that he needed a sexy stage name, rechristening him "Johnny Cougar." Mellencamp quickly came to despise that moniker, though he nonetheless continued to project James Deanish mannerisms onstage. Most of his music was effective in an obvious kind of way, as he attempted, with a modicum of success on albums such as *American Fool,* to create blue-collar anthems of the type Bruce Springsteen was, in the early eighties, doing to perfection. Interestingly enough, his single film to date suggests that a side of him wished for country-western stardom.

Because Mellencamp's one shot at movie stardom also marked his attempt to become an auteur: he directed the film from a script he'd also contributed to, creating a character who, like himself, hailed from Indiana, but Bud Parks, his character, is a twangy country boy rather than an urban blue-collar rocker. The story line, amazingly close to the one employed at roughly the same time for George Strait's similar *Pure Country,* was yet another tired, predictable tale of a performer who visits his hometown for a family event, in this case his grandfather's eightieth birthday. While there, he realizes that he's become too involved in the big business of creating hit records, totally losing touch with the grassroots feelings that inspired him in the first place. Still, Bud finds time to have an affair with his old flame, now married to his brother. Mariel Hemingway, who couldn't act, and Kay Lenz, who could, were the women in his life. Though the final script was credited to Larry McMurtry, this was no *Lonesome Dove,* and Mellencamp hasn't acted since.

175

GEORGE STRAIT
Pure Country (1992)

George Strait as Dusty, the country performer whose success causes him to straddle two worlds. (photo by Ron Phillips, courtesy Warner Bros.)

The most tried, true, and tired of all movie plots to serve as showcases for popular singers turned aspiring actors is the traditional morality tale of a onetime innocent boy, elevated to the big leagues of the music business, who is vaguely unhappy but doesn't realize how far he's drifted from his roots. Then, circumstances cause him to visit his old hometown, where he at last senses what he's lost while out there in the honky-tonk world and sets about trying to reclaim something of his lost youth. That scenario has served everyone from Elvis Presley (*Loving You*) to John Mellencamp (*Falling From Grace*). When "western-swing" revivalist George Strait took a shot at mainstream movie stardom, he also opted for that most predictable of plots, playing Dusty. With Lesley Ann Warren chewing the scenery in retro–Lizabeth Scott fashion as his overbearing manager, Dusty heads home to visit his sweetheart (Isabel Glasser) and her upright father, played (in his final role) by onetime B-movie cowboy star Rory Calhoun.

In real life, Strait's hometown was Pearsall, Texas, where as the son of a junior-high teacher, he early on played rock 'n' roll in his garage, eloped with his high school girlfriend, and joined the U.S. Army. While stationed in Hawaii, Strait alleviated his homesickness by performing the country-western songs his father dearly loved. George stuck with that music after returning to the mainland, eventually winning a Nashville recording contract and turning out hits such as "All My Ex's Live in Texas." Strait has, career-wise, taken his cue from the title of his only film to date, performing a relatively pure country sound rather than giving in to the current trend for mainstream pop with a country undercurrent that's become the style for most gentrified "New Country" performers.

28
FAR SIDE OF THE CAMERA

Directors know more about acting than most actors do and are often responsible for their stars' finest moments; sometimes, they also step in front of the camera and put everyone around them to shame.

RAOUL WALSH

Sadie Thompson (1928)

Somerset Maugham's morality play about a carefree prostitute who arrives in the tropics and outrages a stern, hypocritical reformer while charming a rugged, honest Marine is a staple of Hollywood storytelling. *Rain, Dirty Gertie From Harlem,* and *Miss Sadie Thompson* are among the best-known variations, though the most effective at conveying the author's vision was this intense version starring (with Gloria Swanson and Lionel Barrymore) and directed by Raoul Walsh. In fact, Walsh had actually begun his film career as a bit player of sorts. The former soldier of fortune (born in New York City, 1887) had sailed on a trading ship to Cuba, worked as a wrangler in Mexico, then tried his hand on the fading frontier at everything from surgeon's assistant to undertaker before being hired to care for horses on B westerns, then appeared in several ersatz oaters when the Eastern actors couldn't convey cowboy charisma.

Graduating to the big leagues where he assisted D. W. Griffith, Walsh played the outlaw leader as a youth in *The Life of Villa* and John Wilkes Booth in Griffith's *Birth of a Nation.* But *Sadie* was to be his first and last starring role. After this single leading part established him as a ruggedly handsome leading man, Walsh lost an eye in a freak auto accident while scouting locations for his next feature. From then on, the black-patched tough guy remained behind the camera, proving a great favorite with rugged stars, who appreciated his simple, uncluttered, at times profound storytelling style: most notably, John Wayne in *The Big Trail,* Victor McLaglen in *What Price Glory?,* Humphrey Bogart in *High Sierra,* James Cagney in

The Strawberry Blonde, and Errol Flynn in *They Died With Their Boots On.* Owing to his early experiences, Walsh's action films made clear that the man behind the camera was not some cinematic snob but a person who had lived the very kinds of adventure stories that, for the better part of half a century, he told so very well.

SIDNEY LUMET
One Third of a Nation (1939)

Though Sidney Lumet would eventually become one of the most successful directors of American films, he had originally set out to become an actor. The Philadelphia-born youth was appearing in New York's Yiddish theater at age four, then made his Broadway debut in 1939's *Dead End,* the socially realistic classic about slum life that had an impact on Lumet's entire career. Shortly thereafter, he starred in his one and only Hollywood role, the part of Joey Rogers in *One Third of a Nation,* which like *Dead End* concerned downtrodden denizens of the big cities. Lumet was cast as the younger brother of a poor girl (Sylvia Sidney) who wants to move up and out of the tenements. Lumet may well have become one of Hollywood's more respected character actors were it not for the war, in which he served in the Army with the Signal Corps, where he learned the basics of communications and media that determined his career.

Afterward, he returned to Broadway where he became interested in directing. He was in the right place at the right time to produce and direct live TV during the golden age of drama, on such revered shows as *The Play of the Week.* When one particularly fine televised drama he hadn't directed, *12 Angry Men* (Reginald Rose's courtroom morality play), was brought to the screen in 1957, Lumet was given the go-ahead to bridge the gap between small and big screen, earning himself an Oscar nomination for Best Director. Over the years, his finest work would include movies that stood squarely within the socially realistic tradition he'd grown up in: *The Pawnbroker, Serpico, Dog Day Afternoon, Network,* and *The Verdict* among them. However, whenever Lumet attempted to branch out and do something more lighthearted, the results were disastrous: *Murder on the Orient Express, The Wiz,* and *Just Tell Me What You Want* made clear his total inability to do sophisticated thrillers, musicals, or comedies.

CECIL B. DeMILLE
Sunset Boulevard (1950)

One of Cecil Blount's earliest memories was, as a child, accompanying his father to a theater where a sad play that the elder DeMille and theatrical entrepreneur David Belasco had coproduced was in progress. The boy, handed a molasses bar, simultaneously chewed and cried, the tears and candy running together down his chin. No sooner had the born-to-show-business (in 1881) DeMille entered the emerging realm of motion pictures than he set out to make films that would move the great American unwashed in precisely that manner, mixing heady sermonizing and heart-wrenching sentimentality, operatic set designs and melodramatic conventions, in such cast-of-thousands spectacles as *The King of Kings, Cleopatra,* and *The Ten Commandments.* Though DeMille (who had pioneered such elements as feature-length films, sound, and color) would continue working well into the 1950s, he would always be most closely associated with silent pictures.

That qualified DeMille as Billy Wilder's one and only choice for the role of the onetime pioneer director, still working, in *Sunset Boulevard.* The film concerned Norma Desmond, long-faded silent star who sits alone in her crumbling mansion, delusionally dreaming about returning to pictures. The fictional Desmond was played by former star Gloria Swanson, who would spend the rest of her life insisting she was nothing like the character. Norma is attended by a once-popular, now-obscure director (Erich von Stroheim, playing a part painfully close to his own experience) now her valet/chauffeur. At one point, Desmond insists he drive her to the old studio, where her favorite director, who has passed the test of time in a way she hasn't, is shooting his latest film. DeMille's eyes project respect, sadness, and pity for the woman who helped him invent motion pictures. In her macabre finale, Norma (totally removed from reality after killing her young lover, William Holden) approaches the newsreel cameras, believing her long-sought comeback is at hand, cooing the now legendary line, "I'm ready for my close-up, Mr. DeMille."

FEDERICO FELLINI

Alex in Wonderland (1970)

When he was twelve years old, Federico Fellini ran away from the town of Rimini, where his father was a prominent businessman, and joined a circus. That was in 1932; a few years later, he made the rounds of Rome hotels, knocking out quick caricatures of diners. His early film projects allowed little room for such key influences, as he worked on the scripts for Roberto Rossellini's neorealist masterpieces including *Open City,* which brought the grim, understated style of newsreels to feature films. Then Fellini struck out on his own. First with *La Strada,* then *La Dolce Vita* and *8½,* he surged light-years beyond the limits of any single "movement" to develop his own immediately recognizable, strikingly personal style of poetic cinema: dreamlike, surreal, and metaphoric, always including elments of the circus atmosphere while relying heavily on the art of caricature. He inspired like-minded moviemakers around

the world: every would-be auteur who has ever wanted to write and direct a film that shares his personal vision with the public—Woody Allen's *Stardust Memories*, Blake Edwards's *That's Life!*, Richard Pryor's *Jo Jo Dancer, Your Life Is Calling*—admits to being inspired by the world-class Fellini.

Fellini did cameos in several of his works, but appeared in only a single American movie, Paul Mazursky's *Alex in Wonderland*, one more of those numerous attempts to create a Fellini-esque work within the American studio mainstream. Donald Sutherland starred as a young filmmaker very similar to Mazursky himself, who wants to move beyond the routine synthetic product and emerge as a truly singular voice like his idol. Throughout the film, the title character attempts to turn his experiences into art that he can share with the public, much as Fellini did. Occasionally, he even fantasizes

The young filmmaker Alex (Donald Sutherland, left) gets the thrill of meeting his idol, Federico Fellini. (courtesy Metro-Goldwyn-Mayer)

that Fellini is there beside him, guiding Alex on. Then, by chance, Alex comes face-to-face with his idol, who proves generous and offers some sage advice on how Alex ought to be Alex, and not just a carbon-copy Fellini.

WILLIAM CASTLE

Day of the Locust (1975)

In the 1950s, William Castle lavished more time and money on the marketing of his movies than he did on the making of them. Castle became the Orson Welles of exploitation flicks. In fact, when Welles went to Hollywood to make *Citizen Kane* in 1939, it was Castle—like Welles, twenty-five years old at the time—who assumed control of the Mercury Theatre's stock company at Stony Creek, Connecticut. Born and raised in New York, Castle had entered show business ten years earlier by passing himself off as the nephew of legendary producer Samuel Goldwyn, then at age eighteen had mounted a revival of *Dracula*, establishing him as the youngest director in Broadway history to that date. Hired as a contract director of B pictures for Columbia and later Universal, Castle sensed which way the wind was blowing; owing to television, the majors were concentrating on big projects. Castle understood that inexpensive fare for drive-ins and second-rate theaters would shortly be the realm of independents, so he formed his own company in 1955. Most of his movies—*Strait-Jacket, The Night Walker, House on Haunted Hill*—were at best ordinary, leaving the viewer searching for scares that weren't there. But Castle drew in the teen crowd with ever-wilder gimmicks: Lloyds of London life-insurance policies for anyone brave enough to buy a ticket for *Macabre,* a fright break allowing people to get their money back before the final reel of *Homicidal,* seats that were wired to shock young viewers for *The Tingler,* special glasses

William Castle as a Hollywood director—part Orson Welles, part Alfred Hitchcock, all William Castle—provided a marvelous in-joke for the film Day of the Locust. *(courtesy Paramount Pictures)*

necessary to see the title creatures in *13 Ghosts.* Years later, the Castle canon would be lovingly satirized in *Matinee* with John Goodman offering a thinly disguised portrait of the veteran showman.

But Castle had already offered a portrait of himself. In *Day of the Locust,* John Schlesinger's critically acclaimed 1975 adaptation of Nathanael West's classic satire on Hollywood, the arrogant, obnoxious, cigar-chomping director is played by none other than William Castle himself. Castle's book, *Step Right Up! I'm Gonna Scare the Pants Off America* was published in 1976, one year before the filmmaker died of a heart attack at age sixty-three.

JOSEPH BROOKS

You Light Up My Life (1977)

"You've got a lot to live," the popular jingle went, "and Pepsi's got a lot to give." That simple but effective advertisement may have been the most hummed sung of the 1970s. Its composer, Joseph Brooks, proudly boasted that he'd composed it and so many other "fifty-second hits" that he outranked even Barry Manilow as the uncrowned king of commercial corn. The New York City native, a child prodigy who was playing piano at age five and went on to master twenty-five instruments, eventually enjoyed the distinction of being the only person ever to win five major awards—the Oscar, the Grammy, Golden Globe, People's Choice, and the American Music Award—in one year, for "You Light Up My Life," the theme to his first film as writer-director. That movie, budgeted at $1.1 million, had been turned down by virtually every major and independent studio in Hollywood, while record stores originally nixed the song. Undaunted, Brooks put $350,000 of his own money into the project, raised more from friends in the advertising business, then paid out-of-pocket expenses for test screenings in lesser markets like Seattle. When the movie made a mint, and *Billboard* named the theme as "most successful single of all time," Brooks found himself in the catbird seat with those very Hollywood producers who'd earlier scoffed at his efforts.

"I refused to fail," he later explained. Brooks then starred in, as well as wrote, directed, produced, and musically scored *If Ever I See You Again,* casting himself as Bobby Morrison, a thinly disguised autobiographical role ("the Mozart of Madison Avenue"), who romantically if relentlessly pursues the young woman (Shelley Hack) he loved and lost at college. According to critic Stephen Farber, the film "takes a very provocative theme but reduces it to the level of a treacly pop ditty." Brooks boasted that his "shameless sentimentality" would click in the American heartlands, where people were, in his view, considerably less sophisticated than out-of-touch Hollywood types believed them to be. "I know the public, because I *am* them," Brooks announced. In fact, his second opus was not a hit, so shortly he headed for England, where he wrote and directed (but did not star in) films such as *Invitation to a Wedding.* His pièce de résistance, a stage-musical version of Fritz Lang's milestone film *Metropolis,* bombed in London's West End. Joe Brooks was little heard from following that fiasco.

KING VIDOR

Love and Money (1982)

When King Wallis Vidor was a high schooler in Galveston, Texas, he accepted a job as ticket-taker and sometimes projectionist at the city's first nickelodeon so he could witness firsthand the new medium that, in the early 1910s, had already captured his imagination. Though the pay was a mere $3.50 a week, Vidor had the opportunity to see a two-reel Italian version of *Ben Hur* a whopping 147 times. At first, he had watched awestruck, overpowered by the magic and spectacle. Eventually, though, he considered the film more critically, noting how it had been edited for emotional impact, how individual shots were carefully organized like fine paintings, how the actors played their roles to maximum effect, while also making mental notes about what he would have done differently had he been the director. Though Vidor couldn't know it at the time, this was his film school. When a few years later he talked his way into a job at the recently formed MGM, Vidor made use of what he'd learned, directing movies about his favorite subject, the common man: the common man at war in *The Big Parade,* the common man at work in *The Crowd,* the common man as African American in *Hallelujah.*

Years after his retirement, King Vidor had the opportunity to play just such a common man in *Love and Money,* James Toback's 1982 thriller about an ordinary guy (Ray Sharkey) involved with the international money-laundering scheme of a corrupt businessman (Klaus Kinsky) after being seduced by the villain's number one temptress (Ornella Muti). Vidor

King Vidor (left) *deals with his grandson's obvious corruption in James Toback's* Love and Money.

provided strength of character as Sharkey's senile but still spirited grandfather, the man who—even though incapacitated—shows the misguided young man how to square himself with the world around him. Indeed, Vidor's performance was so powerful that many viewers simply assumed he must actually have been senile. Hardly! In fact, no senile person could ever play senility so convincingly; the gifted director was showing that, had he chosen a slightly different route, he could also have been a gifted actor.

JERZY SKOLIMOWSKI

White Nights (1985)

This Taylor Hackford film was put into production just before the terms *perestroika* and *glasnost* entered the popular idiom. It's one of the last Russia-bashing films of the Reagan era, seeming terribly dated shortly after its release owing to its strident anti-Soviet stance, which felt all wrong at a time when the two countries were embarking on an era of mutual cooperation and greater understanding. Simply,

183

Jerzy Skolimowski (right) *as Colonel Chaiko, seen here with Isabella Rossellini and Mikhail Baryshnikov. (courtesy Columbia Pictures, Inc.)*

the movie was a victim of future shock: times changing so quickly that a piece of work appears passé by the time it is completed. Mikhail Baryshnikov was perfectly cast as a ballet star who had earlier defected to the United States, only to find himself forced back into the land of socialist tyranny when the plane in which he's traveling must make an unscheduled landing. Gregory Hines was cast as an American expatriate with whom he forms an uneasy alliance, while Isabella Rossellini played a contrived role as the woman torn between them.

Lending the film an element of *Les Misérables* was Jerzy Skolimowski, in his only Hollywood movie, as the unbending Colonel Chaiko, a harsh KGB agent who relentlessly hounds the hero. The accomplished writer, director, and actor was happy to play the role, since his own films express a similar antisocialist attitude, though in an esoteric art-house manner. The Warsaw-born filmmaker was second only to Roman Polanski as the most influential Polish filmmaker to appear during the 1960s, inspired by the work of slightly older countrymen such as Andre Wajda, though taking a more cynical, even pessimistic approach than the previous generation had done. Skolimowski cowrote *Knife in the Water* with Polanski, then attended the Lodz film school, going on to write, direct, and act in the films *Rysopis* and *Walkover* as a typical young person in Poland, trying to remain optimistic about life while suffering from the dictates of a repressive social system. Admittedly influenced by France's Jean-Luc Godard, with his radical form of editing and deceptively simple storytelling style, Skolimowski embraced the values of Western Europe and America, commenting on his unhappy home life in such films as *The Shout* and *Moonlighting*. His portrait of Colonel Chaiko is anything but autobiographical, and more than just a chilling characterization: it stands as a living symbol for everything that Jerzy Skolimowski most hates.

29
A HINT OF SCANDAL

Becoming notorious can ruin a movie star's career or make a star out of an unknown; the following cases offer a little bit of both.

SALLY RAND

Bolero (1934)

She was born Billie Beck somewhere in rural Kentucky and, shortly after her family moved to Hickory County, Missouri, changed her name to Sally Rand. After completing a degree program at Christina College in Columbia, Sally pursued a career in show business. Early on, she had bit parts in famous films, including Cecil B. DeMille's *The King of Kings* and Howard Hawks's *A Girl in Every Port,* though if you blinked, you missed her. Giving up on movie stardom, Sally went on the road with theater companies; in 1932, she found herself stranded in Chicago after a show suddenly closed. Practically penniless, Sally agreed to dance in a South Side club for $75 a week, but the bosses insisted she first buy her own costume. All Sally could afford were some ostrich plumes, which she assembled on two large fans. With them, she suggestively concealed, rather than graphically revealed, her form, which was in fact covered by a body stocking. All the while, evocatively colored lights set an exotic, rather than vulgar, mood; Debussy's "Clair de Lune" made clear this was a class act.

When turned down for a slot at the 1933 Chicago's World Fair, "the fan dancer" rented a white horse and, uninvited, rode through the "Streets of Paris" pavilion as Lady Godiva. The press covered her routine with cover pictures and an aroused public insisted she be allowed to perform. She was, and soon Sally Rand was the hit of that year's exposition. Then, in 1934, she returned to Hollywood, this time as a star. Sally performed her fan dance once, and only once, on film in *Bolero,* featuring George Raft and Carole Lombard as club dancers who can't decide if they love or hate each other. For the rest of her life, Sally Rand divided her time between

her then-controversial dancing (she was arrested several times for "indecent exposure") and her family, lavishing her love on son Sean and, later, her two grandchildren. Sally Rand was still dancing more than forty years later; ironically, in the age of *Deep Throat,* her act was considered charmingly nostalgic by the very blue bloods who once howled that she ought to be run out of town on a rail. She died, age seventy-five, in 1979, shortly after dancing—as slender and elegant as ever—for the benefit of a Kansas City theater that had been named a national landmark.

LILI ST. CYR
The Naked and the Dead (1958)

By the mid-1950s, Lili St. Cyr had dethroned legendary Gypsy Rose Lee as current Queen of the Strippers, ranking as the highest-paid ecdysiast in the country. Her contract with Las Vegas' El Rancho hotel guaranteed her ten weeks' work a year annually, though St. Cyr had her sights set on a Hollywood career. The Minneapolis native (real name, Marie Van Schaak)

Lili St. Cyr as the stripper adored by various Marines, including Aldo Ray and Cliff Robertson, in The Naked and the Dead.

had moved to Eagle Rock, California, with her parents when she was eight, attending school in nearby Pasadena and taking dancing lessons. Teenage Lili stepped into the chorus of Nils T. Granlund's Florentine Gardens in Hollywood, at the time populated by such future movie stars as Yvonne DeCarlo, Marie "The Body" MacDonald, and Jean Wallace. She graduated to burlesque at San Diego's Hollywood Theatre, where her 38-24-36 figure made Lili St. Cyr a sensation. Her stage moniker was derived from those of such glamorous though notorious show women of the past as Lily Langtry and Lillian Russell combined with a last name from a romantic story set in Paris she'd once read. She survived five bad marriages in a row, and by 1953 her name was placed over the marquee at Ciro's. RKO slipped her into a harem costume as part of the decorative backdrop in their mini-epic *Son of Sinbad*.

Even at this point, Lili was nervous about her past professional work. She publicly announced that her upcoming marriage to aspiring actor Ted Jordan would be indefinitely postponed because "there would be a certain amount of antagonism toward [Ted] if he were married to a stripteaser." Nonetheless, they were married; Jordan's acting career failed to take off, though Lili was hoping to do giddy comedy in the style of Judy Holliday and had one opportunity to combine that ability with exotic dancing. In Raoul Walsh's big-budget film version of Normal Mailer's *The Naked and the Dead*, she was effectively typecast as the stripper adored by Aldo Ray, Cliff Robertson, and Joey Bishop. Between toned-down, modestly revealing dance sequences, Lili also verbally sparred with the boys in lighthearted bits that preceded the Marines' heading off to war. Shortly after the film's release, Lili separated from Jordan, and then while appearing in Vegas, she took an overdose of sleeping pills in an apparent suicide attempt. The thirty-four-year-old Lili did recover, though the bad publicity diminished any hope for other film roles. Lili's act remained highly popular for another decade, until mainstream pornography ended her classy, old-fashioned dancing.

BEVERLY AADLAND

Cuban Rebel Girls (1959)

The fading superstar Errol Flynn had two major reasons for appearing in what proved to be his final film: it was both a tax write-off and a showcase for his teenage mistress. The film was shot in the Havana environs and gave the star an opportunity to interview Fidel Castro. His dispatches about the Castro struggle to overthrow Battista's regime appeared in the American press. While in Havana, Flynn and Beverly Aadland visited a casino fronted by another former Hollywood star, George Raft, only to witness rebel troops arrive, guns ablaze, reality imitating the movies.

Aadland had met Flynn two years earlier while dancing in the chorus of Warner Bros. backstage drama *Marjorie Morningstar*. Flynn, hanging around the edges of the set and eyeing young blondes, proposed a dinner date, whisking the virtual child off to millionaire Huntington Hartford's estate where he seduced the virgin on a bearskin rug. Then, to the indignation of his wife, actress Patricia Wymore, Flynn flew with Aadland to Africa so he could enjoy her company during the shooting of John Huston's *The Roots of Heaven*, Flynn's final respectable motion picture.

Cuban Rebel Girls, on the other hand, was a bad sixty-eight-minute B movie. In the role of Flynn's giddy teenage companion, Aadland projects a simmeringly sleazy sexuality, suggesting the makings of another Mamie Van Doren. But

187

that was not to be. When filming was completed, Aadland traveled to Vancouver with Flynn on a business-pleasure trip and was with him when he suddenly died. Though he named her as an heir, the will was contested by his children and declared invalid. Less than a year later, Beverly's mother, Florence, became incensed that her still underage daughter was nightclubbing with a thirty-two-year-old scuba diver named Jack Dulin. Late one night, Florence banged on the man's apartment door; Dulin whipped out an antique English dueling pistol and fired at Florence. When the police arrived, only Mrs. Aadland was arrested, on a drunk and disorderly charge. Then a young, out-of-work actor, William Stanciu, was found dead in Beverly's apartment. She claimed he'd been playing Russian roulette after repeatedly raping her, yet his relatives insisted on foul play, since Stanciu's fingerprints were not on the weapon. A lengthy police investigation ended inconclusively. Aadland eventually married a construction supervisor and moved with him to a small desert town where they raised their daughter together.

Barry Sadler poses in full Green Beret regalia; in Dayton's Devils, he was not called upon to wear the uniform, though he did get to shoot a great many people. (courtesy Photofest)

BARRY SADLER

Dayton's Devils (1968)

In 1966, most of the music playing on Top Forty radio heralded the upcoming peace-and-love era, with one notable exception: Sgt. Barry Sadler's "Ballad of the Green Berets." With sales of 9 million singles and albums, Sadler's ditty was the No. 1 song in the country for five straight weeks. John Wayne was impressed enough to use it as the theme for his motion picture *The Green Berets,* just then going into production. In hindsight, it's surprising that the Duke didn't invite

Sadler—who had already expressed an interest in becoming an actor—to appear in his pro-war diatribe. Instead, Sadler was relegated to moviedom's minor leagues, costarring in *Dayton's Devils,* a cheapie actioner headlined by the poor man's Wayne, Rory Calhoun, as the leader of thieves scheming to rob an Air Force base with the help of Lainie Kazan, Leslie Nielsen, and Sadler. Other than a guest appearance on TV's *Death Valley Days,* that was as far as Sadler's acting career went. As a onetime business associate reflected, "He just didn't take off like Audie Murphy."

With good reason. Unlike the charmingly boyish Murphy, Sadler was smug, sardonic, and self-righteous. Though his clean-cut good looks initially impressed the silent majority, Barry Sadler was anything but the boy next door. In 1978, he fatally shot another songwriter (the estranged boyfriend of a woman Sadler was then seeing) in the forehead. Though he was found guilty of voluntary manslaughter and sentenced to five years in a Tennessee penitentiary, the judge (perhaps a fan of Sadler's song) reduced the sentence to thirty days and two years' probation. Sadler then began work on a series of books about a mythical superhero named Casca, condemned by a less-than-forgiving Jesus on the cross to roam the world for eternity as a mercenary. The novels, blatantly racist (the monstrous villains were all people of color), sold briskly. But Sadler felt the need to get back into action again, heading for Guatemala, where he trained contra rebels in warfare. Caught in a crossfire, he was critically wounded. Sadler died at Alvin C. York Medical Center in 1989 at age forty-nine.

SACHEEN LITTLEFEATHER
The Trial of Billy Jack (1974)

Sacheen Littlefeather starred in the third Billy Jack film, at 175 minutes the most belabored, tiresome, and obvious of Tom Laughlin's trilogy about a Vietnam vet who defends Native Americans from white racists. Littlefeather played a beautiful Indian woman in peril. Her lines in the film were not very different from those she had spoken at the 1973 Oscar ceremonies, when the then twenty-six-year-old woman flabbergasted presenters Roger Moore and Liv Ullman by stepping up to the podium, in buckskin clothing, to refuse Marlon Brando's Best Actor award for *The Godfather* at the actor's request. She has, over the years, alternately insisted that "I went up there thinking I could make a difference" through social protest and "I'm not a political person, and I'm not a militant." Not surprisingly, Sacheen has been widely attacked as an opportunist (even by other Indians) rather than a dedicated spokesperson for Native American causes. Why else, critics reason, would she have capitalized on her Warholian fifteen minutes at the Oscar ceremony by immediately agreeing to pose nude for *Playboy*?

In full Native American regalia, Sacheen addresses the 1973 Oscar ceremony, seen by some 80 million people—about 79.9 million more than saw her in Trial of Billy Jack. *(courtesy Photofest)*

Littlefeather had been acting all her life, beginning at age four when she communicated with her deaf-mute father, an Apache, by performing her thoughts. This lasted only a short while, since he was so brutal and abusive to Marie (Sacheen's given name) and her mother (she was white) that the two females ran away to Sacheen's maternal grandparents, the Barnetts, who raised her as a Catholic. On a whim, she entered a bizarre beauty pageant, Miss Vampire of America, 1969, and won, later showing up in Manhattan to confound the panelists on TV's *To Tell the Truth* with that dubious distinction. Then came the Oscar incident, which Sacheen believed would propel her into the big time. "I was very naive," she reflected in 1990. "I told people about oppression. They said, 'You're ruining our evening.'" After the fiasco of *Trial,* the best she could get were bit parts in minor movies such as *Fire Cloud.* Lately, she has been active with various groups that promote nutrition and discourage alcoholism among Native Americans. About the speculation that her Oscar appearance was based more on ambition than sincerity, she continues to insist, "I am not a fraud."

190

30
PLAYING BALL WITH HOLLYWOOD

From baseball, basketball, and football came more sports celebrities who thought it might be fun to carry a ball across the screen.

RED GRANGE

One Minute to Play (1926)

Harold Edward "Red" Grange of Forksville, Pennsylvania, won his nickname when sportswriter Grantland Rice referred to the University of Illinois halfback as "the Galloping Ghost," owing to Grange's remarkable ability to change speed and direction during a wild run that left potential tacklers lost as to where Grange was at any moment. His kicking, running, passing, and maneuvering were responsible for all of the Illinois points in their legendary 1924 win against archrival Michigan, causing Grange to be named all-American that year and again in 1925. Though pro ball was at the time considered an unsavory endeavor, Grange joined the Chicago Bears after graduation and, owing to the loyalty of devoted fans, almost single-handedly made pro football more respectable by his presence. He was responsible for the first-ever football sellout in the history of Wrigley Field.

A living sports legend, Red then starred in his only theatrical feature, the 1926 silent sports epic *One Minute to Play*. The *New York Times* commented: "In his first screen touchdown 'Red' Grange demonstrated his ability to tackle the role of a college hero and portray it far more convincingly than most of those handsome young men who are thoroughly accustomed to greasepaint and facing the camera," noting that he was "pleasingly natural" with an "ingratiating appearance." Grange played "Red" Wade, whose father initially opposes the boy's desire to play college football but eventually relents and allows him to play in the big game between Parmalee and Caxton. Red wins his father over thanks to a pretty girlfriend (Mary McAllister) and his own cute dog in this Sam Wood film. With his Hollywood premiere behind him, Grange then attempted (and failed) to create his own "Grange League" but was knocked out of pro ball by a 1928 leg injury. Grange did momentarily relive his glory days thanks to a twelve-chapter 1931 Mascot sound serial, *The Galloping Ghost,* which made extensive use of preexisting gridiron footage, though he was never again tapped for a mainstream feature.

DOC BLANCHARD AND GLENN DAVIS
The Spirit of West Point (1947)

"The touchdown twins" is what football fans of the 1940s lovingly nicknamed Felix "Doc" Blanchard and Glenn Davis, West Point's star players. This film purported to tell their "true" stories, though much of the plot (about the endless attempts of pro-ball managers to lure them away from the military academy with promises of big bucks) was fanciful, to say the least. The great value of *The Spirit of West Point* is the opportunity to see the duo in the flesh (along with Tom Harmon, who put in a guest appearance), preserved forever as they were in their prime, as well as some scintillating gridiron footage. Doc hailed from South Carolina and received his nickname because his father, Felix senior, was a physician, so the neighborhood kids always called the son Little Doc. At high school age he weighed 180 pounds and was dedicated to football, playing at the St. Stanislaus Prep School and the University of North Carolina before entering The Point.

There, he met the man who would become his backfield running mate during Army's 1944 and '45 undefeated seasons. Glenn Davis could dash around the end and outrun the defense even as Blanchard charged directly forward like (as one sportswriter put it) "a wild buffalo." Their nicknames were, appropriately enough, Mr. Inside and Mr. Outside; together, they scored ninety-seven touchdowns and 585 points for Army. Davis came to The Point from Claremont, California, where he'd excelled at track (as a high schooler, he won the Knute Rockne Trophy and was named southern California's best high school track performer in '43) as well as football. Glenn was twice named all-American; in 1945, he won the Heisman Trophy. After leaving The Point, Glenn served out his required term in the Army, then entered pro ball, while Doc made the Army a lifetime career, retiring in 1971 as brigadier general.

SATCHEL PAIGE
The Wonderful Country (1959)

Robert Parrish's colorful western, taken from a Tom Lea novel, featured Robert Mitchum as a serape-clad *americano* running guns across the border into Mexico. Gary Merrill played a dedicated Army officer trying to track down the desperado.

The cavalryman was assisted by a strong, dignified "buffalo solider," one of those black troopers who had first begun making their presence felt during the Civil War and continued their courageous activities out West during the 1870s. Actually, this forgotten western predates John Ford's better-known *Sergeant Rutledge* (with Woody Strode) of one year later as the first mainstream movie to depict in a positive light the role of the African-American soldier.

For such a significant part, a man whose very presence could communicate the essential dignity and code of honor was needed. Parrish could not have chosen better than to cast Leroy Robert Paige in that part. Confined to an Alabama reform school for juvenile delinquency in 1918 at age twelve, Paige started playing ball during his five years there and immediately sensed he possessed a special talent for the game. Upon his release, Paige left crime behind him forever and joined the Negro Leagues as a pitcher, distinguishing himself with the Mobile Tigers and the Birmingham Black Barons through his ultrafast "bee ball" that literally hummed past stunned batters. Though baseball was still segregated at the time, Satchel played in exhibition games against whites and beat such luminaries as Dizzy Dean and Bob Feller, paving the way for Jackie Robinson to cross the color barrier. When that was accomplished, Satchel spent his last several seasons with the newly integrated Cleveland Indians and St. Louis Browns; at age forty-eight, he was the oldest rookie ever to play in the major leagues. Following that, Paige proved quietly effective as the cinema's first black cavalryman in *The Wonderful Country*.

MICKEY MANTLE AND ROGER MARIS

Safe at Home! (1962)

In this appealing little B movie, Bryan Russell (older brother of Kurt) was cast as a Little Leaguer who fibs to his pals about knowing Mickey Mantle and Roger Maris; as could only happen in a movie, the living legends show up to save the day. Not many athletes are naturals in front of the camera, and Mantle and Maris were no exceptions, freezing up the moment that the director called "Action." Mickey hailed from Oklahoma where, shortly after his birth in 1931, he'd absorbed his father Elvin's love of baseball. Yankee scout Tom Greenwade spotted him playing on an amateur team in Kansas; shortly Mickey was on the Yankees' farm team, proving his prowess and skipping the minors to join the Yankees for the 1951 World Series as an outfielder, the following year replacing Joe DiMaggio in center field. When, over the next twelve years, he hit eighteen home runs in the twelve World Series he'd been instrumental in helping his team enter, Mantle became a legitimate baseball legend, despite the heavy drinking that always threatened his career and finally led to his death in the summer of 1995.

Three years younger than Mickey, Roger Maris hailed from Hibbing, Minnesota, where he excelled at football and was offered a college scholarship, which he turned down owing to his intense dislike of studies. Instead, Roger played bush-league baseball for the Cleveland Indians. While still in the minors, he had the good fortune to fall under the tutelage of manager Jo Jo White, who convinced the left-handed right fielder to develop the slashing "power hitting" toward right field at which he would always excel. In 1959 he became a Yankee, and was named the American League's Most Valuable Player in 1960 and 1961, owing to his .283 average, 39 home runs, and 112 RBIs. Nineteen sixty-one was the banner year for Mantle and Maris, as each went out to beat Babe Ruth's 60-homer season record, Mickey coming in with 54 and Roger beating him (and the Babe) with 61; that cinched their shot at movie stardom. *Safe at Home!* also features appearances by two other baseball greats, Whitey Ford and Ralph Houk, in small supporting roles. That same year, Mantle and Maris also provided brief cameos in the Cary Grant–Doris Day comedy *That Touch of Mink*. But Mantle was near the end of his golden years and his performance soon went downhill. He retired in 1969, being inducted into the National Baseball Hall of Fame in 1974.

JIM BOUTON

The Long Goodbye (1973)

When Robert Altman set out to adapt Raymond Chandler's classic detective novel to the screen, he took the decidedly eccentric approach one would expect from our most idiosyncratic filmmaker. Instead of a California character strolling through 1940s L.A., Philip Marlowe was transformed into a New York Jewish schlep (in the person of Elliott Gould) harboring an internal value system a full quarter century behind the times, causing him to flounder in the superficial 1970s. As always, Altman opted for the most offbeat casting imaginable, including Nina Van Pallandt (then fresh from her infamous Clifford Irving scandal) as the shady lady, fellow director Mark Rydell as a nasty hood, *Laugh-In* comic Henry Gibson as an oddball doctor, and pro-ball player turned TV sports commentator and best-selling author Jim Bouton as Terry Lennox. The slick, athletic character at first appears to be Marlowe's only true friend, but in the end turns out to be manipulating a complicated criminal plot to destroy the gumshoe.

Bouton, originally from Newark but raised in Chicago, had not been particularly athletic as a child, then hit his stride in 1957 after entering Western Michigan University and proving his prowess as a college team pitcher. Shortly thereafter, he was scooped up by the Yankees, first playing in the minors, then in 1962 joining the A team in New York where for three years he excelled, until his arm failed. During his final season in pro ball, relying on a tricky knuckleball to see him through, Bouton revealed his own offbeat side, attending antiwar rallies for Eugene McCarthy and keeping notes on team players. The resultant book, *Ball Four,* took a caustic, cynically comic approach toward the human side of a sport most writers approach with sentimental, smarmy hero worship. Literary critics applauded the tome, though the baseball establishment derided the wise guy–ish depiction of drug addiction, sexual foibles, and mean-spirited contract negotiations. Shortly, Bouton was hired as a sports commentator for WABC-TV, though he had been bitten by the acting bug. An attempt to turn *Ball Four* into a 1976 NBC comedy series starring and written by Bouton lasted little more than a month.

JULIUS ERVING AND MEADOWLARK LEMON
The Fish That Saved Pittsburgh (1979)

Julius Erving was a natural for the role of a top basketball player, though the sports star who had always been with the winners was for this fictional piece placed on a team that just couldn't seem to win. Moses Guthrie was portrayed by the athlete who had affectionately been named Dr. J. by his fans for his endless court successes, though, as the title suggested, that doesn't happen here until the Pittsburgh Pythons' water boy (James Bond III) recommends the guys consult an astrologer. Stockard Channing played Mona Mondieu, who helps the star-crossed team finally get lucky by insisting they play under a single zodiac sign and become the Pisces. The story wasn't much, but every time Erving and other real-life basketball stars (including Kareem Abdul-Jabbar, as himself) headed out onto

195

Julius Erving as Pittsburgh player Moses Guthrie.
(courtesy United Artists)

the court, the film took off—at least, for sports fans. Also around was that other great basketball star of the late 1970s, Meadowlark Lemon, here cast in the supporting role of Rev. Grady Jackson, a preacher who can also perform a mean turn on a court when goaded to do so for a good cause.

Julius Winfield Erving II, a Long Island native, a child of near-poverty, used basketball as his way out via touring games with the Salvation Army's team. While a student at Roosevelt High he won his nickname, the Doctor. Julius soon had a scholarship to the University of Massachusetts, where he averaged 26.9 points and 19.5 rebounds in his junior year. Erving didn't graduate, though, as the ABA's Virginia Squires offered him a four-year contract if he'd join in 1971. In addition to the phenomenal points and rebounds that earned him best-player-in-the-league status, Erving was a master showman on the court, dazzling fans with moves that were as delicate as they were difficult, always managing to make them appear easy and effortless. He continued his efforts with the New York Nets and, after the ABA folded, with the NBA's Philadelphia 76ers, winning the association's Most Valuable Player award in 1981. But in his only film lead, it was a losing Pittsburgh team that stunk worse than rotten fish for which he played.

WILT CHAMBERLAIN

Conan the Destroyer (1984)

Though "Wilt the Stilt" may be a one-shot wonder so far as movies are concerned, his sex life is another matter. Turning author to tell his own life story, Chamberlain claimed to have made love to more than twenty thousand women. Nonetheless, film footage of this immodest seven-foot-one-inch basketball legend is confined to a single action-adventure epic, the second in a proposed series based on Robert E. Howard's epic fantasy novels. John Milius brought the alternative world of the Hyborian Age to life in his 1982 film *Conan the Barbarian*, making a superstar of Arnold Schwarzenegger. Unhappy with the way Universal had recut his film, Milius passed on the opportunity to do a sequel. Richard Fleischer, who had seemingly proven his ability to do grand-scale adventure back in the 1950s with *The Vikings*, was hired, though his clunky approach did not jive with the 1980s aura of glibness and state-of-the-art special effects that ultimately detracted from, rather than enhanced, Howard's material. One intriguing element added for the sequel, however, was black heroes, whereas in the first film, the only notable black character had been James Earl Jones as the evil emperor. The reasoning was more practical than enlightened: market research revealed the first *Conan* had been popular with African-American males, but would have scored even higher with black characters for that audience to root for.

Wilt Chamberlain as Bombaata, guard to the princess Jehnna and uneasy ally of the title character in Conan the Destroyer. *(courtesy Universal City Studios)*

So Grace Jones and Wilt Chamberlain joined the cast as fellow good guys on a quest to save pretty princess Jehnna. Chamberlain's character, Bombaata, was the warrior who had been assigned to protect Jehnna at her birth and had been a loyal bodyguard ever since, striking an uneasy alliance with Conan. A Philadelphia native, Chamberlain had discovered basketball early on; when his height spurted at age fourteen, he realized how perfect he was for this sport. While attending the University of Kansas, Chamberlain changed his major from math to communications, hosting a radio talk show when not playing for the team, though averaging 30 points per game when he did. Leaving school after only three years, Wilt toured with the Harlem Globetrotters worldwide, then joined the Philadelphia Warriors and, in his first season of NBA competition, set an all-time single-season scoring record. If his autobiography is to be believed, that wasn't the only scoring record Wilt Chamberlain set.

197

31

TWO-SHOT WONDERS

H[ere's]{} a special category for those stars who beat the one-shot curse and starred in two major films, then slipped off the screen if not out of our shared memories.

BABE RUTH

Headin' Home (1920)   *Pride of the Yankees* (1942)

William Bendix and John Goodman each attempted to portray the Sultan of Swat on film. But the man who was born George Herman Ehrhardt in 1895 had over the past century become such a vivid icon in the public imagination that no actor, however talented, could successfully sit in for the large, lugubrious, lovable home-run king who transcended sports to become a veritable American institution. So when RKO Pictures cast Gary Cooper as the late Lou Gehrig (Ruth's runner-up for batting honors) in the biopic *Pride of the Yankees,* there was only one choice for the key supporting role of Babe Ruth, and that was the retired athlete himself. In fact, he'd stepped up to Hollywood's plate and batted a home run some twenty-two years earlier, in the silent feature *Headin' Home,* in which he played "Bugs" Baer, a small-town boy who accidentally becomes a baseball star but longs only to return to his roots.

Though Hollywood's 1948 and 1992 biopics about the Babe's life failed to capture the essence of this special man's American-dream success story, that rags-to-riches tale sounds in summation like Hollywood's ultimate Horatio Alger scenario. The offspring of an abusive father who tended bar in a Baltimore water-front dive, the seven-year-old understandably displayed a bad attitude. Authorities determined to relocate him to St. Mary's Industrial School, where dedicated Catholic priests administered an industrial-arts education designed to turn bad boys' lives around. George proved to have a larger chip on his shoulder than most others, so an understanding mentor, Brother Gilbert (one pictures Spencer Tracy

198

playing him in an A movie or Pat O'Brien in a B feature), decided athletics might be the way to involve George with peers. Noticing the growing boy's spectacular accomplishments, Brother Gilbert contacted Jack Dunn, manager of the Baltimore Orioles, who watched the kid play and gave him a shot. Ruth was so young when he showed up for spring training that other minor leaguers referred to him as Jack's "babe in the woods." A move up to pitching with the Red Sox proved a mere prelude to a lifetime career with the New York Yankees. Ruth led the American League in home runs every year for the next decade, excepting 1925 when he failed to play owing to illness. Big and ugly in a cuddly kind of way, Ruth was a born pop hero, so it was only natural he'd be tapped for movies, in which he proved supremely natural—far more so than any of the Hollywood stars who have tried to capture Ruth's essence on film.

Babe Ruth as himself in one of his two starring roles, with Gary Cooper as Lou Gehrig in Pride of the Yankees. *(courtesy RKO Radio Pictures)*

RISË STEVENS
The Chocolate Soldier (1941)   *Going My Way* (1944)

The tall, stunning brunette from Long Island named Rïsa Steenbjorg boasted such a strikingly rich mezzo-soprano voice, in addition to striking looks and natural acting ability, that she was offered a coveted contract with the Metropolitan Opera the moment she graduated from Juilliard, which she'd attended on scholarship. But the star-in-embryo believed she needed more experience before making a New York debut and, incredibly enough, turned the offer down. Rechristening herself Risë Stevens, she headed for Europe, where in Salzburg and Switzerland she played in *Mignon* and *Carmen,* eventually returning home satisfied that she was ready. In 1938, at age twenty-five, she became the toast of Manhattan, particularly when playing temptresses, such as the female lead in *Samson and Delila.*

    MGM scouts caught her and soon she was signed to a long-term contract, though there would be but two films, neither of which allowed Risë to do the femme-fatale roles that opera addicts loved her in. First came *The Chocolate Soldier,* which, despite the title, wasn't a film version of the Oscar Straus operetta of that name but rather a remake of Ferenc Molnar's *The Guardsman,* with Risë as the singing star whose husband tests her loyalty by masquerading as a handsome stranger, then attempting to seduce her. Stevens here replaced Jeanette MacDonald as Nelson Eddy's love interest. Two years later, there was the Oscar-winning Best Picture of the Year, *Going My Way,* in which Risë helped idealistic young priest Bing Crosby win over both his curmudgeonly supervisor Barry Fitzgerald and a tough group of Dead End–type kids. Though the film included such pleasant ditties as "Swinging on a Star," Stevens longed for the serious music she'd cut her teeth on, as well as the bad-girl roles that grand opera allowed her to incarnate, and thereafter returned to the legitimate stage.

EDDIE FISHER

Bundle of Joy (1956)   *Butterfield 8* (1960)

In 1956, Eddie Fisher appeared to be on top of the world. He hosted a popular TV show, *Coke Time,* had a string of records to his credit, including the No. 1 hit "Oh! My Papa," and had even received star billing in a little comedy called *Bundle of Joy* in which he costarred with his bubbly actress-singer wife, Debbie Reynolds. What more could anyone ask for? Apparently, the answer to that was Elizabeth Taylor. When her husband (and Eddie's best friend), mega-producer Mike Todd, was killed in a plane crash, Eddie comforted Liz beyond the realm of friendly responsibility. Shortly, he was involved in an affair that, had he backed away from it in time, his career might have survived.

Instead, he unwisely dumped his wife and family, causing his TV sponsors to likewise dump him, being less than thrilled that the spokesperson for America's family beverage had deserted his own. Undaunted, Eddie married Elizabeth, starring opposite her in *Butterfield 8,* which won her an Oscar as a high-priced call girl (there was a strong sympathy vote, seeing as Liz was near death at voting time) while making abundantly clear to everyone that Eddie Fisher couldn't act his way out of a paper bag. Eddie accompanied Liz to the foreign *Cleopatra* sets and swiftly moved from lover to lackey, tending to her needs while Liz threw herself into Richard Burton's arms. After Elizabeth unceremoniously dumped Eddie for Dick, Fisher spent the rest of his life attempting comebacks, singing in Vegas, but never again trying for Hollywood stardom. One lingering question remains: While married to Connie Stevens, why didn't he also do a movie with her and make it three on a match?

TOMMY TUNE

Hello, Dolly! (1969)
The Boy Friend (1971)

Tommy Tune teams with best pal and favorite dancing partner Twiggy for The Boy Friend. *(courtesy Metro-Goldwyn-Mayer/EMI Entertainment)*

In 1968, Thomas James Tune was flown from New York to Hollywood for a screen test after 20th Century–Fox talent scouts insisted the twenty-nine-year-old dancer would easily become the next great star of musical movies. At six foot six, weighing less than 160 pounds, this appealingly boyish scarecrow with remarkably rubbery yet agile legs had already appeared in the Broadway musicals *Baker Street* and *A Joyful Noise.* There was little doubt in Tinseltown that his zany style combined the best qualities of Fred Astaire, Ray Bolger, and Buddy Ebsen. Then came *Easy Rider, Midnight Cowboy,* and *Taxi Driver.* As movies became ever more reality-based, the all-singing', all-dancin' musicals that would have provided Tune with his perfect vehicles disappeared.

He made an impressive debut in the overblown period piece *Hello, Dolly!* with Barbra Streisand, in the role of the naive swain Ambrose Kemper. But such a big, brassy film was now the exception, not the rule. Afterward, Tune found work where he could get it, as assistant choreographer for NBC's *The Dean Martin Show,* occasionally getting to dance on TV. His second shot at movie stardom occurred three years later, when the reprehensible director Ken Russell set out to undermine rather than adapt *The Boy Friend,* Sandy Wilson's sweet-spirited stage parody of early movie-musical clichés. The piece was transformed by Russell into a mean-spirited attack on Hollywood vulgarity that was itself more vulgar than anything Hollywood had ever produced. Tune and his dancing partner, model-turned-actress Twiggy, ignored Russell's theater-of-cruelty approach. Critics considered their joyous joint effort the best thing in this otherwise unpleasant film that set out to trash the very entertainments Tune had loved ever since his boyhood days near Houston, Texas. Tune returned to Broadway as a director of stage musicals, bringing equal elements of enthusiasm, innovation, and eccentricity to such now-classic shows as *The Best Little Whorehouse in Texas* and *Nine*, finally performing again in 1983 when *My One and Only*, a reworking of the 1927 George and Ira Gershwin musical *Funny Face*, reunited him with pal and partner Twiggy.

HELEN REDDY

Airport 1975 (1974)   Pete's Dragon (1977)

Despite a flat singing voice without notable vocal range and an obvious lack of vir-

Helen Reddy (right) as "the flying, singing nun" in Airport 1975. *(courtesy Universal Pictures)*

tuoso technique or heartfelt emotion, Helen Reddy rose to the top of the female vocalist ranks in the early 1970s. Incredibly enough, she was named number one artist in her category by *Billboard, Cash Box,* and *Record World* in 1973. Such accolades were due more to a miracle of timing than talent. The women's liberation movement had just hit the mainstream big-time in the early seventies; desperately needed now was an anthem. Thirty-year-old Reddy, who had arrived from Melbourne in pursuit of a still-elusive show business career, penned a power-of-positive-thinking ditty that included the line "I am strong/ I am invincible," impulsively adding at the last moment, "I am woman!" Meanwhile, movie producer Mike Frankovich was searching for a proper theme song for his feminist film *Stand Up and Be Counted.* When he caught Reddy on *The Flip Wilson Show,* Frankovich knew he'd found his song; an ersatz star was stillborn.

Hollywood cast her in a pair of films that revealed Reddy's utter lack of charisma. In *Airport 1975,* she was the nun who calms down an endangered plane-load of people just before a crash. "I was the flying, singing nun," Reddy later recalled, evoking two pop icons of the day. The Walt Disney company cast her as the female lead in *Pete's Dragon,* a musical in which Reddy played the lighthouse keeper's daughter awaiting her true love's return from the sea. Made during an awkward period—after Disney's death but before the Michael Eisner regime—the combination of mediocre live action and chintzy animation was a far cry from *Mary Poppins*. Reddy did not work again in films.

HAROLD RUSSELL
The Best Years of Our Lives (1946)   *Inside Moves* (1980)

A fitting note on which to end this book is provided by Harold Russell, whose fascinating career proves the old adage that it's not over till it's over. In 1946, Russell enjoyed the distinction of being the only performer in the history of the Academy Awards ever to win two Oscars for the same performance. He received that year's Best Supporting Actor statuette for his role in *The Best Years of Our Lives* as Homer Parrish, a GI who has lost both hands in combat only to have them replaced by metal claws, in this memorable movie about postwar angst from producer Samuel Goldwyn and director William Wyler. Russell was also awarded a special statuette for bringing "hope and courage to fellow veterans." The reasoning for each of the awards was simple and decent enough: Russell, a nonactor, had indeed lost both his hands to a hand grenade. In truth, Russell's performance—considered from today's less emotionally charged perspective—boasted far more sincerity than skill. The Oscar people have always been known for sentiment, and this would stand as the most extreme example of that until Dr. Haing S. Ngor won in the same category for *The Killing Fields* some forty years later.

Russell had been born in 1914 in Sydney, Nova Scotia, then raised in the Boston area. He joined the army at the outset of World War II. When it was over, he appeared in a documentary film prepared by the War Department, *Diary of a Soldier,* in which he was enlisted to help other soldiers, all facing their own physical and emotional problems, few quite so extreme as Russell's, in adjusting to civilian life. This work led Russell to be chosen for his major movie role, after which he (with no show business ambitions and obviously difficult to cast) became a business executive. In 1964, Russell served on President Johnson's committee for treating problems of the handicapped. If ever someone seemed perfect for the concept of one-shot wonder, it was Harold Russell. Then, in 1980, he came out of self-imposed retirement to appear in *Inside Moves,* Richard Donner's film about a group of disabled people, most of them confined to wheelchairs, trying to make something of their lives. Russell stole the show as an old-timer who helps a young would-be suicide (John Savage) learn the meaning of hope and survival.

ABOUT THE AUTHOR

Prof. Douglas Brode teaches the Film Directors course at the Newhouse School of Communications at Syracuse University and serves as Coordinator of the Cinema Studies Program at Onondaga College. His books include the college text *Crossroads to the Cinema* and, for Citadel Press, *Films of the Fifties, Films of the Sixties, The Films of Dustin Hoffman, Woody Allen: His Films and Career, The Films of Jack Nicholson, Lost Films of the Fifties, Films of the Eighties, The Films of Woody Allen, The Films of Robert De Niro, The Films of Steven Spielberg* and *Money, Women and Guns: Crime Films From "Bonnie and Clyde" to the Present.* His articles have appeared in such popular magazines as Rolling Stone and TV Guide, as well as more esoteric journals such as *Cineaste* and *Television Quarterly.* His original play *Heartbreaker* has been professionally produced, and his original screenplay *Midnight Blue* was filmed in the fall of 1995 by the Motion Picture Corporation of America.